Praise for *Creative Filmmaking from the Inside Out*

"This is a smart book on the filmmaking process. It stresses the [...] of ideas instead of the usual 'How to Break Into Hollywood' or 'Write a Script in 48 Hours' nonsense. *Creative Filmmaking* challenges you to think before you shoot."

—Larry Karaszewski, screenwriter of *Ed Wood, The People vs. Larry Flynt* and *Man on the Moon* and producer of *Auto Focus*

"This is the only book I know of that relates the creative process to every key filmmaking role. Whether the reader is, or wants to be, a writer, director, producer, production designer, cinematographer, actor, editor, sound designer, composer, animator or documentary filmmaker, *Creative Filmmaking* offers insights and advice that should lead to work of greater freshness and individuality."

—James Hindman, Codirector and Chief Operating Officer of the American Film Institute

"An essential tool for bringing out the artists in today's student filmmakers."
—Stacey Sher, producer of *Get Shorty, Out of Sight* and *Erin Brockovich*

"Reading *Creative Filmmaking* reinspired my own teaching. Dannenbaum, Hodge and Mayer tackle the tricky issue of creativity with freshness and accessibility. Grounded in the experiences of successful film artists, their understanding of creativity brilliantly maps out the balance between intuition and intellect, the individual voice and the collective process. The exercises will energize your students' films, and free them from clichéd thinking. This book is a must for anyone making films or teaching the filmmaking process."

—Michelle Citron, filmmaker, author, Professor in the Department of Radio/Television/Film at Northwestern University and Director of the Center for Interdisciplinary Research in the Arts

"In *Creative Filmmaking from the Inside Out,* a carefully chosen group of today's best filmmakers describe their working methods in illuminating detail. The insights in this book are valuable for anyone interested in the art of filmmaking. The suggested exercises are a wonderful bonus for young filmmakers who want to get their creative juices flowing."

—Dan Kleinman, Chair of the Film Division at Columbia University School of the Arts

"This is a very good and necessary book, a lantern taken into the darker corners of the creative process."

—Michael Rabiger, filmmaker, author and former Chair of the Film/Video Department at Columbia College, Chicago

"*Creative Filmmaking* is entirely fresh and different and welcomed. It has caused me to reconsider the content of a documentary course I have been conducting for NYU undergraduates for three decades."

—George Stoney, filmmaker and Paulette Goddard Professor of Film and Television at New York University's Tisch School of the Arts

"The authors have woven a rich collection of personal reflections from talented filmmakers into a valuable and thoroughly enjoyable guidebook through the creative process. Indispensable reading for students and professionals alike."

—Victoria Riskin, screenwriter and President of the Writers Guild of America, west

creativefilmmaking
from the inside out

Five Keys to the Art of
Making Inspired Movies
and Television

Jed Dannenbaum, Carroll Hodge and Doe Mayer

A Fireside Book

Published by Simon & Schuster

New York

London

Toronto

Sydney

Singapore

In remembrance of those who first sparked our creativity and our love for film:
Jed's grandmother Peggy Haetten and his sister Maggy Dannenbaum
Carroll's parents Gordon and Frances Hodge
Doe's grandparents Arthur and Lillie Mayer

FIRESIDE
Rockefeller Center
1230 Avenue of the Americas
New York, NY 10020

Copyright © 2003 by Jed Dannenbaum, Carroll Hodge and Doe Mayer
All rights reserved, including the right of reproduction in whole or in part in any form.

FIRESIDE and colophon are registered trademarks of Simon & Schuster Inc.

For information regarding special discounts for bulk purchases,
please contact Simon & Schuster Special Sales at 1-800-456-6798
or business@simonandschuster.com

Designed by Chris Welch

Manufactured in the United States of America

Photo credits appear on page 203.

10 9 8 7 6 5 4 3 2 1

Library of Congress Cataloging-in-Publication Data

Dannenbaum, Jed.
    Creative filmmaking : from the inside out : five keys to the art of making inspired
movies and television / Jed Dannenbaum, Carroll Hodge and Doe Mayer.
        p.   cm.
    "A fireside book."
    Includes filmography.
    Includes bibliographical references and index.
    1. Motion pictures—Production and direction. 2. Television—Production and
direction I. Hodge, Carroll. II. Mayer, Doe. III. Title.
PN1995.9.P7 D37 2003
791.43'0233—dc21   2002190756
ISBN 0-7432-2319-5

contents

acknowledgments

Over the five years that this book evolved, many people significantly aided and influenced its development. It is a pleasure now to have the opportunity to thank them for their help.

Elizabeth Daley, Dean of the University of Southern California School of Cinema-Television and Executive Director of the Annenberg Center for Communication, provided vital financial and institutional support, as well as her personal encouragement and enthusiasm for the project.

Universal Studios provided research funding, under the auspices of Deborah Rosen. Our remarkable agent Barbara Lowenstein has not only represented the book with great effectiveness, but at a key early point encouraged us to structure it very differently, making it much better than it would have been, and more satisfying to write. We have also benefited from the knowledge, experience, good taste and collaborative spirit of Cherise Grant, our editor at Simon & Schuster. Thanks as well to Allyson Edelhertz, production editor Daniel Cuddy, interior design head Joy O'Meara, art director Cherlynne Li, publicist Lisa Sciambra and all the others at Simon & Schuster whose expertise has served the book so well.

We are very fortunate to have had outstanding student researchers. Jennifer Waldo calmly and skillfully saw the book through its intense final year, and gave us valuable feedback, especially on the efficacy of the *limberings* and *workouts*. Scott Foundas, Steven Jacobson, Myles Sorensen and Susan Vaill all added their insights to the book and assisted diligently over substantial periods of time. We received exceptional help as well from Allison Seoyoung Lee, Nikki Riley and Angela Rodriguez. David Landau ably negotiated the licenses and releases for the photos in the book. Grace Rutledge did a superb job transcribing the interviews.

Many filmmaking and teaching colleagues, students and friends provided careful readings of the manuscript along the way, and were astonishingly generous with their time and ideas. Michael Rabiger inspired us with his book *Developing Story Ideas* and gave us a particularly helpful and detailed critique of ours. He, as well as Patsy Asch, Michelle Fellner, Pablo Frasconi, Mark Harris, Jeremy Kagan, Nicky Phillips and Chris Terrio, not only read the manuscript but helped the project in other key ways. In its various drafts, our revisions were aided greatly by the comments of Tom Backer, Warren Bennis, Bronwyn Barkan, Manuel Bermudez, David Bondelevitch, S. Leo Chiang, Peter Clarke, Michelle Citron, Matthew Cohen, Barbara Corday, Midge Costin, Kathleen Dowdey, Susan Evans, Deirdre Gainor, Michael Gonzales, Sara Hartley, Helaine Head, Stuart Hirotsu, Joe Janeti, Antonia Kao, Phyllis Laughlin, Samantha Laughlin, Lisa Leeman, Roberta Levitow, Mildred Lewis, Stephen Lighthill, Karen Ludwig, Darren McInerney, Billy Mernit, Woody Omens, Amanda Pope, Vivian Price, Al Rollins, Dee Hahn Rollins, Becky Rolnick, Chris Rowley, Rob Sabal, Kris Samuelson, Craig Storper, Meg Tilly, Monique Zavistovski and Bonnie Zimmerman. Our Critical Studies colleagues Marsha Kinder, David James and Michael Renov advised and guided us at an early stage. Erika Surat Andersen, Wendy Apple, Don Bohlinger, Cynthia Cohn, Erin Crystall, Bob Estrin, Brenda Goodman, David Howard, Art Nomura, Emiko Omori and John Tarver read a draft of a preliminary conception of the book and helped us rethink where we wanted to go. Steve Carr, Geoff Cowan, Bill Dill, Deborah Fort, Chap Freeman, Meg Moritz and George Stoney participated in developing an even earlier proposal for what would have been a very differ-

ent book—although that project did not materialize, the process provided intellectual and emotional momentum that led to this one.

Bonnie Arnold, Ron Bozman, Marty Kaplan, Kyle McCarthy, Sarah Pillsbury and Steve Robman all helped in the process of contacting potential interviewees. The University of Southern California Annenberg School for Communication supported development of the book's website. Facing History and Ourselves, under Dan Alba, Director of the Los Angeles Region, played an important role in a series of workshops that were related to, and aided the thinking behind, this book; and Duke Underwood supported another series of seminars through the Summer Production Workshop at USC. Stephen Nachmanovitch generously discussed his ideas about creativity, and Amy Kravitz offered helpful examples of creative exercises. John Levy and Victoria Westhead lent us their beautiful home in rural Connecticut during the summer of 1998 for a serene and productive writers' retreat. And thanks to all the friends and family who have patiently continued to ask "how's the book going?" and then helped us with their good questions and comments.

Jed would like to thank Bob Friedman for his mentoring; Laura Davis, the ideal creative orchestrator-collaborator; Cecilia Woloch for her friendship and advice; and his sister Liz Dannenbaum for love, encouragement and being there when it counts. He and Doe are delighted, and grateful to one another, that their coauthoring experience has enriched and deepened their marriage. Jed and Carroll both thank Deena Metzger, for her specific guidance and for the creative stimulus of her writing groups. Doe wishes to thank her extended family but especially her parents, Janet and Michael, for their constant interest, enthusiasm and support for this book throughout its various incarnations. Carroll is grateful to her creative colleague, Molly Smith, for the insights realized in the making of *Raven's Blood*. And she has been blessed in this writing process more than once with the steadfast support and love of her life partner, Amy Rosenberg.

We are immensely grateful to the fifteen wonderfully creative and very busy filmmakers who were willing to speak with us so thoughtfully and at such length. Finally, we want to thank all our students at USC over the years, who have continually stimulated and inspired us and from whom we have learned so much.

introduction

This is a book about the creative process of filmmaking—the mysterious transformation of mere glimmers of thought into coherent stories, characters, images and sounds. As filmmakers ourselves and as teachers of film and video production at the University of Southern California, we are passionate about films and fascinated by the challenges of making them well (we use the word "film" in this book to include all story-based moving image media). Inevitably, we have written a book shaped by our own tastes—we're drawn to films that feel fresh, multilayered and authentic, that bear the distinct imprints of the people who made them, and that have a strong impact on audiences who see them. These are qualities that can be hard to pin down, but we sorely feel their absence in those films that seem to have come off an assembly line: hollow-feeling cut-and-paste pastiches of other movies and TV shows, filled with clichéd characters, cookie-cutter plots, hackneyed dialogue and imitative stylistic flourishes.

We have written this book to be appropriate for those learning filmmaking on their own as well as for students in a production class or program. We teach in a film school and see its great value in providing structure, contact with diverse tastes and approaches, a collaborative environment, a wide range of hands-on experience, faculty mentoring and many other benefits. We're also aware that film school is not for everyone and that many outstanding filmmakers never went to film school, including a majority of those interviewed for this book. We have therefore tried to make this a resource that would be informative and inspiring, whether used by an individual reader or as an assigned text in a course. (Teachers using this book in classes and workshops, as well as individual readers, may wish to refer to our website, creativefilmmaking.com, for additional suggestions.) Although we designed the book with developing filmmakers foremost in mind, the aspects of creativity it highlights and clarifies are ones that even the most experienced professionals continue to explore throughout their careers. We wrote a book that we ourselves learned a great deal from, and we believe that it will have rewards for anyone working in the field.

It's often said that no one sets out to make a bad film. So, assuming you share something of our taste and want to make films that are inspired, original and resonant, what's the foolproof, surefire formula for great filmmaking? Of course, there is no such thing. Paint-by-numbers formulas—"put a plot point on page 'x' of the screenplay, use lens 'y' and camera move 'z' for shooting a certain kind of scene"—cannot produce the kind of inventive, surprising filmmaking we admire. Doing good work is always a risky, unpredictable, paradoxical process even for the very best filmmakers. We used the word "mysterious" above to describe the creative process of filmmaking; so it is and so it shall remain.

Yet what you *can* learn, and what we emphasize in this book, is how best to prepare yourself, and how to approach your work, so that your inherent creativity has the greatest opportunity to emerge and flourish. *Creative Filmmaking from the Inside Out* describes an approach that begins with preparation that is largely individual and internal—recognizing and strengthening your own unique point of view. As you learn to rely on rather than suppress your passions, idiosyncrasies, intuitive responses, values and personal connections to the material, you will develop a more confident inner voice. You can then bring that clarity to your collaborations with fellow filmmakers, to interpreting the responses of audiences, and to wrestling with your responsibilities as a creator of powerful art, without losing your way or diluting the integrity of your intent. Whatever the results, you will have a much better internal gauge for assessing and learning from each experience as you move on to your next creative project.

We have broken down the overall process described in *Creative Filmmaking from the Inside Out* into five chapters, each exploring one of what we call the "Five I's": **Introspection, Inquiry, Intuition, Interaction** and **Impact.** Although we had to put the chapters in a linear order, in reality the "Five I's" are all interwoven throughout the creative process. You might intersperse working from your own point of view (introspection) and brainstorming with a colleague (interaction). You may be in the middle of research (inquiry) and have a provocative dream (intuition). You may start with an idea of what a film is really about (impact), but find that your idea changes and develops throughout the filmmaking process.

The book begins with **Introspection,** a consideration of how the act of looking within ourselves can help us draw on who we are and how we see the world. The chapter looks at how we might discover the specific kind of work we have a passion for and are particularly well-suited to do; the importance of seeking personal connections in the material we choose to work on; and how we can reference and draw on our own specific experiences, including the darker, more difficult aspects of our lives, weaving bits of ourselves into what we create in order to deepen our sense of connection and authorship.

In addition to working from our own experience, we need as filmmakers to be able to draw on the entire spectrum of human thought and behavior, including those facets we have not yet directly encountered. In **Inquiry,** we see the importance of having a broad knowledge of the other arts and diverse fields of knowledge; the value of seeking direct firsthand experience of the world of a story; and the need for research, looking deeply into a subject, a setting, a culture, or an era in a way that enriches our understanding and point of view.

Our strange, elusive communications with the nonconscious parts of our mind are often the most spontaneously creative. **Intuition** is neither guesswork nor supernatural insight—it is dependable in proportion to the extent that we have prepared ourselves well through education, observation, research and life experience. We can strengthen our receptiveness to our nonconscious inventiveness by connecting more deeply to our ability to dream, daydream, and become lost in play. Intuitive creativity can even require that we turn our conscious attention entirely away from our work for a while, as part of a problem-solving process.

Film is a profoundly collaborative art, and through **Interaction** we can draw effectively on the ideas and responses of others. Our filmmakers show how collaboration can be an open, fluid process that allows for the integration of many voices, with the director serving as the orchestrator of these varied contributions. When "creative differences" emerge, the resultant give-and-take can enhance rather than derail the process. Much of the success of interaction depends on establishing a genuinely open creative environment, insulated as much as possible from outside commercial forces.

In the fifth chapter, we look at how we create films that have an **Impact** on an audience. We see how discovering the deeper layers of a film—its "undercurrent"—can guide us in making choices that give a film power, resonance and universality. We also see how filmmakers use test audiences as part of the creative process, gauging if a film is having its desired impact. Finally, we explore how the powerful effect of films on audiences also brings with it complex questions of responsibility for the images we create, leading us back to introspection.

At the end of each chapter we include numerous practical yet playful **Limbering Up** explorations to stimulate and enhance creativity. These *limberings* are just that—ways to loosen up and get your creative juices flowing. Most can be done in five minutes or less, and all are appropriate no matter what kind of work you are doing, anytime you want to get your head into a more innovative place.

The structure of the **Workout** section at the end of the book, by contrast, follows the specific tasks and various stages of the production process, from originating ideas and writing ("Down on the Page"), through pre-production and production ("Into the Can"), and post-production and audience response ("Up on the Screen"). This final section gives you explorations of greater depth that will connect to any current film project you may be working on.

Good filmmaking is passionate and risk-taking. Throughout this book, we encourage a certain level of conscious self-awareness and intentionality in filmmaking, but the probing and thoughtful explorations we describe are antithetical to approaches that over-systematize or over-intellectualize the essential emotionality and unpredictability of art. Intuitive leaps, serendipitous discoveries, continual exploration and surprise, and even long-after-the-fact realizations are all part of the mystery of the best creative work. The ultimate goal of this book is to help you attune your mind to the unexpected truths of your heart and gut.

listed in **Selected Filmographies.** We also wanted to represent the continuing emergence of a greater diversity of filmmakers in terms of gender, ethnicity and sexual orientation (although the Hollywood studios are lagging badly in this regard), as well as include voices with a more international perspective.

In addition to their remarkable range of background and experience, why did we choose this particular group of filmmakers? We believe they exemplify the honest and deep creativity we are attempting to describe and promote. And while there is no definitive measure of what constitutes "good" filmmaking—tastes vary widely and also change over time—we sought those who are widely acclaimed at the top of their professions, and whose work has been recognized by the major critics' associations, their respective guilds and the Television and Motion Picture Academies. As a group, they have won or been nominated for thirty-nine Oscars and twenty-seven Emmys.

Finally, we looked for filmmakers who are passionate and enthusiastic. There are, of course, filmmakers who willingly embrace the often dismal commercialism and synthetic filmmaking that seems to dominate Hollywood. And there are others who are deeply cynical or bitter in their attitudes, defeated by the obstacles that challenge anyone who seeks to preserve their sense of integrity in a world of bottom-line thinking. Although all our filmmakers have had their share of frustrations, doubts and disappointments, by and large they are role models for the possibility of establishing successful careers, in many cases entirely within the Hollywood mainstream, while keeping to the priorities of artistry and authenticity.

Indeed, central to this book is the belief that developing one's creativity can be both personally satisfying and at the same time a practical means to professional success. In our experience and observations, even the most mainstream parts of the entertainment industry are hungry for people who are genuinely creative. Once hired, it's true, such people are likely to encounter pressure to be more formulaic and clichéd. But the more they have learned to work from their own distinctive taste and point of view, the better they will be able to hold on to those qualities through all the stages and pressures of the production process. And when fresh, innovative filmmaking does reach the theatrical or television screen, it usually makes the responsible filmmakers very much in demand.

Although we are coauthoring this book as longtime friends and teaching colleagues, we are three quite different individuals and have our own points

Our own understanding of this process has come from more than thirt
five years of collective experience as teachers and mentors for literally tho
sands of student productions, and is also grounded in our work as acti
professional filmmakers—writers, producers, directors and editors of bo
fiction and documentary films.

For this book, we sought to enlarge our perspective by going to the be
sources possible: professional filmmakers whose work has been acclaime
for its originality and authenticity. We talked at length with fifteen outstan
ing filmmakers who have held key creative positions on some of the mo
beloved and highly regarded movies and television programs of our tim
American Beauty, Apocalypse Now, Boys Don't Cry, The English Patient, E
Into the Arms of Strangers, L.A. Confidential, Picket Fences, The Remains
the Day, The Right Stuff, The Sixth Sense, Toy Story, The West Wing ar
many others.

Although these professionals had been interviewed many times befor
we set out to get a different perspective, choosing not to cover such famili
ground as working with movie stars, the technology of special effects, or ar
ecdotal production stories ("ten straight days of rain"). Instead, we aske
them to focus on their own creative process, and to give us concrete exan
ples of why they approached specific scenes, sequences, characters, loc
tions, and visual, sound or music motifs in the way they did.

Another way this book is unique is that everything in it is applicable t
every creative role at every stage of the filmmaking process. We sought un
versal aspects of creativity that will be meaningful to you whether you ar
looking for a story idea, choosing a location, casting an actor, deciding wher
to place the camera, making an edit, or selecting a music cue. To achiev
this level of universality, we interviewed a wide range of creators, both i
terms of their professional position and their area of the industry. Write
Hanif Kureishi, writer-director Anthony Minghella, writer-director Kim
berly Peirce, producer Ismail Merchant, production designer Jeannin
Oppewall, cinematographer Conrad Hall, editor Lisa Fruchtman, soun
designer and film editor Walter Murch and composer James Newto
Howard have all worked primarily in live-action features, and write
producer-director John Lasseter is known for feature animation. Write
producer John Wells, writer Pamela Douglas, and actor Kathy Baker hav
worked extensively in television. Director-producer Renee Tajima-Peña an
editor Kate Amend have specialized in documentary filmmaking. They ar
all introduced in **The Filmmakers,** and their major credits and awards ar

of view and distinct professional filmmaking experiences to draw on: Carroll in independent feature filmmaking, Doe in media designed to promote and encourage social change in developing countries, and Jed in behind-the-scenes programs about Hollywood productions. Because all our varied experiences as filmmakers, teachers, workshop leaders and in our personal lives have shaped our views, we try to reference in the book what we have individually observed and learned. It is a challenge to have three authors and yet write in the personal tone we prefer. We try, in effect, to become three additional "characters"—Carroll, Doe and Jed—in this story of creative filmmaking from the inside out, mixing our own examples with those of the filmmakers we interviewed in the pages to follow.

the filmmakers

Hanif Kureishi
Writer

Your point of view, which is your voice, your person, isn't something you have to get. It's something you uncover.

Born in Bromley, England, the son of an English mother and a Pakistani immigrant father, Hanif had direct experience with the racial and cultural conflicts that inform much of his work. He knew he wanted to be a writer from a very young age, completing his first novel while still a teenager. While reading philosophy at London's King's College, Hanif fell in love with the theater. *Soaking the Heat*, his first play, was staged in 1976 at the Royal Court Theater Upstairs, and was followed by numerous other theater productions. His first screenplay was *My Beautiful Laundrette*, and his other film credits include *Sammy and Rosie Get Laid*; *London Kills Me* (which he also directed); *My Son, the Fanatic*; *Intimacy* (based on his stories) and the BBC drama *The Buddha of Suburbia*. He has also published several novels and a collection of short stories.

Pamela Douglas
Writer

I've let go of preconceptions about what you're supposed to write and what you're allowed to write.

Pamela grew up in New York City with a father who always resented abandoning his creative life as a musician, a path she vowed not to follow. Some of the characters she knew struggling to survive in the city have surfaced in her just-completed book of stories. It's the latest in a twenty-year writing career that spans journalism and award-winning dramas for television. In addition to her original movies, she was a creator of the series *Ghostwriter* and story editor of *Frank's Place*. Her many other series credits include *A Year in the Life* and *Star Trek: The Next Generation*. After majoring in English at Vassar, Pamela earned a master's degree in art at Columbia University, and continues to paint as well as write. She has been a member of the board of directors of the Writers Guild of America, and is currently an associate professor at the University of Southern California, where she teaches screenwriting.

Anthony Minghella
Writer-Director

When I'm at work on a film, I'm much more likely to be in thrall to a painting or a poem than to a shot in another movie.

Born and raised on Great Britain's Isle of Wight, the son of an Italian ice-cream merchant, Anthony's path to filmmaking began with a love for music, and as a teenager he performed in local folk clubs and rock venues. While still an undergraduate at the University of Hull in Yorkshire, he wrote some dialogue to connect several of his songs into a musical, and as a result was commissioned to write a play, which led to success as a playwright. *Truly, Madly, Deeply,* his feature film directing debut, was a surprise international hit. Anthony is the writer-director of *The English Patient, The Talented Mr. Ripley* and *Cold Mountain.*

Kimberly Peirce
Writer-Director

You've subjected yourself to every character, to what they want and need. . . . You follow your intuition, but you also want to know and follow your craft because making a movie is like being an archaeologist—you've got to dig out what's been buried, the underlying emotional truth.

Kimberly was born in Harrisburg, Pennsylvania. She earned a B.A. in English and Japanese literature from the University of Chicago, and worked in Japan for two years as a photographer, taking pictures of sumo wrestlers, geisha and yakuza. As an M.F.A. student in film at Columbia University, she learned about the murder of Brandon Teena, formerly known as Teena Brandon. Kimberly traveled to Falls City, Nebraska, where Brandon had lived, and began the research that five years later culminated in her first feature as a director, *Boys Don't Cry,* cowritten with Andy Bienen. She and Bienen have written a murder mystery based on a true story set in Hollywood in the 1920s, which she will also direct. She is working with writer Rafael Yglesias on *Childhood's End* and with David Mamet on *Dillinger.*

John Lasseter
Writer-Director-Producer

Filmmaking is the most collaborative artistic medium there is. One thing I've found is that you never know where the good idea is going to come from.

Executive Vice President/Creative at Pixar Animation Studios, John was born in Hollywood and grew up in Whittier, California. The director of *Toy Story, Toy Story 2* and *A Bug's Life,* and executive producer of *Monsters, Inc.,* John fell in love with animation at an early age. As a high school student, he wrote a letter to The Walt Disney Studios describing his passion for drawing and cartoons. Disney was setting up an innovative program in animation at CalArts (California Institute of the Arts) and John became the second student admitted to the program. After graduation, he worked at Disney for five years before his interest in combining computer graphics and traditional animation techniques led him to Pixar.

John Wells
Writer-Producer

There were five or six people centrally involved in creating ER. *We got excited and we started bouncing off each other. It's like a basketball team where it's all working, people are passing, everybody's hitting shots, and you feel the rhythm. It's selfless.*

John was a writer, supervising producer and then co-executive producer of the television series *China Beach* and is executive producer of *ER, The West Wing* and *Third Watch.* John has been president of the Writers Guild of America, West, playing a central role in contract negotiations between studios and writers in the summer of 2001. Born in Alexandria, Virginia, he completed his undergraduate degree at Carnegie-Mellon University in Pittsburgh. He went on to graduate studies at the University of Southern California School of Cinema-Television and is currently a member of its Television Executive Advisory Council. Although best known for his television work, John has served as producer or executive producer on several features, including *White Oleander, One Hour Photo* and *Far From Heaven.*

Renee Tajima-Peña
Director-Producer

Most times, I'm really pissed off and that's why I make a movie. I was pissed off about race, probably from the time I was very young. It really just drove every- thing I did. So I made films dealing with race.

Renee's documentary credits include *Who Killed Vincent Chin?, My America . . . or, Honk if You Love Buddha, The Last Beat Movie, The Best Hotel on Skid Row* and *Jennifer's in Jail*. Her work has been broadcast on PBS, HBO, The Sundance Channel and Lifetime. Born in Chicago and raised in Southern California, Renee graduated cum laude in East Asian Studies and Sociology from Harvard-Radcliffe College. In addition to her film work, she has been a commentator for National Public Radio, a film critic for *The Village Voice* and associate editor of *The Independent Film & Video Monthly*. Renee writes and lectures on Asian-American and inde- pendent film, and she is currently working on two documentaries about immigrant labor.

Ismail Merchant
Producer

We share the sensibilities and the creativity together, but we never impose our will, that this has to be done this way, because each artist has an independent idea, and their contribution is larger if they're left free.

Born in Bombay, India, Ismail has spent most of his adult life in the West, with his formal education culminating in an M.B.A. from New York University. On his way to the Cannes Film Festival in 1961 with his short film *The Creation of Woman,* he met James Ivory, and the two started a partnership, Merchant Ivory Productions, that has been in operation for over forty years and produced dozens of internationally acclaimed films, most of them written by Ruth Prawer Jhabvala. His credits include *Shakespeare Wallah, Roseland, The Europeans, Heat and Dust, The Bostonians, Maurice, A Room with a View, Howards End* and *The Remains of the Day.* He has also written several books, including cookbooks such as *Ismail Merchant's Florence: Filming and Feasting in Tuscany* and *Ismail Merchant's Passionate Meals.*

Jeannine Claudia Oppewall
Production Designer

Designers are sort of shamans. You can walk by a rock, a tree, a building and they each have a spirit. If you're sensitive and aware, you know what that spirit is and you respond to it, you know when to use it, know how to manipulate elements that add to that spirit. It's something that comes from years of being an observer, a careful observer of life and nature and the constructed universe.

Jeannine grew up in Massachusetts and earned her master's degree in medieval studies at Bryn Mawr. She started out working with the famed designers Charles and Ray Eames. Her film credits include *Tender Mercies; Corrina, Corrina; Maria's Lovers; Ironweed; The Bridges of Madison County; Pleasantville; L.A. Confidential; Snow Falling on Cedars; Wonder Boys* and *The Sum of All Fears.* Jeannine has produced radio documentaries about the Calvinist faith she grew up with. She also has an avid interest in entomology and has written scholarly articles about insects.

Conrad L. Hall, A.S.C.
Cinematographer

It's finding the soul of the story, and deciding what that is. And then all of the scenes develop from the roots of this tree.

Conrad was born into a storytelling tradition—his father, James Norman Hall, coauthored *Mutiny on the Bounty*. Conrad at first thought he might follow in his father's footsteps as a writer, but changed course after taking a cinema class at the University of Southern California. Upon graduation, he and two fellow students started their own production company and bought the rights to a story for their first feature, *Running Target*. They drew lots to decide who would be the producer, director and cinematographer and Conrad drew the cinematographer's lot. His use of desaturated color, lens flares and other innovative techniques in *Butch Cassidy and the Sundance Kid* greatly influenced subsequent films. His many other credits include *Morituri, Incubus, The Professionals, In Cold Blood, The Day of the Locust, Cool Hand Luke, Marathon Man, Searching for Bobby Fischer, A Civil Action, American Beauty* and *Road to Perdition*.

Kathy Baker
Actor

I decided when I was five that I wanted to be an actor. . . . It wasn't about performance—it came from the written word. We always had books around. I wanted to be the people in the stories my mother was reading to me.

Kathy played Dr. Jill Brock on the long-running television series *Picket Fences* and Mrs. Peters on *Boston Public*. Her many film credits include *The Right Stuff, Street Smart, Clean and Sober, Jacknife, Edward Scissorhands, The Cider House Rules* and *Cold Mountain*. On stage, she originated the role of May in *Fool for Love*. Born in Midland, Texas, and raised in Albuquerque, New Mexico, Kathy earned a degree in French at the University of California, Berkeley, and studied cooking at Le Cordon Bleu in Paris.

Walter Murch
Sound Designer-Editor

Something deep in me responds to sound as a language, as a way of communicating with people. It's a mystery where that comes from.

Walter was studying art history and romance languages in Paris when his passion for French New Wave cinema convinced him to enroll in USC's School of Cinema-Television. He earned his first feature credits doing the sound for Francis Ford Coppola's *The Rain People* (1968) and George Lucas's *THX 1138* (1970). In 1969, the three filmmakers formed their own production company, American Zoetrope, and based themselves in the San Francisco Bay Area. Walter is one of the few filmmakers to master both sound design and picture editing. Among his films are *The Conversation; Apocalypse Now; Julia; American Graffiti; The Rain People; The Unbearable Lightness of Being; The Godfather, Part III; Crumb; The English Patient; The Talented Mr. Ripley; Apocalypse Now Redux* and the revised version of *Touch of Evil*. Walter also cowrote and directed *Return to Oz*.

Lisa Fruchtman
Editor

If you allow yourself to play with the material, put it together in a way that isn't the most obvious, and then it clicks, there's that tremendous 'aha' moment like they talk about in science.

Lisa graduated from the University of Chicago with a B.A. in the history and philosophy of science. She began her professional career in film as a documentary editor at the National Film Board of Canada. After moving to San Francisco, Lisa was hired as an assistant editor on *The Godfather, Part II.* Her credits as editor include *Apocalypse Now; The Right Stuff; The Godfather, Part III; Heaven's Gate; Children of a Lesser God; The Doctor; My Best Friend's Wedding* and the HBO features *Truman, Witness Protection* and *Normal.* Lisa has participated in the American Film Institute's Directing Workshop for Women and is developing several projects as a producer and director.

Kate Amend
Editor

I love those hours of just poring over the material and looking at it over and over and over again . . . You're outside of time, just totally focused on the creative process, making something exist that didn't exist before.

Among Kate's credits are the documentaries *Into The Arms of Strangers: Stories of the Kindertransport; The Long Way Home; Skinheads, USA; The Girl Next Door* and *PANDEMIC: FACING AIDS.* Her work has appeared on PBS, HBO, NBC, Lifetime, the History Channel and the Sundance Channel. Kate is also an administrator and historian for Judy Chicago's monumental art exhibit *The Dinner Party,* and has produced several videos about Chicago's art, including *From Darkness into Light, Creating the Holocaust Project.* She holds degrees from San Francisco State University and the University of California, Berkeley, and is an adjunct professor at the University of Southern California.

James Newton Howard
Composer

I think a big part of it for me has been recognizing that moment when you've written something promising, and not letting it escape. . . . That one little moment of spark is where a lot of the magic lives.

James's grandmother played violin in the Pittsburgh Symphony, and he began playing classical music at an early age, later studying at Santa Barbara's Music Academy of the West and the University of Southern California School of Music. James has scored over seventy feature films, but his career did not begin with film music. After playing with the band Mama Lion in the early 1970s, James became Elton John's regular album keyboardist. He went on to produce recordings for Cher, Barbra Streisand, Randy Newman and many others, and didn't try film composing until 1985. His film credits include *The Fugitive, The Prince of Tides, My Best Friend's Wedding, Grand Canyon, Snow Falling on Cedars, The Sixth Sense* and the theme for the television series *ER*.

one introspection

inquiry

intuition

interaction

impact

workout

The artist Edward Hopper said that "a personal vision of the world" is the essential ingredient of great art. We are all likely, when reading this, to hear a faint nagging voice within saying "A personal vision? Damn, that sounds heavy! Am I really going to be able to get one of those?"

The fact is, the essence of that vision is already in you. It *is* you. As screenwriter Hanif Kureishi said to us, "Your point of view, which is your voice, your person, isn't something you have to get. It's something you uncover." The goal of this chapter is to help you uncover your voice, and learn to draw on who you are and how you see the world; the essential starting points for all that you do creatively. The first of our "Five I's," therefore, is **Introspection,** the act of looking within. As a creative filmmaker working from the inside out, your own innate tendencies and individual experiences will profoundly affect the kind of creative work you choose to do, the stories you seek to tell, and the distinctive contributions you make to those stories.

Inherent in each of us is a distinct individuality, the result of an intricate dance between our unique heredity and our equally unique set of life experiences. We begin life with a one-of-a-kind set of genes (except for identical twins). Then, even while we are still in the womb, our innate tendencies begin to interact with our environment. Our genetic predispositions both shape, and are in turn shaped by, the environment in which we grow and develop—our relationships with our family members, lovers, friends and acquaintances; our nutrition, health care, illnesses and accidents; our encounters with places, images, sounds and stories; our education and our assimilation of the mores of our culture and the zeitgeist of our era; and myriad other influences. Some haunt us, some are invisible to us, and some have vanished from our memories.

As we grow, we develop our own specific behavior patterns, emotional triggers, mental templates, our own way of looking at and responding to the world. We learn lessons and we acquire values. Our brains, arguably the most complex and mysterious objects in all of nature, become etched with an unimaginably vast and intricate web of trillions of neural connections. From all this comes who we are—our loves and hates, dreams and obsessions, passions and demons, insights and blind spots. Each of us has a vision that is distinctly ours, and ours alone.

Our initial goal, then, in developing our creativity is to look for what is unique about our own way of seeing and then strengthen its expression. In the first film/video production course at the University of Southern California, each student, on their own, writes, produces, directs, shoots and edits five short films, one every three weeks. At the beginning of this course, many students have never picked up a camera before. Yet, with practically no technical training, their films usually have a distinctive quality right from the outset. Even when the five films a student makes cover a wide range in terms of form, subject matter, genre or tone, there's a mysterious "something" in each film that only that person would have come up with, the glimmer of their own cinematic voice, there to be developed.

It may seem obvious that, as creative people, we need to begin with our own tastes, interests, values, and personal frames of reference. But too often, we fall into a mindset of thinking first about what is the familiar way to do something, or what is easy, or what others expect, or what will "sell." Young filmmakers looking for work in the industry frequently adopt an attitude of "I'll do anything now, take any work I can get, then be choosier later on when I'm more established." But many of our filmmakers made the point to us that if they can't find a connection to the material, they're not able to do their best creative work. We believe that, at any stage of a career, finding projects that speak to you in some way, and job opportunities that provide an opening to develop your own voice, should be a high priority.

Most challenging of all, exposing ourselves creatively is likely to make us feel profoundly and often frighteningly vulnerable. Our fears can intensify if others reject our early attempts at self-expression. At some point in your life, you may have had some very personal creative effort casually dismissed or condescended to or even ridiculed. You may have been taught that publicly revealing your private feelings is unseemly. And you may have ended up believing that you are an uncreative person with nothing important to say, or that the only "safe" way to be creative is to replicate what has already been done rather than expose yourself. When we prejudge and filter our creative ideas in this way, before they have a chance to breathe and develop, they are likely by default to become bland and formulaic.

The insights and real-life examples from our filmmakers that follow, along with the *limbering ups* at the end of the chapter, explore three key ways in which introspection can help you turn up the volume of your own creative voice so you can hear it more clearly and have it reverberate in your filmmaking. We see how, and when, these filmmakers found the kind of creative work that speaks to them most powerfully in **A Mysterious Predisposition: *Discovering Your Creative Field*;** how they seek material to work on that they can connect to on a personal level in **Finding the Resonance: *Choosing the Stories You Want to Tell*;** and how they bring bits of their own lives into a project to deepen their relationship to it in **A Private World: *Drawing on Personal Memories.***

A Mysterious Predisposition: *Discovering Your Creative Field*

As children and adults, our filmmakers made discoveries about their tastes, talents and life experiences that led them into specific life paths, guided their selection of material, and influenced their approach to their work. "I think people are always who they are," screenwriter Pamela Douglas told us.

"They come into the world much more fully formed than we think. Of course, you can take that potential and drown it or maximize it." These filmmakers have been successful in part because they have been able to amplify their innate potential. To begin with, they were either self-aware enough to recognize, or fortunate enough to fall into, a field that resonates with some essential aspect of who they are.

"Gerald McBoing Boing" was a 1950s cartoon character who spoke entirely in sound effects. It also became the childhood nickname of sound designer and editor Walter Murch by the time he was age three or four. Walter sees in himself "a mysterious predisposition from a very early age" toward being creative with sound. "Something deep in me responds to sound as a language, as a way of communicating with people. It's a mystery where that came from." By age ten, Walter was obsessed with the reel-to-reel tape recorders just then coming onto the consumer market: "The father of one of my friends had one for business reasons. I'd go over to his place and say, 'Let's play with the tape recorder,' and then I would spend the next three or four hours just recording things and playing them back. I learned all of the tricks at a very early age, that you can manipulate reality by recording sound fast and then playing it back slow, doing the opposite, recording it in one direction, playing it back in another, and then, ultimately, the idea of chopping it up into bits and taping it together in a different order."

Gerald McBoing Boing

Walter's attraction to sound seems to be something that was just part of his own distinctive nature from a very early age. Not all children have an innate predisposition as singular as his, but when we spend time with children, we quickly see how pronounced their interests are and how distinctive their responses are as soon as they begin to interact in a complex way with the world.

Despite Walter's early fascination with sound, it never occurred to him as a child that he would make a career out of this inclination. Kathy Baker, however, decided when she was only five years old that she wanted to be an actor. She describes the moment as "like an epiphany—if you made a film of it, a shaft of light would come down, and the music would swell. I'm in the bedroom I shared with my sister in our house in Albuquerque. It's a sunny day, and I'm sort of performing in my own little world. I was that kind of child—I had imaginary friends and little worlds to myself. I'm trying some dress on, or some scarf or hat, and I . . . I just decided."

At the time, Kathy's family didn't own a television, and she was barely aware of movies. Her interest in acting, she believes, "wasn't about performance—it came from the written word. We always had books around. I wanted to be the people in the stories my mother was reading to me, Madeleine, or Anne of Green Gables." Because she was not a child who liked to perform in front of others, she thought her desire to be an actor was a secret that was hers alone. "Then at age ten, my mother said to me, 'Kathy, would you like to take acting lessons?' I give myself goose bumps saying it because how did she know that's what I wanted to be? Of course, now that I'm a mother, I understand that my own mother knew perfectly well."

Kathy Baker at age five

ANTHONY MINGHELLA, writer-director

I grew up in a very small seaside resort on the Isle of Wight, an island off the coast of England. In retrospect, it was a wonderful place to grow up, but at the time, all I could think about were ways of escaping. I would stand on the beach, dreaming of going to London. I was a very miserable teenager—extremely dislocated from my family. My father was an Italian ice-cream seller, a very hardworking and typical immigrant. He and my mother still go to work every day selling ice cream on the Isle of Wight. As a kid, I was very conscious of the fact that we had a completely different culture to all of my friends. It was an extremely homogeneous society, except for us.

I had a piano in my bedroom that I had abandoned playing when I was younger, but as a teenager, I slowly returned to it and realized that I could unwind my frustration in some way by banging the piano and singing. I started to write songs, and to feel incredibly empowered by that. I didn't do it very well, but I did it with enormous gusto and enthusiasm. It was something I could do that nobody else had any authority over. I think that was the thing—it was something that was mine.

Music turned out to be the passport for me into a creative world. The University of Hull accepted me not on the basis of having any great academic qualification, but because I could play music and I could also paint. When I got to university, I discovered that I'd come into an environment where what had previously been a problem, my sort of idiosyncratic take on things, suddenly was incredibly encouraged. I went from being

"It's the Time When I Feel Most Like Myself"

a very detached and uncommitted student to becoming the most tediously passionate and attentive child for three years. And I ended up winning the university prize and getting a job teaching.

What had started off as an interest in music became an interest in music for the theater. I was able to think of some way of threading songs into an evening in the theater by writing some text around the songs. That text was, I suppose, something like a play. Then I was offered a commission to write a play. And so I stumbled, with no compass but with massive serendipity, from the piano in my bedroom to becoming, a few years later, a playwright. And what I discovered—and this has never changed—was the epiphany that however long it took me to come to writing as an activity, that is the activity which has most defined me, and continues to define me. If you ask me what I do, I would say I'm a writer who directs, rather than a director who writes. I love writing. I find it very difficult, but it's the time when I'm most comfortable with myself, oddly, or I feel most like myself.

I'd never thought of myself as a particularly creative person. I had one instinct, which was to find some escape route from wearing a yellow nylon jacket and selling Minghella's Ice Cream for the rest of my life.

Another of our filmmakers, Ismail Merchant, also was still a child when he discovered his particular fascination with and talent for producing. He remembers growing up in Bombay, "working with artists from the age of nine. In school, I would put on theater charity programs." The only boy among seven children, at age seventeen he found himself the "producer" of a large wedding for his older sister. "My father was not very keen on her marrying outside the community. So I organized the reception and paid for it with money I earned putting on variety programs—music, theater. And all my friends were there. My father had only invited four friends, and I'd invited something like a hundred." Ismail found he had a talent not only for staging large productions, but for their creative promotion as well: "The invitations for the theater events had to be very special invitations, that maybe opened like a lotus flower."

Animation writer-director John Lasseter as a child "was just a nut for cartoons. I'd rush home from school to watch Bugs Bunny cartoons. And although I wasn't a morning person at all, Saturday I was up, boom, in front of the TV." Most kids love cartoon programs, but John's attraction went a step farther. "I started drawing cartoons and cartoon characters, and then created the world they lived in, this incredible treehouse that was a hollow tree that went down underground, with this big cave right next to it. It was like my dream land. I loved to play in that world."

John Lasseter's "mysterious predisposition" was in turn enhanced by his life experiences. His mother was an art teacher who surrounded her children with art materials. "Whenever we would go on trips, she would bring stuff with us camping, and we would paint rocks. Once at the beach, she told us to collect a bunch of shells and whatever. Then she said, 'Dig out a hole in the wet sand, and put shapes at the bottom.' She mixed plaster of Paris and poured it into the sand mold, and once it hardened, we pulled it out and it was covered with all our shells and stuff. And it was, like, 'Ah, this is cool!' It was so interesting, as a kid, to be thinking about negative space."

John also had a third grade teacher who showed the class reproductions of paintings by Picasso and Monet, as well as Georges Seurat's pointillist *Sunday Afternoon on the Island of La Grande Jatte.* "She got us to look at it closely, and it was made up of a lot of little points, a bunch of different colors, and it made an image. Teachers like that educate our creative minds, as well as our logical minds."

Parents don't need to be art teachers to help spark the creativity of their children. Television writer-producer John Wells (our other filmmaker named John) grew up surrounded by "the tremendous amount of ceremony and creative arts" taking place in the Episcopalian church where his father was a minister. It was also a family environment in which "stories, parables, and ideas were important in the way in which we were raised. The Bible, the New and Old Testaments, are really stories, moral stories, ways in which to live your life."

Sunday Afternoon on the Island of La Grande Jatte, by Georges Seurat, a painting that John Lasseter remembers seeing in the third grade

John's father was part of the political and creative ferment of the 1960s and early '70s, a time John remembers as "a little 'hippie-ish.' We were around street performers, and artists, and people who were protesting. My father and the church itself were very involved in those things. It was a very fertile period for music in the church, and for new rituals, and performance." Within this morally sensitized and theatrical context, John's parents taught their children to think for themselves, to wrestle with an issue's complexities and arrive at their own conclusions. "There was a lot of emphasis on caring about things, having opinions and getting them across to others. If you didn't have opinions, you got them, because my father would say, 'What do you think?' or 'You're just reciting something that somebody else told you. Defend your position.' "

Of course, not all childhood experiences are nurturing. The darker, more painful events of growing up also shape us as creative people. Writer-director Kimberly Peirce remembers a "chaotic environment. My parents were, like, fifteen years old when they had me. They split up and I lived with lots of different people." Her predisposition for certain kinds of imaginative activities allowed her to "just tune out" the chaos around her, and feel that she was designing and controlling her own "special worlds that were calming and clarifying. I was an architect and builder in a strange way. For example, I wanted my dogs to have a perfect environment, so I would draw sketches, and figure out how much space they needed and where their entranceways and exitways would be." She also wrote and drew comic books for herself and her friends, and eventually began to draw cartoons and film them with a Super 8 camera. On her family's regular trips to Disney World, "I would always try to go behind the scenes to find out who was creating and controlling all this."

Film composer James Newton Howard also escaped from childhood problems into creativity: "I was in tremendous conflict with my father. My mother did her best to protect me from him, but she couldn't really. And I think that when I heard music, when my grandmother would play the piano, or when I heard my mom playing certain records, or I heard the radio, it felt like a wonderful, protective bubble that I could go in. It was a way I experienced joy, and I don't think I experienced a lot of joy as a child."

For most of our filmmakers, the creative path they took was shaped not only by their overall childhood environments but also by chance moments and serendipitous discoveries. Despite John Lasseter's combination of innate inclination and creatively supportive life experiences, for example, his talents might not have found such an appropriate outlet if he hadn't come across a book in his high school library during his freshman year. "I found *The Art of Animation*, by Bob Thomas. I opened it up, started thumbing through it, and there was this realization. It was, like, 'Wait a minute! People make cartoons for a living.' I'd never considered that people actually do that. And it was, like, 'That's it! That's perfect.' I knew that's what I wanted to do."

Perhaps you remember having loved specific creative activities as a child, but for whatever reason didn't develop or pursue those interests. Maybe you just didn't have the right chance encounter with a library book or a friend's tape recorder that enabled your innate propensities to crystalize. You may now be feeling a longing to experience a child's creative joy again, or experiencing a lack of satisfaction in another pursuit or career path. If you are questioning whether you might have overlooked a course in life that would be more rewarding, you would not be unusual. Even our filmmakers who described vivid childhood predispositions did not necessarily follow a direct path into filmmaking.

In fact, Kimberly Peirce set out to be a photojournalist and got a job with *Time* magazine, only to discover that it "didn't seem right." Walter Murch at first planned to be an architect, then an oceanographer. He next turned to art history and romance languages. During a junior year abroad in Paris in 1963, at the height of New Wave cinema, he "got infected with the film bug" and applied to the University of Southern California for graduate school, but without any expectation of working in sound. "I did not make the connection with sound until I learned that the soundtrack of a film was a fabricated thing, that it didn't just automatically come with the picture. You can take things out of context and run things backwards and upside down—it is a very manipulable art, the core of which I was already familiar with from my preteen experiences."

Kathy Baker, despite her decision at age five to become an actor and her years taking acting classes and performing in school plays, "also wanted to be a wife and mother, and I didn't know how to exactly do that." She decided to keep her dream of a career in acting "in my secret heart." After majoring in French at Berkeley, she studied cooking at Le Cordon Bleu in Paris, but found herself still taking acting roles whatever else she was doing. "It's always been kind of in spite of myself that I continued to act." The turning point came when she was about to start a job at a San Francisco restaurant. That very morning "I'm reading the paper, and there's a notice: 'Audition at The Magic Theatre.' I go, 'Hmm, Kathy, you're about to be thirty, you always wanted to be an actor, why don't you just go to that audition first.' I go to the audition, get the damn job, and I never made it to the restaurant." At that point, she said, " 'Okay, okay, God, I get it. I'm supposed to be an actor. I *will* be an actor.' And I do invoke God, or a higher power, that I have to do what I was meant to do."

Cinematographer Conrad Hall's discovery of creative filmmaking was even more serendipitous since he started as a journalism major at USC, "to see if there were any genes rattling around from my father, who was a novelist and wrote a lot of books. I found out very quickly that there weren't." Paging through the liberal arts and sciences catalog, he stopped, more out of curiosity than anything else, when he came to the listing for cinema. He enrolled in a class taught by the legendary montagist Slavko Vorkapich. Conrad recalls that Vorkapich "engendered in us the sense that we were involved in an art form, that we were not businessmen out to make money. He was not teaching us how to be a cameraman or director or editor, but how to tell stories visually." Conrad remembers doing a class exercise "in overlapping action and editing, a [Sergei] Eisenstein-ish kind of endeavor. And when I put this together and saw it on the screen, it struck me that I'd found a new language for myself. It was overwhelming."

You may still be thinking as you read this chapter "I don't think I displayed any 'mysterious predisposition' in my childhood and I haven't yet had any revelation as an adult. Maybe I just don't have what it takes to be a creative filmmaker." Yet several of our filmmakers had no clues to their creative focus until they were already well on their way to other careers. Although chance still played a role in their discoveries, it was chance fed by their restless seeking for more satisfying creative outlets and their willingness to try new paths. Editor Lisa Fruchtman majored in the history and philosophy of science at the University of Chicago, then found in film an "escape from who I was at the time. I was very intellectual, very academic. Filmmaking meant exploring a more playful side of myself." It was the early '70s, and Lisa thought that getting involved in making socially conscious documentaries would be a good outlet for her strong political feelings. After starting out at the National Film Board of Canada, she moved to San Francisco and fell into work as an assistant editor on *The Godfather, Part II*. Gradually, she found to her surprise "that editing utilized a particular kind of brain that I have, an odd combination of analytic and creative. It's not the same as the writer facing the blank page. It's more a talent for recombining existing elements and making something new. It's a talent I didn't know I had, but once I discovered it, it was exhilarating."

James Newton Howard knew from childhood that he wanted to be a musician, but his love of film composing took him completely by surprise. "I had done so many things in the music world. I knew I wasn't going to be a concert pianist, even though I was a pretty good one. I had toured with rock and roll bands, I'd produced records, I'd been a session musician, I had orchestrated." But it seemed like no specific area was just the right fit. James had never considered film music, or even been a fan of the genre, until by chance he was offered a scoring job. "When I started to write for the very first scene I ever did, I experienced the same kind of exhilaration I had felt when I was kid. I really, at that moment, felt home, felt connected to some locked-up part of me that just was liberated. But why I felt that kind of connection is still a complete mystery to me."

James Newton Howard looking over scoring sheets at a recording session

Documentary editor Kate Amend had been a college humanities and women's studies teacher for five years when she experienced a life-changing moment of realization. Feeling creatively restless, she had signed up for an introductory film course at the City College of San Francisco. "And one night, editing my five-minute Super 8 film, I had an epiphany that I had never been so happy in my life, sitting there splicing this film together." Kate remembers from that night "the kind of concentration and focus where you lose yourself in something. That really happened to me for the first time ever—'I've been doing this for hours and I haven't even noticed.' You're outside of time, just totally focused on the creative process, making something exist that didn't exist before." Kate took the bold step of quitting her teaching job and moving to Los Angeles to look for film work.

You may have experienced similar feelings in your life of being so engrossed in a creative activity, your attention so sharply focused, that you felt extraordinarily unself-conscious and only intermittently aware of time passing. You probably found this sense of "losing yourself" enjoyable, even exhilarating. Researchers have actually studied this state in people, and see it as one of the key aspects of being creative. If you have had these experiences, they may give you some insight into the kind of work that will most appeal to you.

Although our filmmakers may have taken circuitous routes, they all found an area of creativity that they knew was right for them because it made them feel exhilarated and passionate. Jeannine Oppewall told us of a particularly powerful moment of recognition during her first job as a production designer, on *Tender Mercies:* "When I was almost done with it, I had an experience that you go looking for in your life but you know it's only going to happen once or twice, a moment where everything is a metaphor for your internal condition. I was driving past these flat Texas fields with their winter wheat and cotton plumage, and the road rose up to go over a railroad bed. It was very misty and foggy, but there was a bright sunrise coming through a big dead tree. That intense beauty was coupled with the sense of 'Now I'm done with the first movie, and I'm doing what comes naturally to me.' It was one of those immediate moments of intense ephemeral happiness."

Finding a field that can spark your own feelings of passion and exhilaration often requires trying a number of different paths, and some risk-taking, but once you feel creatively excited by what you are doing, you have the first key to creativity "from the inside out." No one feels that excitement all the time—even the most creative work will involve aspects that are taxing and tedious, times that are frustrating and lacking in inspiration. But when you're doing work that is right for you, the periods of intense concentration, the moments of clarity and synthesis, the joy of making something where there was nothing, will more than compensate.

The discovery of work that seems right doesn't mean "end of story." Each new project brings a search for new surprises and challenges. You may even find that life experiences eventually lead you to fresh paths of creativity and new career directions. Coauthor Doe Mayer, after working in Hollywood for many years, visited Africa in 1980 and the trip changed her life. Two years later she went back to Zimbabwe and lived there until 1985, learning how to use media for social change on issues like health, education and women's rights, work that she loves and has specialized in ever since.

Following a similar but more inwardly turning trajectory, Pamela Douglas, after a successful and satisfying career as a television writer, found herself wanting to turn to more deeply personal themes and different forms of writing. When her daughter left for college, she felt herself moving "into the next portion of life, which for many women is very energizing. I've got a lot more time for my own work, I've got a lot of energy, I'm still young and I know much more than I did before." When Pamela began to mine the characters and events she remembered from growing up in New York City, she realized she wanted the stronger authorial voice that prose can offer. *Twigs and Ashes,* a book of fictional linked stories, resulted. "It turned out, oddly, not to be for the screen. That is a twist that I never would have predicted."

No matter what your own creative propensities may be, these examples from our filmmakers should encourage you to develop an openness and responsiveness to what you feel within, and a readiness to explore the opportunities and possibilities that life presents.

Finding the Resonance:
Choosing the Stories You Want to Tell

Finding the kind of creative work you want to do is the first step, but just the first step, in the creative process. We next look at how, as a filmmaker, you must consider what stories you want to tell, what characters and situations, themes and values, structures and genres, questions and mysteries, speak to you, resonate with who you are, challenge you and allow you to stretch creatively.

This doesn't just apply to writers and directors. We believe that in all the major creative roles, filmmakers must be able to draw on their own experiences, tastes, values and concerns if they are to do their best work. Italian cinematographer Vittorio Storaro has described his creative process as "trying to express something within me: my sensibility, my cultural heritage, my formation of being. . . . I am trying to have a parallel story to the actual story so that through the light and color you can feel and understand, consciously or unconsciously, much more clearly what the story is about." If the potential for those resonances can't be discovered somewhere in the screenplay or the footage, it may be a project to turn down. Once you have committed to a project, it will occupy your creative life for months or years to come, represent yourself to others, and influence the opportunities that will come to you later. As Walter Murch notes, "the die is cast when you say 'I will do this film.' "

Kimberly Peirce believes that "you always have to find yourself in the material. To personalize the story, you have to find the point where your through-line, the movie's and the characters' through-lines intersect." This may sound more limiting than it actually is. At Columbia University's graduate film school, Kimberly found that intuitively she personalized everything she worked on. "We had to bring scenes in, whether it was Shakespeare, or Tennessee Williams, or scenes from movies. And you'd be directing this scene, and all of a sudden you'd realize, 'Oh, my God, it's my story.' You'd always manage to position the actors and position the needs so that the story reflected exactly what you were going through at the time."

The subject matter of her first feature, *Boys Don't Cry,* the true story of a young woman, Teena Brandon, who took on the identity of a young man, Brandon Teena, connected to her own sense of being "very independent, very queer, and very much coming off a whole new articulation of my identity. It was the intersection where my personal myth met Brandon's personal myth." The fact that she found Brandon's story to be extraordinarily personal doesn't mean that it was necessarily autobiographical. "We vibrate to certain things, right? I like Jimi Hendrix, or I like Bob Dylan, or I like Neil Young—I like the way they vibrate. They just make me feel right. Well, that's what I need to gravitate to, and that's what I mean by 'personal.'"

Similarly, editor Lisa Fruchtman told us "I always have to find the resonance in myself in order to want to do a film. I'm drawn to some stories and not to others. To explain why, I'd have to go into all the details of who I am." She believes that finding that resonance allowed her to do well when she was just starting as an editor. Working as an assistant on *Apocalypse Now,* Lisa asked for and was given a difficult section of the film to edit herself in her spare time, in addition to her assisting duties. She spent months cutting and recutting it before writer-producer-director Francis Ford Coppola finally approved what she had done and made her one of the film's editors.

Lisa remembers the long process of that first editing assignment: "I'd try this and that. I was almost the monkey at the keyboard. But behind that was a trust that I would know when it finally got to be good, although I didn't know how to get there efficiently. I had that confidence because I connected to the film, to the literal story about Vietnam because I was political, and to the aesthetic vision of what Francis had shot. It was very powerful material, very emotional, very visual. I was able to use those feelings at a time when I didn't have as much craft." By contrast, Lisa believes that if she had tried, at that time, to edit "something like *Die Hard,* pure style or pure action, I wouldn't have been able to do it, because I wouldn't have had any guiding light."

As teachers, we strongly encourage developing filmmakers to find projects they feel passionately about, to discover, in the words of Indian-born filmmaker Mira Nair, "subjects that get under my skin and make my heart beat faster." Willard Motomura, one of coauthor Jed Dannenbaum's graduate students, recounted in the final journal for his second-semester short film project that in advance of the course he had first scripted a dark comedy "that received positive reactions when I told my friends about it." But at the initial class meeting, when Jed suggested that everyone ask themselves "Am I in love with this project? Do I feel deeply engaged with it and passionate about making it?," Willard had known immediately that he wasn't passionate about his comedy. A different story, with "a very personal theme" came to him. "I sat down in front of my computer, turned out the script, and called my mother to tell her about it. The decision to make this film was the best decision I made all semester. My passion also informed my decision-making when it came down to actually shooting and editing the film."

RENEE TAJIMA-PEÑA, documentary director-producer

Most times, I'm really pissed off and that's why I make a movie. I was pissed off about race, probably from the time I was very young. It really just drove everything I did. So I made films dealing with race.

Everywhere I look, something pisses me off. A few years ago, I decided to focus on economic inequality in this era of great prosperity, which is why I'm doing things on poor working families. Here in L.A., I visited a local high school, and they literally could not even find a bench under a tree for me to do my interviews, because they had classes going on in the cafeteria, they had classes going on in the library. They had to kick out the special education class from this little room in the counseling office so I could do these interviews, and it pissed me off, the conditions they had to teach and learn in.

More personally, my husband's mother Rosa lived with us while she was dying of lung cancer. She was just the funniest, most wonderful woman you could ever want to meet. She had worked as a farm worker, she had worked ironing clothes, she had cleaned offices, she always had three jobs at a time, and she raised seven boys on her own. There were no pensions, and half the time they were not jobs that took social security. She just worked all her life. She was an American citizen, born here, and just died really with nothing of her own from all those years of working. When she died, we found a coupon book of food stamps she had held on to. I guess she figured maybe one of us could use it later on. I think that experience of being with her, and just knowing what she went through and then seeing her die the way she died, it really got to me. It just pissed me off, that that can happen in America. So after that, I decided I'm going to focus on women like Rosa.

> "Everywhere I Look, Something Pisses Me Off"

As a creative filmmaker, you not only put something of yourself into any film that you make, but the film in turn becomes part of you, has an impact on you just as it has an impact on an audience, but even more profound because you will spend weeks, months, even years immersed in it. Lisa adds that although she now has the craft to edit any kind of movie, even ones that have no resonance for her, "I don't choose to. I've been offered lots of movies that either I don't respond to at all or I'm offended by them. I just don't want to engage with them. I don't want to lend my talents to them or live in their world for a year, a world that becomes your world, that becomes your dream life, that takes over your brain. I only want to do that with something that's going to nurture me, and give me something back. My collaboration is not only with the director and other editors, but also with the material."

If you are starting out in the film industry, you might feel a necessity to take any job offered. In addition to paying monthly bills, you may have student loans as well. Yet as hard as it may be to turn down credits and money when you're just beginning—or once you're more established, for that matter—it might just be that saying "no" to a disagreeable project or leaving a soul-damaging job could turn out to be the best thing you could do for yourself. Editor Kate Amend, struggling to get work in Los Angeles, first found a job at a sound post-production facility. "One day they asked me to do cue sheets for an ADR (automatic dialogue replacement) session. It was a horrible exploitation film, a rape scene, and I thought, 'What am I doing here?' That was a Wednesday and I quit that job on Friday." Instead, she took a job editing a documentary for deferred pay, and it turned out that her credit as editor on that film "just led to one job after another."

Avoiding projects that are toxic is not to say that we should look for stories to tell that are easy and comfortable. It is also important to find work that makes us stretch creatively and emotionally. Kate herself has edited documentaries on the criminally insane, skinhead racists, and the pornography industry. "Someone once called me the Diane Arbus of editors," she jokes. But in each of those films, she found a chance to get at "serious, complex human questions" that in turn connect to her personal values: "I was always taught to be tolerant and compassionate. That was definitely a family value."

In these topics Kate found a chance to humanize difficult or hard to understand situations: "How can you try to explain this or make it accessible, and do it in a way that people are engaged and want to watch the film? *Skinheads, USA* is about a group of young boys that were sort of adopted by a former Ku Klux Klan leader. He took in wayward boys, runaways, and then indoctrinated them into his racism and his hate-filled philosophies. So the director, Shari Cookson, and I decided to approach this story from the point of view of these young boys. In fact, in the editing room we nicknamed them the Lost Boys. We tried to show that they were troubled, vulnerable kids being manipulated by this guy."

Immersing oneself in painful material isn't easy. "Living with footage of skinheads for six months was not pleasant. And (for *The Long Way Home* and *Into the Arms of Strangers: Stories of the Kindertransport*), looking at Nazi concentration camp footage over and over and over again—that's really a tough, tough subject. I'm still not immune to seeing that footage. I try to forget about it when I come home, but that doesn't always happen. I do dream about the characters in the films I'm working on." Because of her awareness that she is expressing values important to her, Kate finds tackling these stories worthwhile and rewarding. She also finds them challenging, since, as she notes, "most of the films I've worked on are about people who have had experiences so different from mine. I can't imagine what it's like to go to Auschwitz, or to give your children away."

As an actor, Kathy Baker also knows she has to find a way to humanize the characters she plays. People have told her that Mrs. Peters, her bizarre, darkly comic role on the television series *Boston Public,* is " 'creepy.' Well, I think she's great. She might not be my choice for Mother of the Year, or someone I would want as a best friend. But I always have to find a way to like the person that I play." She seeks that connection through "three basic things about them: their sexuality, their intelligence and their sense of humor."

How, as filmmakers working from the inside out, do we find connections to characters, stories and worlds that are quite distant from our own lives? If the material is totally unfamiliar, we may feel there is little to draw on to make our work authentic. On the other hand, if we stay within the narrow range of what we have personally experienced, the range of stories we can tell may start to feel restrictive or stale. Editor and sound designer Walter Murch told us he seeks material balanced between these two extremes. When he reads a script "to decide if I want to do it, I'm looking for things that resonate with me as a person, but don't resonate too much. You want to sense that you are going to be challenged in your assumptions because that's what makes you grow as an artist and a technician. We want to both reveal ourselves and also grow in the process of doing that. If either of those are stunted, you are not well served by the projects you choose and they aren't well served by you, either because it's too on the mark or because it's not anywhere near the mark. You want something that harmonizes."

Coauthor Carroll Hodge recognizes that she has found this harmony in her filmmaking by drawing on a resonant theme of her childhood: her attempts to embrace both the French and English worlds of her home in culturally divided Quebec, Canada. In both her documentary and fictional work, she has chosen projects that repeat this theme, but in a setting less familiar and even more challenging: Alaska, with its divide between indigenous and non-native communities.

Creative filmmaking is *not* synonymous with autobiographical filmmaking. Still, we find that many beginning filmmakers err on the side of choosing stories that have little or no resonance to their own lives. Although we agree with Walter's caution about too much familiarity, we think that finding substantial resonance is where most filmmakers need to place their emphasis. Walter himself listed for us the many connections that drew him to signing on as the editor and sound designer of *The English Patient:* "I was attracted partly because my mother was a Canadian born in Sri Lanka, and Michael Ondaatje [author of the novel *The English Patient*] is a Sri Lankan who has become a Canadian. I speak Italian and I'm interested in Italy, the setting for a major part of the story. I'm very interested in issues of time shifting. It's just a very provocative thing for me. *Godfather, Part II, Julia* and *The English Patient* are all films that have quite challenging time structures, *The English Patient* probably more than the other two put together. I liked [director] Anthony Minghella. I'd worked before with [producer] Saul Zaentz on *The Unbearable Lightness of Being.* That's another thing. Do you like the people you will be working with? It just seemed to be a very rich arena. It also had some questions that I was anxious to know the answer to. Why did these two people fall in love? Why did Katherine Clifton and Almásy have this 'boing' moment where they fell in love? What is that? That's the way I fell in love with my wife also, so there's that issue of how do those moments happen and what does that mean?"

In an intriguing comparison, Anthony Minghella described to us some of the reasons behind his involvement as the screenwriter and director of the same movie. For him, it began with a love of Michael Ondaatje's poetry and, later, his novels. "I'd saved up *The English Patient* as a present to myself, and I read it in one go. The last thing I was doing was looking for a job, but there was an absolute certainty in my mind, well before I'd finished reading it, that I wanted to get involved with it in some way, a greedy feeling of wanting to attach myself to this beautiful thing."

Why did the novel strike such a chord? Anthony believes that *"The English Patient* fed all kinds of interests I have, not least the fact that it was essentially a poem disguised as a novel, and was enormously lyrical. And when I finally met Michael, I realized there were great similarities in our tastes, our sensibilities, and the way that we look at the world." Anthony compares Michael's background as "an uprooted Sri Lankan who's become a Canadian via England" to his own

Anthony Minghella, far left, on the set of *The English Patient*, actress Kristin Scott Thomas (Katherine) in the foreground

"rather over-elaborated sense of being a foreigner in England." That outsider perspective, he thinks, also fed their mutual concern with nationalism, a major theme in both the book and the movie.

Finally, Anthony wanted to pursue his fascination with private behavior "as it is impacted by what's going on in the public landscape outside the window. And I'm interested in what's going on outside, but only as mediated through what's happening in the private world." Michael Ondaatje had etched those connections into the language of the novel, and Anthony was eager to find an equivalent cinematic grammar where "you can cut from the place on a woman's neck to a desert landscape, and it's perfectly agreeable syntax."

Although the specifics are different, both Walter and Anthony mention remarkably similar areas of resonance—family history, cultural background, personal interests, aspects of aesthetics, collaborative considerations, and a sense of connection to the story's thematic questions—that influenced their desire to become part of *The English Patient*. We want to stress that the impact of these personal connections does not stop with the decision to sign on to a project. Rather, the unique fit between a filmmaker's individual contours and those of a film are what end up shaping the film creatively. Anthony concludes: "I know that any version of *The English Patient* that somebody else made would be completely different from mine, even if they were as intoxicated as I was by the book. When I've said that for me filmmaking is personal, it's not that I want to announce how personal these films are, they just are personal, by default."

Our filmmakers, throughout this book, present a somewhat idealized picture, focusing on their best experiences as professionals, but all of them have worked on projects that turned out to be far less fulfilling. Nor can filmmakers starting out their careers expect to find an entry-level position on a film anywhere near as outstanding as *Apocalypse Now,* as happened with Lisa, especially given the realities of the industry today. But in the long run, we have seen that filmmakers who set their own creative priorities and then have the courage to stick to them usually find a more satisfying career path than those who don't.

Producer Ismail Merchant told us that he has gotten offers to make lucrative projects, "exploitation films filled with violence and special effects," and has turned them all down. "Even if someone gave me $20 million as a fee to produce, I would say no to it because there is no meaning to the story. And therefore, there is no excitement for me, no challenge." He and his longtime collaborators director James Ivory and writer Ruth Prawer Jhabvala are personally drawn to stories with subjects such as "the influence of one culture over another culture, the understanding or misunderstanding between two cultures—that has always been a recurring theme in our films." One result of following their own tastes as filmmakers is that their work has developed a loyal audience that has consistently supported their long career of more than twenty features.

Kathy Baker chooses what roles to take "based on the script first, then the director, then the other actors. I never say to myself, 'What's the medium?' or 'How much is it going to make?' " But her way into the story or the character may be quite small and specific: "Robert De Niro said to me 'If you can find one line in the script that means something to you, and that you connect with, take a look at it. Maybe from there it will grow.' But there does have to be a connection. And sometimes you follow your instinct and say no. Listen to your heart and you'll know the ones not to do."

A Private World: *Drawing on Personal Memories*

At the stage of choosing to sign on to a specific project, filmmakers (including screenwriters taking on adaptations or true stories) are responding to elements that already exist in those stories. But once you are actively working on a film, regardless of the creative capacity, you can add new connections, embedding references to your own life experiences in ways that will strengthen the resonance of the material you are working with. New Zealand–born writer-director Jane Campion, for example, has said that she likes to place images in her films that are based on her own early personal memories: "I remember me standing here, or I remember the light, I remember the feel of grass on my legs. I always feel terribly secure if I have an image as basic or as fundamental to myself as that in a movie . . . so that I don't feel that what I'm making up I saw in another movie somewhere." It is this sense of authenticity that is most important to her about these images—she knows that "they are definitely yours, there's nothing derivative about them."

These personal memories can add emotional depth and authenticity without being at all autobiographical in their film context. Glen Keane, the supervising animator of *Tarzan,* has described working on the scene where Tarzan sees Jane for the first time: "It's a 'flesh of my flesh, bone of my bone moment' . . . I remember thinking, 'When have I really felt this in my own life?' I met my wife, Linda, in a line at a movie, and it wasn't that kind of a moment, with that element of self-discovery. Then I remembered holding my daughter Claire when she was just thirty seconds old. This tiny little baby was so soft, I felt like she could melt off either side of my hand. I was just awestruck, looking at her face and seeing the reflection of myself in her.

Jeannine Oppewall's mother's butterfly tray

When I animated Tarzan's eyes in that scene, it wasn't Tarzan looking at Jane, it was me looking at my newborn daughter."

Personal memories can be as central to the film as the original inspiration for the screenplay, or they might be as subtle as the source of a single piece of set dressing. When production designer Jeannine Oppewall was a child, she remembers that she would often look at "a glass tray of embedded butterflies that my mother had collected as a kid and won a prize for as a science project. I thought it was beautiful because I could look through the glassware and see these gorgeous insects. In the film *Corrina, Corrina*, I brought that butterfly tray from my house for a scene in a dining room where this little girl is hiding out from the adult world. She's under the table, just peering out at legs to see what she can see. Something really terrible has happened in her life that she's trying to come to terms with. Whether you see it or not, that tray is in the movie. That's something special for me."

Jeannine sees herself as working "out of the same place that an actor acts or a writer writes, out of some deeply personal set of private experiences that you can and you must share. It's the same instinct in each craft, it's just differentiated." She now puts "butterflies here and there in every movie I work on. It's a way of remembering my mother, my family and who I am. I'm bringing who I am to the film and that's the only way I know how to work."

Bits of personal history may enhance our creative process by opening up emotional connections that better enable us to tap into our intuitive processes. They also strengthen our sense of "co-ownership" of a film by leaving our personal mark hidden in it, a discreet version of Alfred Hitchcock's brief appearances onscreen in the movies he directed. Anthony Minghella used family names for the names of the cafes in *The Talented Mr. Ripley*. He notes that these intimate references "have meaning to me. The fact that they don't communicate that meaning elsewhere is irrelevant. They give me a kind of sense of verisimilitude." At the same time, sometimes these obscure references paradoxically create an emotional response in the audience, even if their literal meanings are not "understood," because of the lifelike specificity they convey.

"Any Experience, Good or Bad, Informs an Actor"

KATHY BAKER, actor

I once had the idea, for some reason, that my character would wear a high-school ring. And so, I wore my own high-school ring. I don't know why, but it helped. I do stuff like that sometimes, little stuff. On *Picket Fences,* I had to have diplomas on the wall, and I said, "Can I pick the middle name?" And I picked "Langley"—it's the maiden name of a friend of mine, and it meant something to me to have it read "Jill Langley Brock." It was a little thing that no one else would know.

Any experience, good or bad, informs an actor. I'm always doing "as if." Some examples of doing that are a little too private, the sad ones. But a simple one would be on *Picket Fences*—when we started, my kids in the show, Zack and Matthew, were seven and twelve. And my own children were five years apart, two and seven. With [actors] Adam [Wylie] and Justin [Shenkarow], all I had to do was just pour out "Mom stuff." The crew used to say, "Oh, we love to watch you when you do the scenes with the kids, it's so fun." I'm, like, "oh, I'm just being Mom—I miss my own kids, and I'm just pouring everything into them."

With crying, or sadness, or anger, you have to go to some awful places in your past, that you don't want to have to go to. There are a couple of things in my past that I won't use. It's just not right. I will not sully that, even in my worst times of feeling "Oh, my God, I can't cry in this scene." That's sacred. It happened, but I'm not going to use it.

I am not particularly an addictive personality. So, when I had to play a coke addict for *Clean and Sober,* I asked my husband—I had never done coke, still have never done coke—and I said, "Well, gosh, I guess I better try coke, huh?" He said, "Well, you just played a prostitute in *Street Smart,* and you didn't . . . you know." So, I said "well, real seriously, what is an addiction that I've had?" You just have to think of something you couldn't live without. For me, it would be love. And that's in all the different forms you can think of.

For characters that are really hard for me to find, I almost always need to pick somebody that I either know, or whom I've watched. For Mrs. Peters on *Boston Public,* it was really hard for me to find "icy." David [E. Kelley, the show's creator and executive producer] had written the stage direction "icy." And I was convinced that I was not a person who came off as icy, and that I wouldn't be able to do it very well. It turned out, of course, that she had a lot more colors, and David didn't really want *just* that one color, but he *did* want "icy." I ended up using someone I know who is icy. And the painful thing is, I have to think about that person a lot now doing the role.

Audiences recognize the emotional touchstones of real life, and that authenticity helps to counteract the inherent artificiality of moviemaking, reducing clichés and stereotypes. When Pamela Douglas wrote *Different Worlds,* a story of interracial love, she drew directly on personal memories of her own mixed background: "It was very, very important to me that I get it right, that the stereotypes not be there. I had to explore this very honestly in my own mind, in terms of what I had heard people say, and have the guts to write it down. That was life research, voices I had really heard in my own life experience." Pamela's phrase "life research" captures an important aspect of this process: we often have to dig deeply into ourselves to uncover the most telling and resonant memories (the *limberings* can help you with this exploration). The familiar stories about ourselves, the ones we have repeated over and over, often lose their emotional intensity and even their authenticity.

Over time we may wonder "did it even happen that way, or has the familiar story entirely replaced the original memory?"

Writers, of course, are well placed to include personal references because they shape the story. But regardless of the creative role, the underlying idea of finding resonance between one's self and the film is the same. When writer Hanif Kureishi describes the real-life experiences that led to his screenplay *My Son, the Fanatic,* his list is surprisingly similar in essence to the one Walter Murch gave in describing his connections to *The English Patient.* Hanif mentions "the *fatwa* (death edict) against Salman Rushdie which made me think about fundamentalism and Islam. There was a trip I made to Pakistan in the early '80s, which was my first visit to a theocratic state. There was also a trip I made in England to Birmingham, where I found that the prostitutes and the Muslim fundamentalists were living in the same part of town and not getting on well together. I've often thought about and written about fathers and sons before, but I wrote this script after my first two children, twins, were born, and so it was the first time that I wrote *as* a father, as opposed to being a son. That was quite a big change for me. I felt that I had a number of elements that kind of suited me at that time, and so with those bits I sat down and started to write, to experiment, to see whether there was a story there."

Om Puri as the father and Akbar Kurtha as the son in *My Son, the Fanatic*

As Hanif's reference to the recurrent theme of fathers and sons in his work makes clear, some of the "bits" of our lives that we weave into our films may draw on potentially painful themes. Hanif suspects that for him "fathers represent all kinds of fears and inhibitions. It may or may not be the case that my father frightened me—he certainly did in some ways—but there are certain wishes he had for me and other wishes he didn't. And I think that writing about my father was very important to me as a writer. And then, writing as a father after he died was very important to me and gave me a new point of view. I could become a father once my own father was gone."

Just as Kate Amend found with the dark subjects she has been drawn to, these deep personal themes are difficult to deal with, yet creatively productive. Hanif believes that often "we are creative because we suffer. Somehow, creativity makes sense of suffering, and our suffering is something that we share with other people in order not to feel so alone." He recognizes that "writing can feel incredibly transgressive. Maybe it should be transgressive, to a certain extent." Transgressive art intends to challenge, provoke and disturb conventional or comfortable ways of thinking and feeling. A filmmaker entering this kind of territory often encounters internal as well as external resistance. Hanif has discovered that such transgressions "can make you feel very fearful of revenge from your friends, from your family, from other imagined enemies. They're usually your parents' voices, and your fantasies of your friends' reactions, people from school, other filmmakers, other novelists, whatever." He finds that with his own writing students, "it's not that the kids are not creative, it's really that their creativity is blocked by their terrors, which come mostly from other adults who they think will punish them for speaking the truth."

These fears are accentuated if we are portraying real people in our films (even if they are partially fictionalized). Then we must also wrestle with complex questions about our responsibilities as ethical artists and human beings. We may even have to get to a certain point in our lives before we can delve fully into these darker themes. Pamela Douglas grew up in a family where "we had problems with not having enough to eat. I'd keep sugar cubes in my pocket because if I started to faint from hunger, I could suck on the sugar cubes." In recent years, she has found that for the first time in her life, she can write about her childhood: "I don't think that when I was younger I could have handled a lot of these subjects. I didn't handle them. But you come to peace with yourself, and the things that you might have been embarrassed to write or talk about, finally, who cares what anybody thinks? I've let go of preconceptions about what you're supposed to write and what you're allowed to write."

Deeply personal aspects of our lives can embed themes in our work that we may be only partly aware of, or recognize after the fact. Renee Tajima-Peña's older brother was killed by a hit-and-run driver when she was twenty. Now in retrospect she realizes that one response to his death has been to ask through her filmmaking "how people respond to a tragedy like that. I think in every film I've done, somebody has been changed by the death of a young man. It's such an intense loss, because you know what might have been. So somehow, you find others who have been through the same thing. I don't know if I'm doing it consciously or unconsciously at this point." She also believes that the losses she has experienced in her life feed her creative energy and drive. "I've seen a lot of people die, so I know life doesn't last too long. I have a very keen appreciation for the finite moments in life and I just don't want to waste it."

James Newton Howard thinks that his painful longings in childhood and adolescence have shaped his strengths as a composer. "I write about all the things I didn't have. I was painfully lonely as a kid, so I think I can write music that deals with aloneness effectively. I also think I'm particularly good at writing love themes because, as an adolescent, I was so completely screwed up that I never really enjoyed a great relationship with a girl." James still carries in his head a fantasy of a kind of perfect rite of passage into young manhood that would have involved meeting and falling in love with a beautiful girl when he was sixteen. "I'm very happily married, I have incredibly great kids. But there's a part of me that still is very much in a yearning kind of place, still in love with the ideal of the young woman I never met when I was in high school. So, that's easy for me to write. It's a wellspring of past experience that is still very much alive in me, and the way I contact it is through music."

You may be fortunate enough to have not experienced an unhappy childhood or a deeply painful loss in your life. Yet everyone has felt moments of grief, anger, jealousy, arrogance, fear, revenge, defeat, shame, longing, rage, rejection, envy, guilt—all the dark emotions that humans struggle with. These are the emotions at the center of most stories, even comedies. Of course they are usually set in contrast to love, trust, selflessness, compassion, tolerance, generosity, courage, and the other emotional traits we see as noble and honorable. You won't be able to connect deeply to the story, however, unless you can bring a recognition of your own shadow emotions to the creative process.

When Conrad Hall read the script for *American Beauty,* his first reaction was that he didn't like the dysfunctional characters. When he voiced his concern, he recalls director Sam Mendes responding "Well, Conrad, just examine your own soul, your own psyche. Aren't there dark corners in there that you think about, but don't necessarily act upon?" Conrad was able to remind himself that "we all are filled with these dark corners. And as soon as I had that in mind, then I could get to like the characters even if they were dysfunctional, because the way they behave is fascinating."

As we begin to recognize, through introspection, our own creative finger-prints, we also see that our unique personal history is inextricably inter-woven with the culture and history of the era we grew up in and the broader questions of identity we face. Hanif, for example, remembers that in the England of his youth in the 1960s, he felt the cultural impact of rock musi-cians like the Beatles, the Rolling Stones, the Who and Jimi Hendrix. They shaped in him a desire "to be a writer who was like a musician." He also found that the writers he connected with were "mostly Americans, actually. Kerouac, Roth, Bellow, Mailer, Salinger particularly, Sylvia Plath. The loony ones—Anne Sexton, those kind of people. They saw society from the out-side in some way. They were Jewish, they were gay, they were adolescent, they were rebels—the characters, too. Holden Caulfield in *The Catcher in the Rye*. You think, 'That's me, pal.' " These reflections of his experience as a Pakistani-British outsider in turn influenced his desire to write about life "the way that it is, not only the good bits, but failure, conflict, unhappiness, death, decay, which is part of our humanity as well."

A painting in our childhood home or music we first loved as a teenager may play a different, more emotional and deeply rooted role in our creativity than research we do in the pres-ent (which we look at as part of **Inquiry** in the next chapter). Reading *The Catcher in the Rye* because you are about to make a film about adolescence is not the same as having read it at a key formative moment in the past. Renee, for example, remembers coming across a collection of plays in her family's bookshelves as a pivotal event in her life: "I used to ditch school and go to the beach and just take plays." She became a voracious reader and soon discovered specific works

Renee Tajima-Peña as a child visiting the Statue of Liberty with her family

that spoke to her deeply, including a particularly intense connection to Jack Kerouac's novel *On the Road*. Her experience as an Asian-American seemed related to Kerouac's persona as "an outsider who nevertheless had this in-credible love of America. I thought 'it's almost like an Asian-American book,' because I always felt like I was an outsider, especially in the sixties when my family would travel around the country and we'd be the only Asian family on the road. But I just loved going out into America. My father used to pack us into the Ford or the Buick and take us all over. That's how I discovered America as a child."

Kerouac's book and Renee's associations with it became the emotional and structural touchstone for her documentary *My America . . . or, Honk if You Love Buddha,* an on-the-road exploration of Asian-American identity and diversity. Renee discovered that part of her voice as a filmmaker is to find "literary kinds of sources to shape the making of documentaries. There's probably this library somewhere in my head or in my heart, just waiting to be made into documentaries."

It's worth noting that for a documentary filmmaker like Renee, drawing on her own voice is just as central to her creative process as it is for someone working in fiction. Developing filmmakers sometimes try to embrace the notion that nonfiction filmmaking can or should be a dispassionate, objective recording of reality unaffected by the intercession of the filmmaker. But as documentary filmmaker and film historian Eric Barnouw wrote, "the documentarist makes endless choices. He selects topics, people, vistas, angles, lenses, juxtaposition, sounds, words. Each selection is an expression of his point of view, whether he is aware of it or not, whether he acknowledges it or not."

A central paradox of creating from the inside out is that by working from our own voice and our deeply personal connections to the material, we make films that are profoundly universal. Kimberly Peirce told us that finding the personal meaning "creates the impulse to do what you're going to do, but then the discipline of the craft says, 'okay, good, now let's tell a story that everybody can understand. It's not just my story, it's *the* story.' There are still moments when you suddenly realize what a reflection of yourself it is—you think 'Oh, my God, it's me.' But then the director of photography thinks it's him, so who's to say? It's a multi-refracting mirror, which is kind of great. You're in search of what's in yourself that you find reflected in the world. The mystery is first directed inward, and then it's directed outward."

LIMBERING UP

We have designed each *Limbering Up* to be a short, enjoyable mental stretch, a stimulant to get your mind in a more intimate and spontaneous place. Many can be done in five minutes or less, wherever you happen to be. Let them take you in a direction that feels comfortable for you, and yet has the potential to surprise you—there are no rules or "correct" outcomes.

You may want to try out these limberings as you're reading this book, or you may wish to mark ones to come back to when you're about to engage in creative work. Try recording your responses in a journal or file that can then become a source of future cinematic ideas. And if you are planning or working on a specific film project, you may also wish to try the **Workouts** in Chapter Six.

Before you begin any of these limberings, close your eyes and breathe deeply for a minute, relaxing your whole body.

1) Rediscovering the Roots of Your Creativity

What memories do you have of being creative as a child? Perhaps you remember making up stories, creating imaginary worlds, constructing secret places, performing your own experiments, building contraptions, dressing up in costumes or parent's clothing, or having conversations with your pets. Remember what creative play felt like for you. Do you remember when you stopped doing these things, or why?

For five minutes, do something you used to love to do as a child or take the next opportunity of being with a young child, and really play. Pull out the crayons or paints, sing songs you loved, build bridges out of straws or towers out of cookies. Look at bugs and flowers through a magnifying glass. Consider your reactions to this play. How did it feel? How do you remember it feeling as a child? Might thinking more deeply about your creativity as a child help get you past any obstacles of self-judgment or self-consciousness you feel in the present? Or perhaps give you additional clues about your creative talents and predispositions?

2) "Everywhere I Look, Something Pisses Me Off"

Coauthor Doe Mayer has a bumper sticker on her car that reads "If You're Not Outraged, You're Not Paying Attention." Write down a list of what outrages you. Next to it, write a list of what inspires you. Stick them both up on your refrigerator and add to them from time to time. Include visual images (political cartoons, advertising, stereotyped photos, etc.) that provoke you. If you want, add captions to your selections. Is there anything on these lists—pissed off or inspiring—that might energize you to want to make or work on a film that deals with that topic or issue?

3) Exploring Family Archives

Our old photographs may contain evocative clues to who we are, and were. Take out some family photos that include you as a child—try to find ones that are candid and spontaneous rather than posed. Imagine that you have just found these photographs in a secondhand store and that the people in them are total strangers. If you find this difficult, try squinting your eyes to blur the image and make its subjects less familiar. What information can you glean from such cues as body language, expression, clothing, hairstyle and the proximity of individuals to one another? How similar or dissimilar are you to the child you once were? What characteristics did you (or do you) share with other family members? In what ways were you (or are you) different? Are some of those characteristics reflected in the work you are doing?

4) Going Home

Think of a place from your childhood that felt very familiar and homelike to you then but which you haven't been inside of for years (perhaps your family kitchen, a secret hiding place, a grandparent's porch). Close your eyes and imagine yourself in this space. Go on a slow mental tour, trying to bring to mind the sense details—the sound of your feet in slippers or boots, the texture of your father's unshaven cheek, the color of the wallpaper, the light through a bedroom window, the smell of the inside of a closet. What are the feelings this brings back for you?

If this place were to be recreated as a location in a film, what elements would be essential to capturing its feel? What details would suggest time period, region, class, culture, family structure? Imagine a key scene set in this location. What would be the emotional tone of this scene if the main character were you as a child back then? What would be the tone if the main character were you revisiting this place now?

introspection

two inquiry

intuition

interaction

impact

workout

We've seen in Introspection the creative importance of exploring and drawing on our own lives. But if filmmakers limited themselves to just their own personal stories, filmmaking would be greatly impoverished. On the other hand, when we try to portray people and worlds we have no real knowledge of, the results are almost invariably clichéd and inauthentic. We can bridge this gap through our second "I," **Inquiry,** a combination of our own firsthand observations of the world and our ability to draw from the vast storehouse of shared human knowledge, wisdom and artistic expression.

Good filmmaking at its most fundamental level is, like all art, a reflection on the questions and mysteries that have always most concerned humanity. We are inquisitive and reflective animals—one of our most distinctly human qualities is that we notice the world around us, and wonder why things happen a certain way, why we behave the way we do, why we exist. Over the centuries, as humanity wrestled with such topics as love, morality, spirituality, fate, beauty, evil, death and the true nature of things, its investigations, distilled insights and creative expressions became the fields of study we call the arts, humanities and sciences. Our better educational institutions enhance our grasp of and appreciation for the human response to these questions, and encourage us to form our own conjectures and opinions. In so doing, they prepare us to be more inquisitive thinkers and less formulaic filmmakers. Our chapter on **Inquiry,** therefore, begins with what we call **Breadth of Knowledge:** *A Preparation in the Liberal Arts.*

In **Getting Out of the Car:** *Observation of the World,* we explore the value of being more attentive to the world around us, developing our own distinct response to its texture, nuance and complexity. By becoming close observers of such things as minute gradations of facial expression, gesture, body language, and tone of voice, and by attuning ourselves to the emotional resonance of light, color, space, sound and movement, we will be better able to create on screen a fresh, vivid representation of the human relationships and sensory experiences that surround us.

Finally, in **Doing the Homework:** *Researching a Film,* we see how each project brings new opportunities to expand our knowledge and understanding. As Kate Amend told us, "I'm always interested in research and learning, and I look at every film as an opportunity to learn something about another world, another culture, another subculture, just another pocket of humanity that I wouldn't know anything about."

Developing as a creative filmmaker means continually exciting your curiosity, expanding your range of experience and knowledge, honing your observational powers, and deepening your comprehension of the world around you. This ongoing, lifelong pursuit can keep you feeling fresh about your own work, and creatively inspired and connected to the world. At the same time, inquiry can enrich and guide your creative choices on any specific film you may work on.

Breadth of Knowledge: *A Preparation in the Liberal Arts*

The educational backgrounds of the filmmakers featured in this book are remarkably varied. Lisa Fruchtman majored in the history and philosophy of science; Walter Murch studied art history and romance languages; Renee Tajima-Peña majored in sociology and East Asian studies; Kate Amend studied and taught humanities; Kimberly Peirce earned her B.A. in English and Japanese literature; Hanif Kureishi majored in philosophy; Pamela Douglas studied English, psychology and art; Jeannine Oppewall has a master's degree in medieval studies; Kathy Baker majored in French literature; and Anthony Minghella majored in drama. Coauthor Jed Dannenbaum has a Ph.D. in American history and taught it before becoming a filmmaker.

Prospective students frequently ask us what they should do to prepare for film school. They often expect us to recommend getting more technical experience with cameras or editing systems, or making their own films (which, with the new technology, they have sometimes been making since they were in junior high school or even earlier). Many are surprised when we encourage them to get a good liberal arts education, to take classes and pursue interests in subjects other than film, and we suggest they try to use a variety of media, not just the written word, for their work in all their courses of study. We also encourage broadening their life experiences and deepening their capacity for empathy through some form of activism or volunteer work meaningful to them, and undertaking travel that involves meaningful cultural contact rather than just sightseeing.

Because each person is unique, the ideal preparation will be different in each case. We have worked with outstanding student filmmakers who focused their prior studies on theatre, anthropology, poetry, astronomy, dance, critical studies, history, photography, literature, medicine, art history, music, quantum physics and psychology. Any discipline can provide a framework for creative and analytical thinking that helps us tackle new challenges. Kathy Baker has found that studying a foreign language has strengthened her work as an actor: "When you learn how people form sentences, you also see how they form thoughts." Sound designer Ben Burtt has said that "Success as an artist, to say something new, ultimately depends on the breadth of your education . . . If film is all you know, you cannot help but make derivative work. I found that what I learned about sound, history, biology, English, physics all goes into the mix."

Literature, music and the visual and performance arts are the fields that connect most directly to filmmaking. We too often treat film as a world of its own, rather than think, as writer-producer John Wells does: "I'm involved in the visual arts—cinema and television are visual arts in the same way that photography and painting are—anything that involves the use of space, and presentation through balance in a frame of some sort is a visual art." He is also, of course, a storyteller, and finds that "most of the people that I know in television and in film are voracious readers." Production designer Jeannine Oppewall says that when she comes to a film, "I see it as a part of a long tradition of visual literature that makes a contribution to our cultural history."

John Wells is drawn to naturalism in art, and owns an extensive collection of black-and-white photographs. Composer James Newton Howard is also an art collector, focusing on American abstract impressionists such as Marsden Hartley and Arthur Dove. He doesn't think of this as a highbrow pursuit, and considers himself "the most average, middle-class, unartistic kind of guy in the world." But living with his own collection, he finds, is "like a palate-cleanser. I don't want to listen to music after writing music. I sit in my study and I look at some of these pictures and it does a good thing for me. I'm very enriched by that." He first became involved in collecting when he visited the home of another collector: "Walking into his house, it wasn't museum-like, it had the wonderful warmth of a home, but, my God, you were just surrounded by the energy of all these paintings around you. It was stunning to me."

Every creative filmmaker we know, not just the ones we interviewed for this book, maintains an active involvement in other art forms by going to some combination of plays, concerts, art and photography exhibitions, poetry readings, dance performances, etc., as well as reading both fiction and nonfiction. Although we're specifically considering the creative process in filmmaking, it's apparent to our filmmakers that creativity in any field has clear and inspiring parallels to the work they do. Kimberly Peirce finds music "incredibly helpful" in providing models of what she would like to do creatively. "Jimi Hendrix is so beautiful and perfect to me, very much like a great filmmaker, or any great artist. He is the instrument, and the stuff just flows through him." Kimberly relates to the "wild and inventive" way he interacted with his guitar, and ponders how he was "such a product of his culture, and yet he produced culture." Like many filmmakers, she listens to music while she works. "I listened to David Bowie the whole time we were editing *Boys Don't Cry*. He'll write a note in some way that you've never conceived of, and it changes the shape of perception. I think that's what you want to do with movies, take an emotional state and create it with new artifacts."

JOHN LASSETER, animation writer-director-producer

When I was going to California Institute of the Arts, and then first working at Disney, I'd go to a museum and fall in love with drawings. That's what I was into, because animation was 2-D. I would see the drawings of some of these great old masters, and study their line work, and be in awe. Picasso can just draw four lines, and it's like, "Ahhhhhhh! Look at that!" And Rembrandt and Da Vinci, and, oh my Gosh, Michelangelo.

Then when I got excited about the possibility of creating a 3-D world through computer animation, I found that when I went to museums, my interests started shifting, becoming 3-D. And now I got really blown away by Honoré Daumier's little caricatured sculptures of politicians, and the sculptures that they have in Paris at the Musée d'Orsay. I started discovering Rodin. I went to Florence and was awed by Michelangelo's statue of David. My inspiration started coming from all over, from anyone who was able to capture beautiful, three-dimensional forms in a way that felt solid. My interest in children's book illustration and painting became much greater. I started loving painting that had really dramatic lighting in it, Georges de La Tour and Rembrandt. And probably one of the biggest inspirations I've had from a lighting standpoint is Maxfield Parrish. If you look at our movies, there are scenes that are very, very Parrish-like in their lighting.

At Pixar [Animation Studios], we want to understand everyone's particular talents and let them do what they do best, but also give them room to grow. We have our own Pixar University, where we have sculpture, drawing, improv acting—and we encourage the computer programmers to take drawing classes and things like that, to try to get this cross-cultural thing going on.

"My Inspiration Started Coming from All Over"

Just as people are drawn to certain creative fields, it's likely that their attraction to other art forms and specific artists will echo their "mysterious predisposition." Walter Murch likes to translate Italian poetry, and has discovered a direct parallel to the work that he does in film. "Much to my delight, the state of mind I'm in when translating text from one language to another is virtually identical to the state of mind when I'm editing or doing sound for a film. On a movie, you're translating the language of the script into the language of time and image and color and sound." Walter notes that in translating poetry, "there are times when the literal meaning of a word is the right meaning—it says *nave* in Italian, you translate it as boat, *nave* equals boat, no problem." But the translator often faces choices about how literal the translation should be. Similarly, in film, "sometimes what the script says is what you do. Other times, what the script says is the last thing you want to do. Or you do it in a different order, putting this first, rather than that. Or you take two words in the script and expand it to twenty seconds, or condense half a page of script into something that's five seconds in the film."

Anthony Minghella wasn't someone who gravitated at first toward film. And still today, as he told us, "when I'm at work on a film, I'm much more likely to be in thrall to a painting or a poem than to a shot in another movie." Anthony's first love was music, and he recalls that the seed idea for *Truly, Madly, Deeply,* "the very first image, was of a Bach duet." He found himself

drawn to this image because "I've never experienced the same kind of joy as when you are able to play music with other people. It's such an intense, and egalitarian, and wonderful experience. And a friend of mine had been very sick, he was a pianist, and he and a clarinet player would meet once a week and play duets. And so, the first idea for the screenplay was not a romantic relationship. It was not about bereavement or ghosts. It was about music."

Producer Ismail Merchant has also drawn on a love for music—in his case, the classical music of India—in films such as *The Householder, Shakespeare Wallah* and *The Guru.* He says that a producer "must know music. Music is one of the most important things." For *Mahatma and the Mad Boy,* a short film he also directed, Ismail explored mixing the Indian and Western cultures he had grown up with by choosing Vivaldi's "Winter" Concerto from *The Four Seasons* as the film's musical theme, but then letting Indian musicians improvise a raga from it using Indian instruments.

Even when filmmakers draw inspiration from books, it is not simply in terms of stories and characters. For *My America,* documentary filmmaker Renee Tajima-Peña reread works by Alexis de Tocqueville and Thomas Jefferson on the character of American society: "As I traveled, it drove my thinking about the whole question of ethnic identity. Those books were the driving intellectual force in the film, even though they're not there explicitly. I didn't want to stop and have a Thomas Jefferson moment in the

Ismail Merchant (foreground) on the set of *Mahatma and the Mad Boy*

film, and probably, unless I talk about it, nobody will notice it. But it's there as the subtext."

Just as Renee, a very forward-looking filmmaker, has found inspiration in books hundreds of years old, the path-breaking video artist Bill Viola counts among his great influences such painters as Giotto, Raphael and Rembrandt. He sees video art as standing "at the bridge between the history of cinema and the history of painting and the visual arts in general."

Of course, many filmmakers also find inspiration in contemporary work in other media. Mexican director Alejandro González Iñárritu has said that his film *Amores Perros* was deeply influenced by both the photography of Nan Goldin and the innovative narrative structures of authors like Jorge Luis Borges and Julio Cortázar. Iñárritu has argued that "cinema has not evolved in step with painting, for example, or music, or literature. I think the structure and the way we tell the stories in cinema have been very conventional, very straightforward. . . . Little by little, we're beginning to accept other ways to tell stories."

Nearly all filmmakers are also students of films and film history. In stressing the importance of a breadth of knowledge, awareness and cultural appreciation, we don't want to minimize the value of understanding the development of film language and aesthetics, and drawing inspiration from specific films that have deeply affected us. When Anthony discovered the films of Italian directors Luchino Visconti, Federico Fellini and Paolo and Vittorio Taviani, he found "a sensibility and temperament that felt organic to me, and I began a very intense love affair with those films, which has never left me." Fellini's *I Vitelloni* had particular resonance for him since it's "about a group of kids growing up in Rimini, an Italian seaside resort, dreaming of Rome," just as he grew up in an English seaside resort on the Isle of Wight dreaming of London. "I've watched it probably fifty times in my life."

Similarly, Renee told us of the deep connection she has to "politicized Hollywood movies like *It's a Wonderful Life* and *Grapes of Wrath*." Kimberly also finds a link between the movies and movie characters she most loves and the themes that she is drawn to. "I think that we each have these undying themes that relate to our personal quest, our conflict that we're trying to work out. And we seek characters who are on similar quests. Some of my favorite characters are Luke in *Cool Hand Luke*, or Sonny in *Dog Day Afternoon*, Jim Stark in *Rebel Without a Cause* and Bonnie and Clyde. To me, the real Brandon [Teena, in *Boys Don't Cry*] resembled all these

American antiheroes. When he failed, he'd get right back up, do it again, get knocked down, do it again—like Jake LaMotta in *Raging Bull*."

Conrad Hall remembers how profoundly *Rashomon* affected him when it first came out: "It was such an interesting way of examining the truth and what the truth means, and how different the truth is from various perspectives, and what is the truth?" He notes that "we all learn so much from each other, from studying other people's films. I go to movies and I'm greatly influenced by the good work that's done by so many wonderful cinematographers, past and present." When he was a student, examining a film closely was harder to do. "Nowadays people can play a video or a DVD, and they can stop and pause and single-frame, and they end up knowing your film better than you know it."

Some filmmakers, while making a film of their own, like to look at other films that connect in some way to their current work. When Kimberly was struggling structurally with how to open *Boys Don't Cry*, it helped her to look again at *Raging Bull*. "I remembered in the opening scene, Jake LaMotta is all alone in the ring, shadow-boxing with himself in slow motion, and it's not really a scene out of the movie. It's a scene in his mind's eye—it's his fantasy of himself." That influenced her to start her film with images of cars on a highway "which is always a strong image for me, the lights passing by. And we specifically cut that so that it's not like a real scene from the movie." Other filmmakers find that having other movies too freshly in their minds can muddy the primacy of their own voice. If Pamela Douglas is "on a project, the absolute last thing I want to do is look at any work that might have something in common because it takes me off my center. I don't refer to movies really at all."

This issue relates to the paradox of wanting to create work that feels fresh, not tired and clichéd, while at the same time recognizing that we necessarily draw from what other filmmakers, artists and writers have done before us. John Wells notes that "in any art form, we build upon other artists. You don't start from scratch, go into a cave somewhere, if you're a painter, and decide you're going to work with sticks of charcoal, and start without any knowledge of any other artists to inform your work." He notes that the television series *ER* "clearly worked off of the form and style of what Steven Bochco, David Milch and a number of other really talented people had done on *Hill Street Blues*, which was really a landmark change in the language of dramatic television. But you're still looking for ideas that seem like you haven't quite seen them before."

Working from the inside out means doing work that is true to ourselves, finding a distinct voice that resonates with our unique sensibilities, even as it draws inspiration from our vast and rich cultural history. Consider how, four hundred years after William Shakespeare wrote *Hamlet,* and after countless productions on stage and on film, artists are still finding original, authentic and vital ways to interpret this work. As Anthony Minghella observes about the originality possible through variation, "John Coltrane played 'My Favorite Things.' It's the same song, but it's not. It's John Coltrane." Our filmmakers have primarily worked within classic dramatic structures, even as they found ways to make their work innovative and surprising.

In fact, working in a deeply personal way leads naturally toward fresh ways of construing established plots and genres. Kimberly described in *Introspection* how, when she directed well-known scenes in film school, she would inevitably end up shaping them into a reflection of her point of view without consciously attempting to do so. But emerging filmmakers who haven't learned to work from their own voice may find themselves overwhelmed by the difficulty of reinvigorating or reinventing the familiar. We have too often seen students resort to novelty for its own sake, filling the screen with stylistic embellishments that may be inventive and attention-getting, but have no deeper resonance or purpose. Or they may simply embrace formula, imitating it as closely as possible. Coauthor Doe Mayer once had an Indonesian student who had loved Hollywood Westerns when he was growing up, and who earnestly set out to make a film of a cowboy gunfight that attempted to replicate every overworked device in that stock scene, right down to a white hat for the hero and a black hat for the villain.

An Indonesian student thoroughly imbued with the conventions of Hollywood exemplifies a hidden danger in drawing creatively on the films we know well. Mainstream Hollywood movies and television have become so dominant throughout the world that their production methods and commercial goals can seem inevitable. Developing filmmakers may have had such little exposure to other approaches that their imaginations are confined to a fairly limited range. We therefore encourage our students to see many films, but to seek out those with perspectives and aesthetic sensibilities that awaken us to the incredibly varied possibilities that exist in filmmaking, from the Danish "Dogme 95" films to contemporary Iranian cinema. As German writer-director Tom Tykwer has said, "We haven't even reached, by far, ten percent of what film language can offer, so why do we think it's coming to an end? We're still at the beginning. We can still discover so many possibilities. If we stick to the idea that strong films are always personal, then there's 5.8 billion possibilities for films, 'cause there's that many people whose views we can share."

Getting Out of the Car: *Observation of the World*

We strengthen our voices through direct, thoughtful observation of the world around us. Sometimes beginning filmmakers believe they can portray something they have never experienced or observed or learned about, just by using their "imagination." But the late French filmmaker Jean Renoir recalled that his father, impressionist painter Auguste Renoir, had "mistrusted imagination." The great artist believed that "if you paint the leaf of a tree without using a model you risk becoming stereotyped, because your imagination will only supply you with a few leaves whereas Nature offers you millions, all on the same tree. No two leaves are exactly the same. The artist who paints only what is in his mind must very soon repeat himself." Jean, as a filmmaker, had made the same discovery—he needed observation as "a point of departure."

Cinematographer Conrad Hall states "I work from what I see. What I use are my observations about life, what I see happening around me." Although many people keep journals, Conrad finds he can recall his "little mental notes. I've been making mental notes from the time I started to study film." As an example, he might see something happen while having breakfast in a restaurant, and then later, working on a scene that requires a certain emotion, a particular mood, "I remember when I was sitting by the window and how that looked and what that made me feel. And then I use what I remember about the light, the composition, all that kind of thing."

Observation isn't just noticing and storing details in a factual, intellectual way. It is visceral, emotional, subjective, and profoundly personal. Each

Jeannine Oppewall's sketch for the library building in *Pleasantville*

BOOK FRIEZE
SIMPLE FRIEZE WITH SOME KIND OF
APPROPRIATE LIBRARY DECORATION — EX.
NAMES OF CULTURAL FIGURES, ETC.

STEPS TO GET WIDER AS THEY COME DOWN
WITH CURVING STONE BALUSTER, POSS.

PORTICO/ENTRY W/ COLUMNS, SIDE ONES ENGAGED?
BASIC RED BRICK W/ STONE TRIM, DK-GRAY ROOF

WINDOWS CAN BE 1 CENTRAL LG. LIGHT W/2
SMALLER SIDE LITES W/ SIMPLE STONE TRIM
ABOVE

SET BACK FROM ST. W/ GRASS LAWN, BUSHES, &
ROOM FOR FLOWERS TO GO COLOR LATER. WINDOWS
HAVE TO LIGHT UP LATER

SMALL ALLEYS ON SIDES BET. OTHER BLDGS.

of us will notice different things among the flood of sensory data our minds receive, and develop our own distinctive store of observations to draw on. Writer Hanif Kureishi finds "a conjunction of observation with personality, with character. I would notice those details, and you would notice different kinds of detail. And it's those details that make it a 'Hanif Kureishi' piece, as opposed to a piece by you, or Scott Fitzgerald, or whoever. What I notice, and the way I invest those details with my personality, is what makes it alive."

Jeannine Oppewall talks about being able to draw, as a production designer, from her own "image bank." "A lot of my ideas come out of my background, my trips through America. They come from things I've remembered, things I've internalized, things I've actually photographed or kept in my garage. Maybe I'll never use them, but they're accessible, so that when I push the right button I can retrieve them, my own personal, private collection of images."

For the buildings in the town of *Pleasantville,* "what I wanted, what I read in the screenplay, was a comment about the meaning of American democracy. The film is about an idealized all-American, middle-American, fantasy culture, and for me that had to do with our down-deep national origins. If you travel through the small towns in the U.S., you notice that the bank, the library, the town hall and a lot of the civic buildings are likely to be neoclassical in their design." Jeannine felt that this style would echo the Jeffersonian idea "that the civic buildings in a democracy should draw on the Greeks, the classics. I think Jefferson even said we borrow that architecture because it has encoded in it the concept of how we should rule ourselves."

For the town library, Jeannine created a building in the style of a scaled-down Palladian villa that evoked these Jeffersonian ideals. The classic design, drawn from what she had observed and studied, still left room for her to add "a subliminal, personal, private" touch: "the frieze of authors around the building—those are my own favorite classical authors."

Because it's the partic-

The library building in *Pleasantville,* with the names Chaucer, Shakespeare, Milton, Hawthorne, Thoreau, Whitman, Melville and Twain visible in the frieze

ularity of what you choose that conveys meaning and point of view, a long catalog of descriptive details is seldom as effective as a few well-chosen ones. Jeannine notes that, in selecting from a wealth of potential visual elements that will create the environment of a film, it's important to resist the temptation to put in too many: "My philosophy is 'take away.' It's much stronger than adding. You can add all the adjectives you like, but at a certain point, you've diluted the subject and the predicate. You need to get back to one or two perfectly chosen adjectives."

Along with visual and aural details, observation can give us character and dramatic story. The late Japanese filmmaker Akira Kurosawa told the story of how he had once met and talked to a man in a bar, and then ten years later realized that a character in the film he had just completed had unconsciously been based on this man, who had been "living inside my head, waiting to come out." Pamela Douglas finds that most writers "are collectors of people, mentally. You collect details as you walk around." When she talked with us, she had recently been to a concert at the Hollywood Bowl: "In the row in front of me was a group of young adults. One young woman was awkward, but she was dressed in a beautiful satin, pastel lime and pink outfit with a ribbon. She had tried so hard to look pretty that day. A young man came by who was smooth and attractive, and she was looking at him, yet trying not to look. Finally he said to her, 'How you doing?' And then he left. I saw her body language fall, and at the same time, I saw her defense against it. Her friends were there, she had brought chicken she had made, and she was going to reassert her self-esteem." Pamela adds that the young woman may not ever be in a script: "It's more about developing an understanding of the dramatic moment. That was a complete dramatic scene: desire, anticipation, struggle, effort, the climactic moment of the scene, and even an aftermath and a reassertion that would lead you to the next scene. It was all there. And if you go around the world as a sponge like that, you see that sort of thing all the time. You get full of these characters."

"A Need for the Experience of Living"

JOHN WELLS, television writer-producer

The work requires that you be aware of what's going on in the world around you. All lives, no matter how apparently mundane, are complex, rich, and interesting, and it's the writer's responsibility, whether it be in film, or television, or on the stage, to take that unexamined life, and examine it in a way that's interesting or useful for the audience. You have to talk to people, listen, read, walk in other people's shoes, try to understand their point of view and see why they would make that decision, that choice. Every time you're confronted with something that seems appalling, I think you're required as a writer to try and figure out what might have put you at that same place. How does someone end up there?

I know very few writers who really get good before they get into their thirties, and it's not because they're not talented. But it's a need for the experience of living—living enough to understand people's motivations, the way in which you make decisions, having enough of your own personal experience to draw upon. On the other hand, as you become more successful, your world becomes more and more insular, and you have less access to what it was you wrote about and were interested in when you began. And so you have to increase the amount of information that's coming to you, to make certain that your work is authentic.

I used to routinely take the Amtrak train from one side of the country to the other because you're in the train for three or four days. And if you're traveling by yourself, you end up being seated with other people for three meals a day. And you just sit and ask people questions, and they tell you the most extraordinary things. There's no place to go. There's time. The world is passing by. And you just hear their stories.

I remember I was coming back from Chicago, and this guy was going to Albuquerque. He was about sixty-five years old, and he had on a big old tooled belt with a big silver belt buckle, old blue jeans, and cowboy boots. He looked like a piece of beef jerky. He said he was going home after being in Chicago for eighteen months. I asked, "What were you doing in Chicago for eighteen months?" And he said, "Watching my son die." I said, "What do you mean?" And he said, "Well, I got a call. I hadn't talked to my son in about fifteen, sixteen years, because he was gay and I'd thrown him out. And I got a call from his lover that he was dying of AIDS. And I went up to Chicago to see him, because my wife, his mother, said that if I didn't go, she'd throw me out. And I went up to see him, and ended up staying and taking care of him until he died." And so you see an entire life—the dichotomies of how people live, the things we do, the mistakes that we make. You don't necessarily want to write a movie about it or do a television show about it. But there's a story in that conversation. And you've got to get that stuff.

Hanif, who grew up in the 1960s and '70s, found himself fascinated but puzzled by the "convolution of stereotype" he was dealing with in *My Son, the Fanatic*—he had always thought of children as being "wilder" than their parents. To understand better the young Muslim fundamentalists he was portraying, he not only read fundamentalist magazines and books, but would "go and see the kids in the mosques, British-Asian kids who were talking about reeducating their parents who were not fundamentalist enough." He listened to their complaints about their families: "They watch

TV all the time. They don't pray. They eat crisps." Eventually, he was able to craft an authentic, and in many ways, sympathetic portrait of the fundamentalist son even though his personal feelings were much more in sync with the liberal father.

John Wells, in his sidebar above, described the danger of achieving success and becoming insular as a result. This can be particularly problematic for actors who, if they become recognizable to the public, find it difficult to observe others unobtrusively. Early in Kathy Baker's career, when she was preparing the role of May in the original stage production of *Fool for Love,* she was able to take "a trip back to New Mexico, where I grew up, to get a feeling for old motels and . . . just to get a feeling. I could really observe people." Now that she is better known, she finds: "I can't stare at people because they're staring at me. If I'm in a restaurant, I can't just watch someone as much as I used to. I don't stroll around a mall observing." Kathy can still manage to go unnoticed in some situations, but she wonders, "*what* happens to *hugely* recognizable people? Does it freeze their instincts?"

Real-life observation is intrinsic to documentary filmmaking, which is one reason we encourage all our film students, even those definitely planning to work in fiction, to take a documentary production class. Renee Tajima-Peña says that "if you're a documentarian, your eyes are always darting around." Everywhere she looks, "people have incredible stories." She finds it particularly important to go beyond distanced observation, to "get out of the car" and talk with people face-to-face, especially when they at first seem baffling or frightening to her, "then I begin to really understand people." She remembers that for *My America,* she and the crew "went into this trailer park that was really scary, and you could see people fighting with beer bottles, and even the guys on the crew were terrified. So we're driving through in the van, wondering, 'Should we get out? Should we try to talk to people?' And then finally we got out, and once you do, it's almost like the air is fresher and cleaner. You're on ground level with people, they greet you hello, and they are so interested, you're a film crew and on eye level, and it's just another neighborhood and people are people."

"Getting out of the car" is not only key to understanding the subjects of our observations, it also brings us face-to-face with the intellectual, emotional, ethical, aesthetic, practical, political and thematic questions that we need to respond to as responsible filmmakers. Renee has written about assigning a group of students a small video project on "non-citizen, legal immigrants who were threatened with loss of public assistance because of welfare reform legislation. More specifically, they were elderly and disabled immigrants, the most vulnerable portion of the population other than children." Renee notes all the questions that should come up for filmmakers as a result: "Even at the very start, as you plan interviews and

Renee Tajima-Peña "getting out of the car" to walk with people along Route 66 during the filming of *My America*

initial filming: who is the audience? How will the final product be used? Whose Rolodex do you use in finding interview subjects? Do you go through a county social worker, an advocacy group, family contacts, the INS, or do you hang around the neighborhood? Although the focus is on immigrants, will your intended audience tolerate subtitles or voiceovers? What kind of 'audition' criteria do you use for choosing subjects? Are they photogenic? Articulate? Are these valid criteria when filming this type of story? Will the media exposure leave your subjects vulnerable to detection by welfare authorities? Can they legally agree to be filmed, especially those who are mentally disabled? If they are housed in a board and care facility, what kind of access will you have? If they are homebound in a small room, how many crew people can you fit in the room? What lens will you use to get a sense of the cramped space? Is there natural light? Is there a noisy, central air conditioning unit that can't be turned off? And with each of these questions, there are sub-questions."

With our own documentary students, we give them a "get out of the car" assignment early in the process of developing their ideas, and see the dramatic difference it makes when they move beyond an intellectual construct of their topic to the flesh-and-blood complexities of real life. They may need to spend many hours with the characters in their films deepening their own understanding, as well as building up a relationship with their subjects. Dylan Robertson, one of coauthor Carroll Hodge's students, had begun production and completed fifteen hours of interviews for his film about women who are fat and not unhappy about it, but he recognized that he "didn't have the film at all yet." He and the crew started spending more time with these women in their daily lives, eventually going with them to a fat acceptance convention. One evening, the crew filmed the women putting on makeup before going to a party. The intimacy of the setting, the associations of the activity with societal attitudes toward appearance, and the relationship of trust that had evolved between the subjects and the crew allowed the women to speak much more from their hearts about the impact on them of negative responses to their being fat. It also triggered a more profound emotional understanding of these issues in Dylan. That night, he later realized, "was the beginning of the real documentary."

Firsthand observations and interactions with real people are vital for fictional films as well as documentaries, if filmmakers are to avoid the pale two-dimensionality of stock stereotypes and recycled plots. We sometimes encounter students writing fictional stories who want to populate their films with characters who are exotic to them, whose appeal is that they seem strange, taboo, transgressive—hit men, prostitutes, drug dealers, homeless people, the mentally ill. The students may have no real knowledge of such people, and base the characterizations on what they've seen in movies and on television, resulting in work that is stale and recycled. As writer-director John Sayles has said, "You get a movie like *Mean Streets,* where the references are to the stuff that went around Marty [Scorsese] when he was a kid living in Little Italy, and then you get twenty-five movies, fifteen years later, where the references are to the movie *Mean Streets,* but not to anything that is real."

Of course, many things in fiction cannot or need not be experienced in a literal sense. Jean Renoir's statement above referred to observation as "a point of departure." A filmmaker full of personal observations translates and reconfigures them as fictional characters, settings and events. In becoming more attentive to the world around us, we not only acquire a storehouse of human insights and evocative details to draw from, we also begin to understand more about the nature of our perception. In effect, we learn to notice what it is that we notice, and to recognize how we process sensory information and turn it into thought, feeling and memory. That heightened awareness in turn can help add the richness of observation to what we imagine. Adam King, one of coauthor Jed Dannenbaum's graduate students, after taking a class based on some of the explorations contained in this book, wrote in his final class journal: "I came to the understanding that creating from experience isn't about simply transcribing the events of one's life into words or paint, it's understanding how you experience, and applying that to a creative process, real or unreal. It's about observing a space that you may or may not know, with all of its details, its colors, and idiosyncrasies. It's about fully experiencing the thing you're creating, whether it's happened to you or not."

Doing the Homework: *Researching a Film*

Having steeped ourselves in "the masters," and having filled our mental notebooks and image banks with personal observations, we nevertheless have not finished the process of Inquiry. When going to work on a specific film, filmmakers still need to fill in many details through research, often the old-fashioned kind where you get books out of the library or find an expert to talk to.

Universally, our filmmakers report how much they relish this focused inquiry. Writer-director Anthony Minghella believes that one reason he has fallen in love with certain projects "is because of a profound ignorance about them. One of the great joys of being a filmmaker is the obligation to keep learning. I'm absolutely dependent on research." When he began his adaptation of the novel *Cold Mountain,* the British-born Minghella knew "nothing about the American Civil War, nothing about that part of the world. And those are the opportunities just to plunge into a lot of books, and listen to a whole new world of music." He found Charles Frazier's novel to be "very palimpsestic"—that is, like a parchment that has been partially erased and overwritten. "It's written over *The Odyssey,* it's also written over a series of personal documents from the Civil War. It's got many, many layers." As a result, Anthony's research went well beyond the history and music of the era. "I went back to *The Odyssey,* to *The Bible,* to medieval journey stories, "Everyman" stories, *Pilgrim's Progress*—anything to feed and nourish those deeper layers."

Anthony sees the time he spends in preparation as part of his creative voice, an aspect of his nature that dictates the process he needs to follow. He offers as a metaphor his memory of being "on holiday some time ago with my family and with a friend. We had a pool, and in the morning, everybody would go down to swim. My son would go running in and bomb the pool. My wife, who is very elegant, would sort of slide into the pool, and go up and down. And my friend would do a beautiful swan dive. And I would walk 'round and 'round and 'round, contemplating. And then eventually, when everybody had had their swim and gone, I would get in. And then I would stay in for a very long time. I feel that's how I am as a writer. I can't just belly-flop in, I have to keep plodding around until I feel I know enough to start."

Despite the time-consuming nature of this sort of research, Anthony has come to realize that "when I'm reading the Book of Job for a day, it's not specious. It's because that's where my own particular journey requires me to be. Or when I'm spending two days examining the Smithsonian collection of early American folk music, it's not just indulgence. It's because there's going to be a clue there somewhere that's going to feed the film."

"I Keep Looking Until I Find the Places That Inspire Me"

JEANNINE OPPEWALL, production designer

I could tell from the minute I talked to Curtis [Hanson, director of *L.A. Confidential*] about the project that he had done his homework. He had gone through old magazines and books and had several photos which were personally inspiring for him, images of people from the era, how they dressed and how they were lit, and some were of places. He had had them blown up for a meeting with executives who were talking about putting the money into the film, and they perceived that he had a feeling, a vision of what he was going after.

As soon as I read the script, I made what I call cheat sheets, which is one page of notes per set listed in the movie. I put the name of the set and a brief outline of the action described, which pretty much tells you the elements you must have for the scene to "solve itself." My cheat sheets for *L.A. Confidential* also had any descriptions from James Ellroy's novel, and anything that Curtis or I had particularly liked about them.

For Lynn Brackman's apartment, I immediately thought of Hollywood-style courtyard apartments, so I hauled out the book *Courtyard Apartments,* and Curtis and I went through it and identified a feeling that we both liked. I wanted the Spanish style because that's the classic L.A. concept, and that's what Lynn Brackman is paid to represent on the surface. I'd always had in mind that the living room set where she played out her public activities dressed as movie star Veronica Lake should be two stories in height, with some kind of balcony and staircase. Anytime you can get the camera out of the precise rectangle of a room, you've got a lot more visual expressiveness available to you.

Then when you go upstairs to her bedroom, it's something completely other—a small world but it's her world. Who is she personally? Well, all you can do is make a few suggestions—painted metal beds, little watercolors of plants and fruits, reds, yellows, oranges, warm colors in her personal space which is very curvy and natural, as opposed to the hard, cobalt-blue, manufactured look downstairs.

When I walked into the house in Hancock Park that the location scout had found, it had what I wanted: two stories, a little balcony, Spanish-style stairs, a sculpted Spanish tile fireplace, a big curvilinear window, an archway, a room beyond and a little closet. I could see immediately how the action would take place. The camera reveals the Veronica Lake movies on a screen, then moves to the bed in the back. I brought in Curtis and Dante Spinotti, the cameraman, and when they walked in, they had big smiles on their faces because they saw the same possibilities I did. If I can't find some poetry in the location, I cannot sell it to the director. I keep looking until I find the places that inspire me.

Research is such a basic part of filmmaking that large projects usually employ professional researchers. John Wells has "a full-time researcher who works for me at the company because we've got so much going on. And then, every individual show has at least two full-time researchers who work between fifty and sixty hours a week, just getting material." In addition, there are research-oriented events for the writing staffs of each show. For *The West Wing,* people come in who have served in the admin-istrations of Presidents Clinton, Carter and Reagan, "and they talk to us extensively about what they did, and that's where a lot of story ideas come from." There's a similar process for *ER,* but with emergency-room doctors and nurses. In addition, every *ER* writer, no matter how long they have been on the show, is expected to spend at least four shifts, ten or twelve hours per

Allison Janney (C. J. Cregg) in *The West Wing*

shift, in a working emergency room every six months. "We look at it as like even if you have your pilot's license, you have to keep going back and getting additional training." John believes that the thing that makes these shows feel authentic is "people who've actually done it, who tell you how it really works. And so, you get that sense of being inside something that you didn't know before." He finds that although audiences may not be familiar with the world you are presenting, they nevertheless "know a fraud when they see it. They know when something seems inauthentic."

We can well imagine that hearing someone talk about life in an emergency room, while greatly informative, is not nearly as vividly detailed or as emotionally profound as spending many hours oneself in an actual emergency room. Although we can get a lot from libraries and experts, we should always try for in-person research whenever possible. Pamela Douglas recalls an early writing assignment on the life of Rosa Parks: "I had a notion of what the historical events were that you can find in any history book, but it's so thin that you really can't get much out of that. So I went to Montgomery [Alabama], and I stayed there for over a week." She interviewed people who had known Ms. Parks during her formative years that led to the Montgomery bus boycott, and they told their personal stories about her, details of character "that are beyond anything in the history books, revelations and insights that could not all fit in the script but which textured the experience for me."

Research isn't just for writers. To develop the visuals for *A Bug's Life,* John Lasseter and his creative team shot closeup, bug's-eye video footage in the grassy areas just outside the Pixar studio. Jeannine Oppewall spent six months taking duplicate photos with two still cameras, one loaded with color film and the other with black and white, to learn how to design the sets of *Pleasantville* so that they would work equally well in the black and white and color portions of the film. While editing *The Right Stuff,* Lisa Fruchtman kept a rocket chart on her editing room wall, so that for any specific launch in the movie she could use NASA archival footage of the correct kind of rocket. Even for film scoring, James Newton Howard has turned to experts in his research. To bring a Japanese flavor to *Snow Falling on Cedars,* a story with Japanese-American characters in the Pacific Northwest, "I worked with the head of the ethnomusicology department at UCLA. We spent many sessions together. He happens to be a shakuhachi master, and I also sampled him playing the shakuhachi." James finds that the post-production schedule requires that he do his research and composing more quickly than he would like, and so he prefers to be involved in a film at an early stage. "What I really love is to have five or six months to work on a score, and immerse myself in it. But usually I have only eight to twelve weeks."

Often the writer, the director and researchers have compiled a significant amount of research by the time other creative collaborators join the production, and the new colleagues can use this body of work to facilitate their contributions. Shared research also aids the process of getting everyone in sync with a cohesive vision of the film that is emerging (while of course still allowing for fluid innovation). For Walter Murch, one attraction of doing a film adapted from another medium is that, as a resource, "you not only have the novel or whatever the source is that the film is based on, you have all of the research material that the author used to write the novel, and all the research that the director or the screenwriter used to convert the novel into pictures—music, documents, firsthand reports of details such as, for *The English Patient,* what it's like to defuse a bomb. All of these things can filter into the decision-making process."

Pamela finds research on the Internet "a wonderful fountain of inspiration. I use it all the time to get detail." But she cautions that "research can give you the illusion that you've done your job when you haven't, because your job is to take the research, internalize it, and then leave it alone and do the creative work." The detailed accuracy of research can help provide a level of authenticity, but often a deeper truth emerges, an authenticity that can transcend the specific information we discover through research.

This may be the case even when working from a true story. To research *Boys Don't Cry,* Kimberly Peirce read the police records of Brandon's arrests, talked with the sheriff and jailer, interviewed the real Lana and her mother, and attended the murder trial. "In 1994, I went back to the farmhouse where Brandon had been killed and I sat there trying to comprehend how and why these people had been able to destroy him. I was trying to get to the epicenter of the pain surrounding his life and death, but I wasn't yet inside it."

Kimberly found she had to go deeper than the real-life story, drawing on her "own experiences of physical violence, living through it and then talking about it," as well as her experience working with rape and incest survivors. She also turned to classical drama, "Aristotle and *Romeo and Juliet.*" Eventually she found that "Brandon became a character that we had invented. He had been inspired by the real character, but there was the real Brandon, there was us, and then there was the 'Brandon' we had created, and that character has its own truth."

Hilary Swank as Brandon

Research may deepen our sense of connection to the subjects we are investigating in such a way as to lead us beyond inquiry into direct participation, an involvement that extends beyond the life of the film project. After producing an independent feature that dealt with domestic violence, for example, coauthor Jed Dannenbaum served for many years on the board of the advocacy and counseling organization that had provided expertise for the film. One of coauthor Doe Mayer's graduate students, Karen Price, after writing and directing a documentary about people involved in animal rescue (*Living by Instinct: Animals and Their Rescuers*), found that she wanted to make an ongoing commitment herself to rescuing and sheltering animals. And Renee has emphasized the extent to which her filmmaking and her social activism almost entirely overlap.

This intertwining of personal involvement and creativity exemplifies the deeper thrust of this chapter on inquiry. The stories, characters and rich details that we uncover are not just fodder for our filmmaking. Their greater value lies in the broadened perspective, questioning mindset, and deeper human empathy they engender. In striving to be creative, we constantly run up against our own blind spots: reflexive assumptions and predispositions ingrained by the culture around us, with all its pressures to conform. Our education must often be a process of *unlearning,* as we develop a facility for probing, skeptical inquisitiveness. Observation is frequently a chance to see—really see for the first time—what is right in front of us. As our life experiences and our research spill over into one another, we grow, first as human beings and then as artists.

LIMBERING UP

1) Finding Intellectual Inspiration

What areas of study other than film have you particularly enjoyed and felt enriched by? What courses have you taken, at any age, that clicked for you? Take a few minutes to think of a class, a research paper, a public lecture, a self-study project, etc., that you found personally satisfying. Dig out and thumb through whatever you may still have in the way of science or art projects, test booklets (blue books), essays and creative writing.

Are there some areas that seem to reawaken an interest, or that surprise you? Choose one and spend another few minutes quickly jotting down (without judgment or editing) ideas about an imaginary film or a character or a scene in a film that would allow you to draw on this specific interest or knowledge that you have.

2) Artistic Nurturing

What visual or performance arts do you enjoy seeing? What do you like to read? Take a few minutes to go through the arts and entertainment section of your local newspaper, and plan to go to something you might not otherwise make time for, performance art perhaps, or a watercolor exhibit, a music concert or a theater production. Or look through your bookshelf and find a good book that you've been wanting to read (or reread), then set aside the time to get started. Spend five minutes looking, really looking, at an artwork (or reproduction) you have in your home, and try to remember your first impressions and what drew you to it. See if you can reconnect with it and see it with fresh eyes. Cultural activities are not frivolous or time away from the film work you need to do, but essential components of both your short-term creative work and your long-term development as a filmmaker. Which ones are most important to you?

3) Cross-fertilization

Use the concepts and creative energy from one area of your interests and apply them to another area. Walter Murch finds that translating Italian poetry exercises the same creative muscles as editing. The paintings in James Newton Howard's study help spark his music composing. According to actor Helena Bonham Carter, Ismail Merchant finds tremendous similarity between filmmaking and cooking: "Just as his films are often hybrids, his dishes are often a cosmopolitan mix of Eastern spices with ingredients indigenous to whichever country he finds himself in. He is speedy to the point of instantaneous; he cooks and invents new concoctions by improvisation, using his wits and trusting his instincts."

As you make this connection from one of your interests to another, don't limit yourself to obvious links—you might try for a much more eccentric relationship. Arrange flowers in a way that seems to capture the rhythms of a piece of music you love. Cook a meal inspired somehow by a favorite poem. Take a photograph of a lover or friend in a pose prompted by some aspect of astronomy or quantum physics.

4) Sensing the World

Close your eyes and pay attention to all the stimuli coming to your other senses. Is there a breeze on your neck? Are the muscles in your legs tightened up? What are you feeling in each part of your body? Is there a dog barking in the distance, a car going by, a bird outside your window? How many different sounds can you hear? How far away are they and what direction are they coming from? Are you aware of any smells in your nose, or tastes in your mouth?

Now open your eyes and carefully look around you. What is the quality of the light? Is there something meaningful in your line of sight that you haven't really looked at or thought about in a long time? Is there a tilted picture of your mother on the wall in front of you?

It is easy to get lost in our busy lives and conscious thought processes, and be oblivious to the actual world around us. You can strengthen your creative work by becoming more aware of the detailed sensory environment that you inhabit. Think about how you might make a habit of noticing life more. For example, choose specific times of day or repeated activities as cues—as soon as you wake up, while you brush your teeth, or as you sit down to a meal. One day you might notice sounds, the next day sensations related to touch and temperature. Apply these perceptions to something you are working on. They will enhance your skills in directing an actor, rewriting a moment, designing a set or rethinking a prop.

5) Taking Note

Start a notebook of observations and keep it handy to write down your impressions and draw sketches that will remind you of what you saw. In his book *Developing Story Ideas,* filmmaker and teacher Michael Rabiger has developed a system for thinking about and keeping track of such observations, under the categories "Characters," "Locations," "Objects," "Situations," "Acts" and "Themes." You may discover other categories that are appropriate for your sensibilities, such as sense impressions, lines of dialogue, moments of humor, titles, conflicts or paradoxes.

introspection

inquiry

three **intuition**

interaction

impact

workout

Filmmakers will frequently describe a particular creative choice as something done "instinctively" or "intuitively," a nonconscious process they can't put into words. Writer-director John Lasseter told us "I reach down and trust my instinct, trust my gut. It just feels right." Editor Lisa Fruchtman often follows "some kind of intuitive hunch that can't even be articulated." Cinematographer Conrad Hall says that "when you do it instinctively, it's hard to articulate what the process really is. I don't know how you can describe 'instinct' except to say that it comes out of . . . well, you don't know where, basically."

The nonconscious parts of our minds are often the most spontaneously creative. We look next at **Intuition,** the ability to know things without using a conscious reasoning process. Intuition may at times seem eerie or mystical, but it's a perfectly natural and understandable part of the way our minds function. Cognitive scientist Steven Pinker has written that "intuitive psychology is still the most useful and complete science of behavior there is. To predict the vast majority of human acts . . . you don't need to crank through a mathematical model, run a computer simulation of a neural network, or hire a professional psychologist; you can just ask your grandmother."

We are wired for intuition, in part because we must sense, evaluate and respond to far more information about ourselves and the world around us than we could ever follow consciously. Rather than try to assess logically every possible choice we could make, usually a vast or even infinite set of options, our intuition helps us preselect the most promising choices. This nonconscious sorting out is crucial to creativity. Even scientists rely on it. Physicist and biologist Leo Szilard wrote that "the creative scientist has much in common with the artist and the poet . . . Those insights in science that have led to a breakthrough were not logically derived from preexisting knowledge: The creative processes on which the progress of science is based operate on the level of the subconscious."

What does relying on this nonconscious part of our minds feel like? We've all had the experience of driving on "autopilot," arriving somewhere and realizing that we've been lost in conversation or thought, yet our nonconscious mind has handled all the driving and navigation tasks, or alerted us if something demanded our conscious attention. We can engage in highly complex activities—play a musical instrument or take part in a sport—without thinking about what we are doing. In fact, if we do try to think consciously about just what it is that we're doing while engaged in such complex activities, we probably can't do them as well.

Not only can we do things physically without thinking about them, we can give our nonconscious minds tasks to do while we turn our attention elsewhere. We might fail to remember a name or a fact, and then minutes or hours later the answer will pop into our conscious minds without our having been aware that we were still trying to recall it. We make judgments about people we are dealing with—are they trustworthy? reliable? sincere?— without being able to explain the basis for our feelings. The list of our nonconscious mental activities could go on and on. In fact, most of our mental functions are carried out beyond the level of our awareness. We might even think of the conscious, self-aware part of our being as a rather specialized function of the mind that focuses our mental attention in a way that is useful in certain situations.

The strange, elusive communications we receive from our nonconscious minds manifest themselves in many ways, from doodles to dreams, from vague hunches to sudden moments of clarity and insight. The inexact, even messy nature of intuition can make it frustrating and even frightening to rely on. Creativity would be easier (if far less interesting) if it were neat and predictable, something we could summon up at will and understand thoroughly. But surprise, unpremeditated leaps and serendipitous discoveries are intrinsic parts of the best creative work.

However mercurial our intuition may be, we can nevertheless learn to strengthen it, stimulate it and be more attuned to its wisdom. In this chapter, we see the importance of learning to encourage and trust the invisible currents of our intuition, harmonizing our conscious minds with the unexpected truths that come from the heart and the gut. In **Open-closedness: *The Link Between Intellect and Intuition,*** we see that intuition is not a mystical shortcut to creativity, but rather the result of extensive experience, preparation and conscious thought. We next look, in **The Dreamer: *Connecting to the Nonconscious Mind,*** at how our filmmakers use dreams, dreaminess and playfulness to encourage their intuition. Finally, **Time at the Desk and Time Running in the Forest: *Enticing Your Intuition*** explores the seemingly paradoxical relationship between intuition and disciplined work, especially with regard to how our filmmakers deal with getting creatively "unstuck."

Open-closedness: *The Link Between Intellect and Intuition*

One problem with trusting our intuition is that it can sometimes be completely wrong. At the end of **Inquiry,** we talked about the reflexive assumptions we inevitably absorb from our culture. These can bias us about everything from our understanding of the cosmos and our place in it (for most of human history, for example, it seemed intuitively obvious to people that the Earth was flat, and the center of the universe) to our intuitions about other people (our initial judgments can turn out to be entirely off the mark, particularly when we unthinkingly apply culturally learned stereotypes).

In creative efforts, what feels like intuition may be nothing more than the first thing that comes to mind, often reflecting an unconscious preference for the familiar, leading back to formula and cliché. As teachers, we encourage our students to trust their intuition, but only in conjunction with the conscious preparation described in **Inquiry.** The education, observation, research and life experience outlined in that chapter train our minds to look past reflexive assumptions to more deeply truthful and original intuitions. If you're learning to play a musical instrument, you first have to be very aware of what you're doing, and practice many long hours, before you can do it well intuitively. In the same way, intuition in creative filmmaking is dependable in proportion to the extent that you have prepared yourself thoroughly with a questioning mindset and a broadened perspective.

Writer-director Anthony Minghella talks about his intuitions as "entirely educated activities, the end of a process where you've narrowed down the course until you can just run along it. You've thought your way—and that's the only way I can describe it. I don't think of it as remotely mystical or spiritual. It's just work." And documentary filmmaker Renee Tajima-Peña told us, "You have to think intuitively, which is why I start with an intellectual framework, so I don't get lost in my own brain synapses."

Actors, when performing, are also relying on intuition that has been fed by careful preparation. Kathy Baker comes onto a production having already worked through the emotional structure of the role through her readings of the script: "Whether or not it's taken me thirty seconds, or three weeks, I've done that by myself." But she still needs to build her characterization through the physical details of appearance and environment: "I've almost always said to the wardrobe people, 'This is where I start, so what is she going to wear?' On *Edward Scissorhands,* I had to see what Joyce was wearing—the pastels—and then get the wig on, and see that little neighborhood—who knew they were going to do that?—and the car she drives, and the light, that bright, flat Florida light. At that point, boom, I'm there. I don't have to think about the character anymore."

Kathy next works through the "geography" of each scene, developing a mental "map" of her performance: "The map has to do with what I'm doing physically, and how the lines fall into that. If we do the scene in the living room or we do it on the front porch, that's part of the map, so that's important to know. It changes the way I do it." Once she is dressed and has worked out her map, Kathy feels the confidence to put all her preparation out of her mind and simply respond in character.

One of the many paradoxes of intuition is that once you have "thought your way" as Anthony describes it, the next step is to stop thinking about what you've worked out and just respond intuitively. When Lisa Fruchtman edits, she tries to be "in a very nonintellectual, intuitive place. I intentionally disarm the intellectual side of my brain, maybe because I have a lot of confidence in it and I know it's going to be operating anyway. Why do I make one editing choice and not the other? I often don't know why. It's the intuitive, rhythmic, aesthetic, visual, emotional component that can't be bottled."

Walter Murch considers intellectual preparation essential for that hallmark of intuition, serendipity, the ability to discover things you weren't consciously seeking. But there is a delicate balance required between intellect and intuition. "One of the essences of filmmaking is that you try to construct the making of the film such that it can take advantage of serendipity. The phrase that I use in these states is a kind of open-closedness or a closed-openness. You can't lock yourself into a pattern in advance, otherwise you can't take advantage of any of the spontaneous things that come up, and you will surely crash. On the other hand, if you have no idea going in, then you're simply a leaf being blown in the wind." Walter uses the mental image of a parachute to represent his intuitive process. "Parachutes only function in a state of open-closedness. If it's completely closed, you fall. If it's completely open you fall as well. It has to be this thing that is both open to the air coming into it and yet closed enough to contain the air."

Walter Murch uses a "picture wall" while editing. He arranges the still frames in the order they were shot, not in the order they appear in the film. This more random display is a way of "stirring the pot" and "avoiding the danger of images sedimenting on the bottom. It's a triggering mechanism."

Maintaining this balanced state can be difficult, in part because the spontaneous ideas Walter describes are unpredictable, and we would like to be able to summon them up at will. James Newton Howard has found that his creativity "derives so completely from the subconscious" that it has been essential for him to learn to trust that it will happen. "And that's something very hard to trust initially, because no matter how hard I sit at a piano and try to conjure up an idea, forcing it or willing it to happen just won't work." What he finds does work is "immersion in a state of mind, an openness to the availability of an idea. I just surrender to whatever the moment is—it sounds very cosmic, but it has really served me well."

"It Comes Out in the Pictures"

C O N R A D H A L L , cinematographer

I prepare for each day of shooting, but I don't have a plan. Or rather, the plan I have is about the scene in relationship to the other scenes, a plan that comes out of understanding the story very well because I've read it over and over again, and put it inside of me. And I reread every scene the night before and think about it. I know what's to be done. Internally, I know all of that.

But I can't plan the specifics before I have a chance to watch what the actors do with the script and have a sense of the vision of the director. I'm living the story at the moment that it's being told, not the moment that it was written, not the moment that I read it. When we go into rehearsals, in the place where we've chosen to play this thing, and at the time of day that we know it occurs in the story, then all of these factors come to bear on me, and I pull out compositionally the light, movement, whether it should be wide-angle or telephoto, and all of the aspects of seeing a film.

For *American Beauty,* the story is not judgmental, even though there are all these dysfunctional things going on. And so I tried not to pass judgment on the characters through the cinematography. I didn't make the father look evil when he was about to consummate his relationship with his daughter's young friend. And I didn't make him saintlike when he realized that she was a virgin and what a fool he was. I just put it in the kind of romantic setting that it deserved, which was a lot of darkness and a sense of being alone in his living room with this storm going on outside, and a little dot of red on the black rose. Sam Mendes, the director, had it pretty well storyboarded that way, too. And the set was beautiful. Everybody is contributing to those pictures and telling the story—the art director, the actors, the costumers—we're all in it together.

Overall, the scenes of *American Beauty* are not stylized in any way. I didn't want to romanticize, or create too surreal an effect for this bizarre family. There is a kind of stylization because the boy sees his part of the story through his video camera, so we have a very different kind of imagery there that is very strong visually in telling the story. But we decided to not go for unusual compositions. It was better to allow their actions to just be in a simple frame, and to have this sort of classic sense of being central, being straightforward in the telling of the tale. For the scene in the dining room, you just move in very slowly to these three people talking, with everything dead center.

Annette Bening, Thora Birch, and Kevin Spacey (Carolyn, Jane, and Lester Burnham) in *American Beauty*

And then we have medium shots of the individual characters right in the center of the frame, very classic compositionally. It allows their behavior to be observed without creating any visual influence upon it.

I like to think about things like surprises, how to create gasps, visual gasps. You don't know exactly what's going to happen and then, wham, something opens up and it becomes wondrous, or beautiful, or magical. Like the scene where Jane [Thora Birch] and Ricky [Wes Bentley] are watching a bag floating around, a drug dealer articulating how beautiful real life is by watching a plastic bag that most people would not think was something wonderful. But after that scene you do think it's something wonderful, rather than a dirty old bag in the wind. You watch the joy of that haphazard kind of art that's happening, and you're realizing that there's something beautiful.

And at the same time, it's a love scene between two people. She's listening to him and she's falling in love. And you can see what an artist he is because he's so passionate about describing what he feels about this bag, and how it pertains to life. And she takes his hand and kisses it, and then says "Are you hungry?" It's such a good scene! And once the scene has gotten to you in the writing, then it comes out in the pictures, you know what I mean?

Jeannine Oppewall described her own version of "open-closedness," telling us that "it's important not to go into a project with ideas set in concrete. If you as a designer approach a project and say 'I have a vision that it has to be exactly this or that,' you deny the material sometimes, deny it coming into its own. You have to let the material breathe." Her metaphor for this is that the material will, in effect, tell you "what it wants to be. It sounds kind of silly, but designers will come into a room and talk about how the wall wants to be red." In developing a creative relationship with the physical world, she has learned to think in terms that sound animistic. "You can walk by a rock, a tree, a building and they each have a spirit. If you're sensitive and aware, you know what that spirit is and you respond to it, you know when to use it, know how to manipulate elements that add to that spirit." Jeannine concludes that "designers are sort of shamans," but she also makes clear that this shaman-like ability is not metaphysical but the result of careful preparation. "It's something that comes from years of being an observer, a careful observer of life and nature and the constructed universe. And it's something that you're trained to notice and take advantage of."

Jeannine's metaphor of being a shaman finding the spirit of an inanimate object is similar to what animator John Lasseter describes as finding the "integrity" of an object. He has discovered that "if you study an inanimate object, you can pull out everything you need to bring it alive." For manufactured objects, he first considers their purpose, why they are made. "A glass is made to hold liquid, so if a glass were alive it would want to hold liquid more than anything else in the world. A full glass is a happy glass." As John talked with us, he picked up his paper coffee cup and contemplated it. "This coffee cup in my hand is very happy, it's full of warm liquid and it's doing a good job. But it's starting to be a little sad because it's getting less warm." He took a sip and then reflected again. "The more I drink, the more it gets worried, because it's losing its liquid. In fact, this is probably one of the saddest characters there is—a cup that's meant to hold liquid just once, and then it's thrown away."

John Lasseter with the collectible toys in his office

John's ability to connect emotionally with inanimate objects led him to the idea for *Toy Story 2.* "My four young boys came into my office and started grabbing the toys off the shelves and playing with them, and I'm, like, 'no, no, no, no, no!' There are a lot of one-of-a-kind toys, prototypes or things that were given to me, that mean a lot to me." Then John started to look at it "from the toy's point of view, and I thought 'how sad it is, a toy that wants to be played with by a child more than anything else, but is autographed by Tom Hanks.' " This caused him to wonder "what would it be like if Woody"—the cowboy doll in *Toy Story*—"actually were a rare, valuable toy. Andy plays with him and loves him, but we find out that he's a rare collectible and he would be discovered by someone who knew his value. He's so valuable that he would be stolen."

If we can imagine the emotions of inanimate objects, not surprisingly we can extend this shaman-like connection to human characters in a film as well. Our filmmakers describe developing an intuitive relationship with the spirit of their characters, getting to a place where the characters seem to take on a life of their own. When Pamela Douglas is writing, she will "sit and actually wait until I hear the characters speak to me. They will not write the scene, they will live the scene. They will be in that place in time, living and breathing, and I will be the fortunate one chosen to write down what it is that they are doing." She sees this intuitive writing as "the reverse of the paper-doll method of manipulating characters, where I move these people around and make them do things. If I'm making them do things, it's probably not genuine." Anthony Minghella told us that when he's at a good place in his writing, "It's not like I elect for somebody to get up and move and do something: They are doing that, and I'm just witnessing it, hurrying up to try and keep up with whatever it is that I know is the right thing to happen."

Kimberly Peirce, working on the screenplay for *Boys Don't Cry*, felt at times as if she were communicating with the real-life Brandon Teena, the murdered central character of her story. "I would wake up in the middle of the night and say, almost as if to Brandon, 'Is this right? Is this how it would have been? Is this how you would have said it?'" She finds that "you start to do that with all your characters, begin to know what might have happened. You just know it." But again, this knowledge is the result of preparation, thought and immersion in the process. "It's because you've subjected yourself to every character, to what they want and need. It takes a while. I have to surrender to the parameters of the characters, the circumstances and the event to begin to know. You follow your intuition, but you also want to know and follow your craft because making a movie is like being an archaeologist— you've got to dig out what's been buried, the underlying emotional truth."

Because the serendipity of intuition is random and accidental, one of the dangers is seeing its products as mistakes or as creatively trivial. We need to be alert and open to recognizing good ideas when they come along. James Newton Howard observes that "anybody who's a decent pianist can improvise and accidentally play a lot of great stuff." What's important, he's found, is "recognizing that moment when you've written something promising, and not letting it escape. It's possible to let some of your best work slip right through your fingers. It might be just a sequence of three notes presented in a certain way, with a tiny little hesitation, and my ear just sort of pricks up and I listen to that. The magic, in a way, is recognizing that moment as it floats by, and saying, 'Oh, there's one. I need that.' That one little moment of spark is where a lot of the magic lives."

James, as an example, told us about coming up with "the theme for 'the sixth sense,'" the supernatural power in the movie of the same name. "I mean, what was the sound that you heard? There's a beneficent quality to this thing. It's not all scary. Night [M. Night Shyamalan, writer-director of *The Sixth Sense*] sent me an e-mail—it said something like, 'Think of it as something alive. It's a force that moves unseen from one room to the next.' It was just the most chilling, crazy e-mail I've ever gotten. And then I realized I'd already written the theme, it was a small part within a cue for when Cole is in the church with Bruce Willis early on. It had just this little kind of quality to it. I went back and expanded it, put it in a different scene by itself, and sure enough, that was it. It was there all along. And it could have been thrown out with the bath water."

The Dreamer: *Connecting to the Nonconscious Mind*

The receptiveness to nonconscious creativity described by our filmmakers can be encouraged by connecting more deeply to those aspects of our lives—dreams, daydreaming, being lost in play—that are the most spontaneous. Several of our filmmakers have already spoken of creating within a dreamy state of consciousness where they lost track of time, of concerns and worries and judgments and expectations, of themselves. Composer John Cage once described to painter Philip Guston how "when you start working, everybody is in your studio—the past, your friends, enemies, the art world, and above all, your own ideas—all are there. But as you continue painting, they start leaving, one by one, and you are left completely alone. Then, if you are lucky, even you leave."

We begin with dreams, those haunting and mysterious landscapes of our nonconscious minds. Artists of all kinds have long used dreams for inspiration, but film is a particularly fertile ground for working from dreams because films themselves have a dreamlike quality. Swedish writer-director Ingmar Bergman wrote about "film as dream," believing that "no form of art goes beyond ordinary consciousness as film does, straight to our emotions, deep into the twilight room of the soul." And the late Luis Buñuel, the Spanish-born filmmaker who first brought surrealism to cinema, said that "film seems to be an involuntary imitation of dream. The darkness that gradually invades the auditorium is the equivalent of closing our eyes."

Walter Murch notes that there is a paradox about edited film, "which is that it presents a continuous reality that is made up of chopped-up pieces, both of sound and of picture, and yet this strikes the viewer as being continuous." He finds this strange, given that "we have no biological experience of visual discontinuity. In our four hundred million years of evolution, we have experienced reality as one long dolly shot." Why, then, has it been easy for us to accept the discontinuity of film? Even though we're not used to looking at something while awake "and then having that thing ripped away instantaneously and replaced by something else," Walter is struck by the fact that in dreams we do have that experience. He speculates that the "swoon" people fall into when they watch a film is literally analogous to our dream state, and perhaps the reason that film editing works.

Whatever the cinematic quality of dreams may be, our filmmakers find their dreams to be a rich source of intuitive inspiration. Renee Tajima-Peña describes being in the middle of making a film, and getting into a state where she is "all stressed out and can't sleep because I'm trying to figure something out." If she can get herself to "sleep for a long time and just dream about it," the answer will often come. But she cautions "you have to make sure you remember your dreams when you wake up."

Kimberly Peirce, an admirer of the dream theories of psychologist Carl Jung, recalls that "dreams were a big, big part of *Boys Don't Cry*." At the beginning of the project, she had recurrent dreams about her skin burning off, which she connects to the research interviews she was doing with transsexuals, some of whom described feeling "on fire, and uncomfortable in their own skin." She believes that her way of both incorporating and emotionally releasing those images "was to dream that I was unzipping my skin, or that it was burning off. I'd wake up in these cold sweats, and then just write it down. It was terrifying to go through all those nightmares, but it was great." These dreams strongly influenced the film, even though they weren't reproduced in any literal way. She finds that a dream image will leave an emotional impression, "and it won't be, 'oh, I want to transpose this image directly onto the film,' but rather 'I want to transpose this emotional state onto the film.' "

Anthony Minghella based a scene in *The Talented Mr. Ripley* on a dream he had that combined an image from the book *The English Patient*—a statue of the Madonna rising out of the water—with the new element of a floating corpse nearby. As with Kimberly, he considers the macabre juxtaposition the result of the preparation he was doing: "I was reading a lot about Gore Vidal and Tennessee Williams, and other displaced Americans working in Europe—what they felt about Europe, and their obsession with the fact that, on the one hand, that period in Italy was about modernism, but it was modernism written over quite pagan ideas and rituals. I'd spent a lot of time in Rome, and Rome is this odd collision of the modern and the ancient. I wanted the film to speak of that, so I was thinking about superstition, and Catholicism, and the fact that the film was about murder, and bodies, and those things just started to float up, I guess, into my subconscious."

Gore Vidal, coincidentally, has said "I write shortly after I wake up because one is closest to the dream world that one has just left." Renee finds that a lot of her ideas "come when I'm asleep, or that half-awake kind of thinking about it." This dreamy, half-awake state is a very energized, active mode, with a sense of being immersed and engaged, quite different from what we mean when we say we're half-asleep, that is, drowsy. Anthony, when he's writing well, is in "some form of trance. I'm in a place where I can't watch the process too much. It's just happening." Kate, in **Introspection,** described editing with "the kind of concentration and focus where you lose yourself."

"It's an Intuitive Process"

LISA FRUCHTMAN, editor

My preferred way of working is quite dreamy. If you allow yourself to play with the material, put it together in a way that isn't the most obvious, and then it clicks, there's that tremendous "aha" moment like they talk about in science. In film, too, you do something, you don't know at first why it really works, but it does. When it's done right, it feels so right. Like it's meant to be cut that way.

When I designed the John Glenn flight for *The Right Stuff,* the sequence had every conceivable element in it—NASA archival footage from that and similar flights, matte paintings, documentary footage from the era such as the shots of Times Square. Phil Kaufman, the director, had shot scenes of the NASA control rooms around the world, with dialogue that was taken from the actual transcripts of the flight. We had the footage of the Aborigines in Australia, and we had Glenn in the capsule with just black outside the window. None of it was scripted as to "this goes here, this goes there."

We went through several months of not having a form for the whole sequence. One idea for a long time was showing what was going on down on Earth as he crossed. I did montages of things that were happening all over the world, and I'd show that and everyone would go, "Uh-huh, well, I guess we don't have it yet." That never worked and all kinds of things never worked.

All the various ways we tried to create the sequence, they were just factual. They achieved the goal of telling the story of orbiting the globe three times, but they had no power. We needed to be true to the facts—the three orbits, what happened to him during the various orbits, the kind of rocket. But what the sequence was about, really, was wonder. It's hard to believe now, because it seems so obvious in retrospect. Yes, he was the first man to orbit the earth, he went around three times, and ultimately, he got into trouble—all those things needed to be in-corporated. But what was extraordinary was the sense of wonder, and the challenge was, how are we going to get to that?

There was a regular special effects department, and a model department and matte paintings. Phil also hired Jordan Belson, an experimental filmmaker of the 1960s. There was nothing outside the capsule window when they shot it, so at each stage, I could decide what would go outside the window—light, or a piece of NASA footage, or a piece of Jordan's footage. The model department would send film of a little capsule on a string, going left to right, right to left, forward and backward, and I would bi-pack two pieces of film—put one piece of film on top of the other on the editing flatbed—to combine the capsule images with the NASA footage or the matte paintings. I would decide, "Okay, it's going to go left to right, and then right to left, and then I need a moonrise." I would call Jordan and say, "I need a moonrise." A couple of weeks later, this beautiful, abstract, gorgeous moonrise would arrive. And that's how the scene was created. Why should the capsule move left to right, or why do I feel like the moon should rise? There are so many elements that have to come together—rhythm, visual impact, story, theme—that in the end you can't say. It's an intuitive process.

Kimberly tries to "spend time in a dream state" as much as possible while awake. "I swim every day, and when I swim, I go to outer space. And I listen to music all day." This allows her to "almost not fully wake up all day long— it's like a waking dream where you can just zone out." When she's doing this successfully, she feels like she's living two lives: "One is the life when you're in that state, not being too distracted by other people, and the other life is when you're dealing with a lot of the B.S." of film production. She tries to do what she can to "decrease the B.S." and limit its ability to "interfere too much with my ability to escape."

Kimberly's sense of "living two lives," one immersed in the practicalities of her work and the other in a creative waking dream, is echoed by Kathy Baker's description of feeling as if she has two people inside her when she performs. She told us about filming a particularly harrowing scene in *Street Smart,* where Morgan Freeman's character, Fast Black, threatens to cut out the eye of her character, Punchy: "I knew Morgan would never hurt me. I didn't even realize until I watched the film later that he not only put the scissors here on my cheek [close to the eye], but he moved the blade up so that it was pushing toward my eye. And people say to me, 'How did you do that?'" Her answer is that she somehow simultaneously knew "I'm Kathy Baker, and Morgan Freeman isn't going to hurt me, and I'm also Punchy, scared out of my fucking mind, because Punchy *knows* that Fast is going to cut her eye out."

As intense as a scene like that is, we can see the connection between acting and the world of make-believe pretending and spontaneous play that children engage in so easily. Hanif believes that "if you're interested in creativity, the best place to start is with children. I suppose being creative is what children do when their parents go out of the room. They start to imagine and make stuff up that hasn't been put into their head by their parents—they make something that wasn't there before." He echoes the idea of "two lives" when he notes that what adults and children have in common when they're playing is "that way of being with yourself and not with yourself—where you don't know quite what you're doing, where you experiment, where you see what happens, where you take various elements and see if they go together, where your mind is open in certain kinds of ways."

Many of our filmmakers talk about the value of "playing" with the material. Renee recalls that with *My America,* "I tried to make the film very intuitively, especially, cutting it very intuitively." Although she doesn't edit her own films, there was a period where she sat down at the editing table and "just played around with it myself." Kate Amend says that while editors need patience and concentration, "you have to be playful. You have to have a sense of adventure and a sense of play. The actual process itself is fun, a big creative adventure. It's play, in a lot of ways."

Time at the Desk and Time Running in the Forest: *Enticing Your Intuition*

Relying on intuition may sound like undisciplined chaos. The word "dreaminess" might seem to imply a lack of focus or an avoidance of disciplined work. But our filmmakers make clear that good intuition and the state of creative dreaminess are closely linked to long, patient hours of creative effort. Hanif Kureishi told us: "I think ideas come when they know you're going to be sitting there waiting for them. Out of the chaos of the rest of my life, I have to create space and time to write." Like most writers he knows, he sits down every morning at the same time and starts writing. Then within that focused structure, he feels free to "play around. If you don't sit down, there's no freedom in the art at all. You need to have discipline in order to be free." Where does this discipline come from? "I love to write, and the love creates the discipline. Everybody has methods to keep themselves at the desk, and keeping yourself at the desk can be quite hard work. But you can only really develop as a writer if you do it consistently."

Anthony Minghella, once he's arrived at the writing stage, isolates himself physically: "I can just go into a zone, and that zone has taken me so long to get to, I get very pernickety about it being invaded in any way. So I've given up trying to write in my own environment. I go to a place in the country, and just lock myself in and don't come out." At this stage he gives himself page targets each day. "I have such a pedestrian process, it's ridiculous. I get into this very strict 'you will get to this point by tonight' mode. It takes me so long to get going, usually a year before I can write anything, that when I start, I will brook no psychic jousting. I tell myself, 'okay, you've screwed around for eleven months, now you're going to write.'"

Lisa describes a focused dreamy state similar to Anthony's zone, and like him she finds that she must spend many hours every day in the editing room to arrive there, and still "can only get to this state if I'm working alone a lot of the time. If I work with a director who insists on being in the room, I have to somehow get around that." When she first worked with director Randa Haines, on *Children of a Lesser God,* Randa wanted to be in the editing room while Lisa worked. "I had to find a way to have public solitude, to ignore the fact that she was in the room—not talk, not be self-conscious that she was watching me, not feel defensive about anything I was trying out. And she had to find a way to watch and not intervene. So we became good friends, and sometimes I was able to say 'you've got to leave.' And sometimes I was able to have an out loud dialogue with her which was not that different from the inner dialogue I would have with myself."

The need for "public solitude" can be particularly challenging for actors, who must intimately bare their souls while surrounded by dozens of people. Kathy has discovered that she can shut out everyone else while filming, but only if, just before she starts to act, she hears the familiar words " 'Rolling. Speed. Marker. Action.' I learned that if they don't say that, I can't do it."

When she encountered new equipment that didn't require a marker, and "the director just said 'action,' I said, 'Wait a minute—you can't just say *action*.'" This sequence of four words, almost like a magical incantation, is such an important and precise mental cue for her that when she worked with a director who politely said "action, please," she had to ask him to not say the word "please."

Walter likes to alternate between periods of solitude and sessions of brainstorming with the director. When he and the director are together, he uses the digital editing system "as a sketch tool to provoke something." Then, working alone on the notes from these sessions, "I will get other ideas that lead me into other areas." As an example of the value of this autonomy, Walter recalls "a scene in *The English Patient* that, as shot, was each member of the party singing 'Yes, We Have No Bananas' in their respective languages. On the page, it looks fine. But the inertia of the film seemed too great. I thought, 'let me abstract it and each will sing one phrase, say there are four phrases of the song, the first will be in English, the second will be in French, the third will be in Italian and the last will be in Arabic and then, you get the idea and it's more dynamic and it's more fun.' And this is kind of a montage, so to speak." He phoned director Anthony Minghella "and I said, 'well, I made a montage.' And he said, 'nothing could make my blood run colder than to hear the word montage.' I said, 'I think you'll like it when you see it.' So I sent him the tape and he called back and said 'I love it.' But that's actually one of those things that if he had been here and I said 'what if I make a montage' and he said 'no, no, no, don't do that,' maybe I wouldn't have gone there."

"I'm Always Problem Solving"

KATE AMEND, editor

My assistants are always amazed that I can stay in the chair for hours and hours. It's just a kind of concentration that I love. I love those hours of just poring over the material, looking at it over and over and over again. If you can't watch footage over and over again, you can't do this kind of work, but I seem to be able to focus that way. It's better to be alone. Even having an assistant in the room, sometimes I'm conscious of them, but usually they just go away and leave me, and work in another room. It feels very creative, a lot of problem solving and trying different things. And just really looking hard, and thinking hard, and being open to trying different things.

Sometimes there's a problem and you're not sure how to fix it. Maybe you don't have the footage to make the scene work. If it involves archival material, you might need to call the researcher and ask for more footage. If there's still shooting to be done, you might talk to the director and put in a request. Or maybe you have to do something with music. Perhaps the scene is just not going to work as a scene—maybe it has to be a montage. Or maybe you just throw it up in the air and try something completely and radically different with it.

Kate Amend editing

But whatever the right idea is, it might not come just then. When I work at home, if there's a scene that's a problem and I'm really not getting anywhere, I can get up and water the tomatoes. Or I go for a walk or a swim. I just put it aside. I'll come back to it the next day, and feel energized again. I'm always problem solving. I like to cook, and when I'm cooking I'll be thinking about the scene. I might be driving. Or in the middle of the night, I'll think of the one thing that will solve it. It's always stored in the back of my mind. It doesn't all happen right in front of the screen.

These filmmakers capture the paradox of diligent dreaminess, focused play. And yet there is one more paradox of creativity inside this one. Although our filmmakers all emphasize the need for putting in the hours at the desk or the editing machine or wherever, they also know that creative ideas can occur anytime, anywhere, and that sometimes you need to get away from the work and the workspace.

Even Hanif, despite his rigorous work schedule, agrees that "there are times when it may be that you shouldn't be at the desk, and there are other things that are more important that you need to do. There's no point in trying to sit at a desk when you really should be running in the forest." He sees the choice to break your work routine or to leave your work area as a difficult one: "Sometimes you say, 'Right, I'm at the desk, but I really want to be going for a walk,' or 'I want to be having a conversation with somebody.' And then you have to make a decision, whether it's better that you should go and have the conversation or whether you should just stay at the desk and carry on with the work." In any event, Hanif finds that "the work is always in your head. When I was walking down the street to get here to the interview, I was thinking about something that I'm working on."

James Newton Howard has learned that "most of the time it happens when I'm in the chair. I think you have to have the time in the chair." But he has also experienced moments "when I'm driving or watching television and I have a very specific feeling that I'm ready to do it. I just know it. And that's a very subtle moment. I'll get up from watching TV and walk into the room where I work, and I'll just start to play, and there it is. With the movie *Dave,* I had a clear, complete idea come to me while I was watching television with my wife. I walked into the other room and, in ten minutes, sort of completed the whole idea." The result was "one of the best themes I've ever written. It wasn't labored or forced, but had a wonderful kind of inevitability about it, which I've sometimes managed to achieve again, and sometimes not."

Pamela Douglas, who writes every day when working on a script, will first close her eyes if she gets stopped in a scene and visualize the world of the movie, the specific place for the scene and the characters moving through it with their needs and fears. If she's still stuck, she'll sometimes take a walk with a notepad "because I find that oxygenating the brain can produce a fresh approach. What I never do is sit and stare at a blank computer screen. I think that's deadening."

Another approach to getting unstuck is to turn to other work, particularly some task that requires less mental effort, and let the problem percolate in your mind. This is easier to do in some areas of film work than in others. Walter Murch notes that "you get stuck all the time." But he has found that the stage he is at in the filmmaking process determines how he confronts these obstacles. On those films he has worked on as a writer, getting stuck "always seems more catastrophic, a wild disproportion between the thing that's getting you stuck and the effect of stuckness." His image for this is "driving an eighteen-wheel juggernaut down the highway, and then suddenly you stop, in an instant. And you look and under the front right wheel is a pebble." In the writing phase, he believes, "you are so early in the process that even a small discontinuity in the story means that you can't go on until you solve the problem." But in editing, there is so much momentum behind what's already been done "that when you get stuck, you don't come to a complete stop. It's more like you're driving along and you feel the engine cough or splutter but the truck continues to move."

It's at this point of being stuck in editing that Walter finds a value in turning to other work. "There's always lots of stuff to do and if you get stuck in one area, what I usually do is just jump over to some other area—'I'll just go over here and smooth out the sound in some backgrounds for a while'—and let the subconscious take its time coming to terms with the problem. Sometimes, there's even some mad inspiration in where I choose to go; it provides me with some little fragment that I use to solve the problem that has got me stuck."

The opportunity to turn to less mentally taxing work while pondering a problem has been affected by technology that has sped up most aspects of the filmmaking process, and created unrealistic expectations about how quickly people should be able to do good creative work. Lisa also will turn to something else while grappling with a problem in editing, and "a lot of times the answer to the other thing will come floating to me." She used to find, with manual editing on a flatbed, a great value to the fact that there was "a lot of built-in down time. While you're looking for the trim, or splicing, or rolling back, or going to get the other roll of film, that's thinking time or associative time." She finds non-linear computerized editing to have many advantages, and she wouldn't want to go back to manual editing, "but the great disadvantage is that people assume you can work as quickly as the machine, and if you can't there's something wrong with you. And I think something is lost—gestating time, time to fool around, for things to reorganize themselves in an inventive way." Lisa tries to recreate that more dreamy, contemplative pace in digital editing. Most important of all, she finds, is that "when I'm stuck, I try to get out of the intellectual framework of 'what should I do now?' I try to get into that free-floating mentality, to let it just appear to me."

This ability to not be too impatient with oneself, but trust that the answer will come, seems crucial. Kimberly has tried to teach herself to "just think, okay, I'm stuck. I'm hitting that blackness. For me, it's not a blank wall, it's just dark. You have to accept it, and remind yourself, 'when it's working, it's working, and it's just not working right now.' It's like my conscious mind has stopped knowing the answer, but it's there somewhere in my subconscious. Sometimes you can go to sleep and the answer will come to you. Sometimes you just indulge your frustration at not yet knowing." When she did become impatient, and turned to producer Christine Vachon for an answer, "Christine would say, 'You know the answer, and I'm not going to tell you.' And then I would always make the right choice. And I would really appreciate that she had allowed me to find it myself."

It seldom works to be impatient with ourselves. And yet our filmmakers report that it does help to have an external deadline. Anthony believes that

"If somebody said to me, 'You know what? It takes you so long, we're not going to give you a deadline,' that would be fatal." Pamela notes that when she's writing on assignment and there's a deadline "there is no possibility of writer's block."

Conrad Hall on the set of
Searching for Bobby Fischer

In the midst of production, the deadlines are non-stop. Kimberly observes that "the funny thing about the set is you don't have time to indulge the moods. So, the blacknesses don't happen, or they happen in a much shorter span, because there's so much pressure to perform." Conrad Hall notes that, as the cinematographer on the set, "when I'm finished lighting, they do the scene and I have to watch it. And then when they're finished doing the scene, they go to the trailers and I have to light the next scene. It's just a constant effort. I'm needed every second of the time." But he finds that the relentless pressure keeps him creatively focused and unstuck. The pressure of production, of needing to be continually in the flow of creativity, can be very appealing to some people compared to the ebb and flow of working in a more solitary creative role. But it can also lead to being so reliant on that pressure that you fall into manufacturing it yourself in order to keep in high gear all the time. Conrad recalls that "in the past, I was sometimes late a little bit, and I wondered why I was late, and I thought to myself, 'it's probably to put myself on edge, so that the adrenaline was already cooking.' I don't like to be late anymore."

Making a film isn't a nine-to-five job, and that's one of its aspects that many filmmakers love. But the intensity of production can also be quite taxing. Conrad finds that the very long days during shooting can eventually become counterproductive: "It's hard to keep creativity at its highest level when everyone's exhausted." James says that he's "learned that even if things are going absolutely perfectly, I'm having no resistance from the director, and it's some of the best music I've ever written, it still takes a lot out of me physically. There's a trade-off for it. By the end of the process, I'm just a wreck. I really need to go away and just physically regenerate." The production process has its own rhythms, with periods of extremely focused effort, followed by slower periods or even hiatuses. It's important to use those more leisurely times to reemerge into the broader world and reconnect with the aspects of life that can make you a more introspective, observant, knowledgeable and intuitive filmmaker: spending more time with family and friends, catching up on reading or theater, engaging in activist causes, traveling, taking a class in watercolor or Russian history, or whatever it might be that will nurture your creativity and humanity as you prepare for the next project.

LIMBERING UP

1) The Emotional Life of Objects

Look around the room you're in, and pick at random four or five inanimate objects. If possible, hold each one in your hands, or go to where it is and run your fingers over it. Imagine you can sense its essence by touching it and looking at it carefully. Think about each object's purpose, its reason for existence. Then imagine an emotional life for the object, and a dramatic conflict it might be facing. Remember John Lasseter's paper cup and its feeling of uselessness when it was drained of coffee. Do those two pictures hanging next to each other on the wall have a deep friendship, a romantic flirtation or perhaps a bitter rivalry? Did the book written in another language have trouble assimilating culturally with the others on the shelf? Is the vase with the big ego fuming because mere daisies were placed in it?

Choose any one of the objects and begin to create the object's "backstory," its history before it came into your life: its politics, attitudes toward sex, relationship to family, feelings toward recycling, career aspirations. Imagine that your object has long dreamed of getting a job as a prop in a film, and that in fact, it wants to play the part of a key metaphor. What metaphoric role does it aspire to? What case would it make for itself in an audition?

2) Daydreaming

What activities help your mind creatively wander? What helps you stop thinking about the mundane plans, deadlines, problems and worries that often occupy our minds? The most helpful activities often require some, but not our full attention, and are largely nonverbal, such as playing or listening to music (especially music without lyrics), gardening, dancing, hiking or lying on your back and gazing at the shapes of passing clouds.

Try to spend several minutes every day in a dreamy state. Observe where your mind drifts, without directing it too much. Let internal "chatter" bubble up and float away. Allow your mind to indulge in thoughts of fantasy, wonder and meaningful memory.

3) Making New Connections

The parts of our brains that "associate" one thing with another, whether words, shapes, colors, sounds or whatever, play a key role in creative activity. One way to access and stimulate this associative response is first to clear and relax your mind and body, then "cluster" words on a page in a free-form manner.

To see how this works, begin with a blank piece of paper, and in the middle put a single word. You can start with any one of the following: window, blue, pillow, noon, toe, escape, snowball or choose one of your own.

Draw a circle around the word. Quickly, playfully, and without censoring or judgment, draw a line or arrow from this word and write down another word or phrase that comes to mind. Circle that word or phrase, and then continue from either of the first two, write down another word, and so on. Feel free to jump around, making new links from any of the words on the page.

After a couple of minutes, you will have a large cluster of words that are linked through associations in your mind. Look over the different areas of connectedness on the page, and see if there is a part of the cluster that feels particularly intriguing to you. Spend a few more minutes jotting down ideas or doodling images that utilize several of the words in this area or from the cluster as a whole. Retrace your chain of thought as well as you can, and notice the associated connections your intuitive mind made.

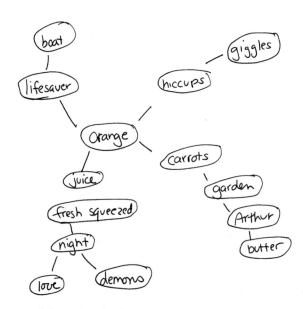

A cluster started with the word "orange"

Use this technique any time you want to get your creative juices flowing, but particularly if you are originating ideas (for a scene, a character, a lighting plan, a color palette, etc.) or feeling stuck at any point in the creative process. (This idea is adapted from Gabrielle Lusser Rico's *Writing the Natural Way*.)

introspection

inquiry

intuition

four interaction

impact

workout

One of the central paradoxes of creative filmmaking from the inside out is that so much of the process is personal and interior, yet somehow each individual voice has to merge into what John Lasseter rightly calls "the most collaborative artistic medium there is." Our fourth "I" is **Interaction,** that sometimes difficult but essential process, whereby your own point of view blends with that of others to create a work that feels like a coherent whole rather than a crazy quilt of mismatched intentions.

In one sense, this harmonizing of separate voices is necessary, because filmmaking is an amalgam of art forms, each one requiring its own expressive skills. And even if one could master all the creative talents involved in filmmaking, the three-ring circus of production almost always requires filmmaking to be a group activity.

But rather than look at this inevitable interaction as an obstacle to creativity to be overcome, we believe, as Walter Murch has written, that collaboration "may be the very thing, if properly encouraged, that allows the

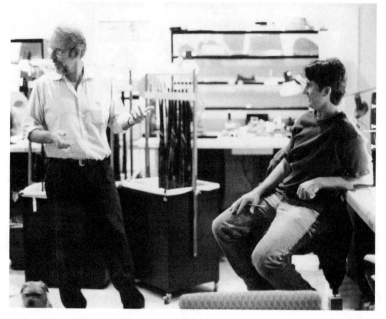

Walter Murch with editing
assistant Michael Struk, who
is conforming Walter's digital
cut to film

work to speak in the most developed way to the largest number of people. Every person who works on a film brings a particular perspective to bear on the subject, and if these perspectives are properly orchestrated by the director, the result will be a multifaceted and yet integrated complexity that will have the greatest chance of catching and sustaining the interest of the audience."

Interaction in filmmaking can be a profoundly creative experience, in which you find yourself stimulated and spurred to do better, your work enriched by the strengths and insights of those around you. John Wells, executive producer of the television series *ER,* notes that "there were five or six people centrally involved in creating *ER.* We got excited and we started bouncing off each other. It's like a basketball team where it's all working, people are passing, everybody's hitting shots and you feel the rhythm. It's selfless."

John also notes, however, that "when you're doing something that's collective, people always want to look to one person, to say 'All right, who really did it?'" In Hollywood, possessory credits on feature films have become common: title cards read "A Jane Doe Film" or "A Film by John Doe." We believe that such credits generally misrepresent and undermine the interactive nature of the creative process in filmmaking.

Yes, usually one person—or a very close partnership—does have primacy as the orchestrator, to use Walter Murch's image, guiding the film to coherence and providing a unifying and overarching vision that everyone else tunes into. (In theatrical features today, that person is almost always the director, while in television it is more often the executive producer. For the purposes of simplicity, we will use the word "director" to mean the person who orchestrates the overall process.) In **Plenty of Rope: *The Fluid Collaboration,*** we see how our filmmakers acknowledge the central role of the director, yet model a process of interaction that, as Hanif Kureishi puts it, "finds a way of making all these voices integrated, without their individuality being lost."

Part of the way this integration of voices occurs is through the push-and-pull, give-and-take debates that take place over the best creative choices. **Arguments Worth Having: *Responding to Creative Differences*** considers how these struggles can play a vital, positive role in shaping a film, so long as the participants focus their disagreements on what is best for the film rather than for their own egos.

Finally, in **Everyone Is Telling the Story: *Establishing a Creative Environment,*** we look at the importance of developing a workplace that is open to and supportive of the contributions of everyone working on a film. We see how those in charge not only need to set the example of encouraging and valuing fluid collaboration, but also must strive to protect the entire production from intrusions by commercial forces that undermine innovation.

Plenty of Rope: *The Fluid Collaboration*

We can look at collaboration in filmmaking as *orchestrated* by the director. The word suggests a process in which the director brings together and guides the distinct contributions of a group of artists. This model is quite different from the mythology of the director as a kind of omniscient dictator (benevolent or otherwise) who either has the finished film envisioned at the very start or else single-handedly determines each key aspect along the way. Everyone else's job then becomes either trying to discern and conform to a predetermined result, or else simply to carry out the director's express bidding as the film progresses.

Walter describes this latter model as "reductive: 'I, the director have a vision of sublime filmmaking, and I know you Lilliputians can never achieve my vision. But if you get, say, eighty-two percent of my idea, then I will allow it in the film.'" In this case, no matter what one does as a collaborator, one's work "is always going to be less than they imagined." Walter, understandably, prefers to work with directors who give their heads of departments "a lot of rope" in taking responsibility and making creative decisions. Or as documentary editor Kate Amend puts it, "if they just want a pair of hands, they don't need me."

A film that was completely foreseen and fixed in the mind of the director from completion of the script on would likely end up seeming pinched and constrained, if not dead and embalmed, on the screen. Federico Fellini, the late Italian writer-director, spoke of the importance of remaining "open to all suggestions, to all changes that occur while the film is growing day to day . . . I prepare everything, more than is necessary, but then I want the film to grow and tell me itself what I must do. . . . I can write a three-page scene which is very beautiful, and then suddenly discover that a certain light accomplishes all that those three pages did." Anthony Minghella also talks about the process of "growing the movie," and recognizes that what he's hoping to achieve as a director "is something much greater than any particular narrow scene that I can manage by myself. I want to have the greatest amount of brain power and creative energy working on the film. The cast and crew are filmmakers in their own right. They're not there to be my servant."

What emerges from our interviews with both directors and their collaborators is a model of interaction with a great deal of autonomy and leeway, but guided by the director, who becomes a kind of human tuning fork from whom the other creative personnel take their cues. Rather than a rigid hub-and-spokes authority structure, our filmmakers see a flowing and intricately interconnected process, where each creative filmmaker responds constantly to the contributions of the other cast and crew members, and spontaneously expands upon them.

Editor Lisa Fruchtman sees the ideal interaction as "a fluid process, and each step has to be fluid. The script has to be great and seem to be rock solid, but when the actors come, if they don't add something unexpected to it, another layer, then it doesn't come alive. Or if the production designer doesn't add something that the director didn't think of, it doesn't come alive. Or if the director of photography doesn't have an inspiration or doesn't respond to things in the moment—the light is different or the location is different than anyone anticipated—then the movie is dead. So each step along the way, there are unforeseen things that happen and unforeseeable combinations that come about."

Lisa cautions that for this to work, "you have to feel that the director is not just flailing around, that the process is one of discovery, not repair. And I think it's a thin line. I'm not interested in working with someone who isn't prepared, hasn't done their work, doesn't have a vision, and I'm going to do all the work. But I'm also not interested in simply executing something that's already figured out." She has found that "very talented directors," such as

Francis Ford Coppola who she worked with on *Apocalypse Now* and *The Godfather, Part III,* can "shoot the movie in a way that allows room for things to happen, where they don't know exactly how it will go together. I don't consider that a limitation but rather a strength. There are people who don't like to work that way. But for me and others that Francis draws to him, that seemingly chaotic atmosphere is very creative. I can genuinely say that when neither I nor anyone else knows what to do, I feel great! My eyes light up!"

Creative fluidity, Lisa says, requires that the filmmakers other than the director tune into the director's guiding vision even as they seek to make their own distinct contribution. In fact, she sees her principal role as "being attuned to the director's vision of the movie, what the movie is really trying to accomplish. It's the vision that I work from—everything springs from it. A huge part of my job is just absorbing the director's vision before I begin." Becoming attuned, for Lisa, is a largely intuitive process. "When I sit in dailies and the director is saying 'Oh, I like that take, and use that take and use this moment,' I have my assistant write all those things down while I'm just trying to absorb what the director's feeling about the material is, and what their sensibility is."

"The best director for me," production designer Jeannine Oppewall told us, "is one who articulates to a certain degree, and then just says 'Here's the rope, go hang yourself, then let me know when you're dead or alive, then come back.'" As with Lisa, this approach for Jeannine requires a director who allows creative leeway, but at the same time is very well prepared. She prefers working with people who "leave me to direct the design aspects of it. Don't ask me how I'm going to do it, because I don't know right now, but when I know, I'll come back and tell you." On the other hand, she expects the director to be involved and informed enough to give her collaborative input. "I've worked with at least one director who didn't really care what was in the background, because the only thing he really understood was moving actors. He could just as easily have imagined a

Jeannine Oppewall with director Curtis Hanson on the set of *L.A. Confidential*

scene taking place in the bathroom as well as in the correct environment. That was a problem, because I get no feedback from that. If I'm getting no feedback, after a while I start to feel drained—you need people around you who can give you food." She describes her working relationship with Curtis Hanson on *L.A. Confidential* as "exceptional, because he is really interested in the history of architecture in Los Angeles. If I mentioned a building or style, he actually knew what I was talking about."

"I Collaborate in Order to Lose Myself"

HANIF KUREISHI, writer

As a writer, I don't have to work with other people, but I do. In a sense, you don't want too much control, you don't want to be omnipotent. You can feel yourself going mad if you do it entirely on your own terms. The point is to have them change you. It's like getting married—you're going to find out who you're going to become after a bit. So I collaborate in order to lose myself, to a certain extent.

Working with a director always drives me in a certain direction. Working with Stephen Frears, who directed *My Beautiful Laundrette,* or Udayan Prasad, who did *My Son, the Fanatic,* or Patrice Chéreau who made *Intimacy*—all those films are different because the directors are different. They're similar because they're my voice and my stories. They're also different, because those are the visions of the director, and of the cameraman, and all the other people involved who are going to change the story.

I find that my own particular terrors and fears are not shared by the director. The director doesn't get uptight at that moment and they can push you past it. Stephen Frears wanted *My Beautiful Laundrette* to be more transgressive, wanted me to be a less nervous writer, so he behaved like a good parent. He's older than me and he said, "You can do that and come back alive. I'm here. You're safe," just like with a kid.

You push each other. "Why don't we do that?" "Can't you do it like that?" "Oh, God, it would be better if you could do that." I mean, these are good arguments. They're arguments worth having. If you have ideas which are the same, then it's dull. And if you have ideas which are too different, too diverse, then you can't work together. There are some collaborations that are a pain in the ass.

James Newton Howard, even when scoring a film late in post-production, looks for a fluid interaction in which he's giving vital collaborative input to the director and the editor: "I watch the movie over and over and over again, and my job is to respond emotionally to what's going on. And if I'm good at it, I'm going to have trouble responding to parts of the movie that, for one reason or another, are not succeeding—when there's a bad edit, when the timing is off, when it's an insincere moment from an actor." James also finds that he unlocks new aspects of the picture "by seeing it a different way, and by laying a piece of music in there that perhaps has a different tempo or cadence or resolution than they imagined. Instead of stopping the music cue before that cut to the next morning, I might carry it over into the next scene so that the moment of them having break-

James Newton Howard at the mixing console during a music scoring session

fast together, that was totally insignificant, all of a sudden takes on a whole new resonance because the music connected it to the previous moment."

Walter calls this fluid approach "progressive rather than reductive, meaning that everything builds on everything else. The film grows organically out of the material that is being supplied." He sees this creative progression as spiral-like in form, where "the cameraman looks at the location and says 'Huh, I didn't expect the production designer to do this, but that's interesting. Okay, well, that gives me an idea. If they're going to do that, I'll do this with the light.' Then the actor comes in and says, 'Hmm, I didn't expect the room to be lit this way—so I'll do that with my acting.' Now the cameraman is shooting the actor, and the actor does a move based on this hidden thing. So the cameraman says, 'I didn't expect him to do that, so I'll zoom in at the same time.' Then the soundman says, 'Huh, he's zooming in at the same time. That's interesting. I'll do this.' The editor sees all this in dailies and says, 'I didn't expect them to do that, but that gives me an idea—maybe we can do this.' And the director sees a first cut of that scene and says, 'Hmm, I didn't expect that, but that gives me an idea for something I'll do in the subsequent scene.' " Walter believes the pattern of this spiral, "I didn't expect, therefore I will do" is "really the only way a film can be made, when you think about it. A film is so complicated that if everything had to be spelled out in advance, it would take you a hundred years. You could never do it. So it can only be done by this game of kind of blind man's bluff, in which people use their intuitions and their assumptions to move forward."

Of course, if this fluidity leads to a sudden or substantial change in plans, colleagues may be thrown off balance at first. Kathy Baker notes that if as an actor she has prepared her "map" of a scene, based on the expectation that it will involve "walking down the street, and I get there and they say, 'No, we're going to actually do it in a small little office, and you'll just be sitting there chatting,' I can get a little nutty for a minute." But once she processes the new setting and reestablishes her sense of the "geography," she usually finds that she enjoys the challenge: "I like going, 'Oh, they're sitting quietly. Okay, so that means . . .' whatever it means. It's fun to find out what it means."

Like other collaborations, the one between director and actor seems to flourish best when there is a balanced combination of creative leeway and well-prepared guidance. As a director, Kimberly Peirce finds that both the cast and crew require the same preparation from her: "They need me to know the emotional landscape of the script, inside and out, the spine of the story, the arcs of the characters, their life needs and their scene needs. If I walk on the set with that and an open mind, then any question they throw at me is in the realm of possibility—I can help them do their job." At the same time, the emotionally volatile self-revelation required of an actor can make their interaction with the director particularly charged. Kimberly recalls the night of shooting the rape scene in *Boys Don't Cry*. For the close-ups of Tom, one of the attackers (played by Brendan Sexton III), the crew had shot two takes "and the form of it was violent, but we still weren't there emotionally. So I took Sexton aside and I said, 'Okay, you've got it physically. I'm terrified. But you're not reaching into who Tom is—Tom's sense of self-hatred, Tom's sense of inadequacy. He has to unleash that on Brandon. You're not unleashing it. You're not yet doing it [raping Brandon] because you *need* to do it.'" On the next take, "he found that place in himself, and he unleashed that violence on Brandon, and that was it—that's the take in the movie."

When the crew was ready for the next take, Kimberly saw that the actor had disap-

Peter Sarsgaard (John), Hilary Swank (Brandon) and Brendan Sexton III (Tom), in *Boy's Don't Cry*

peared from the set. "I followed him, and he saw me coming and he turned away saying 'Kim, I'm sorry. I'm crying. Don't look at me.' And I said 'Well, you shouldn't apologize for crying. That's good. The fact that you're crying means that you're not like Tom. He couldn't cry. Had he cried, he might not have raped.' And then Sexton came back. He was terrified by the potential for violence that he had, and then he also found a well of emotion he hadn't known that he had. It opened him up on both extremes."

As wrenching as a scene like that might be to film, the actor only needed to achieve this state of self-revelation once, and as Kimberly notes, that's the take in the film. Anthony observes that, unlike the theatre, "on film, you don't need ever to have the same moment twice. You just need it once, in focus, without any scratches on the film." That aspect of film acting, ephemeral and unpredictable moments that must be captured by the camera, can make the question of balance between guidance and openness particularly crucial for the director. Anthony has found that actors need to be "sufficiently comfortable that they feel they can be emotionally unadorned," and he tries to create for them "an emotional space in which they can work. You have to determine how much of that space feels comfortable. If it's too big, people feel they're going to fall over—they're not protected. And if it's too tight, some people feel claustrophobic."

Kathy prefers a small space when she does the initial rehearsal on the set, with just the director and her fellow actors present: "You know how babies have to be swaddled, or they feel like they're falling? That's how I feel if they don't give me my cozy rehearsal space." After that initial rehearsal, "you can invite the *world* to watch, and we can rehearse it twenty-seven times, or we can shoot it. But I have to have that cozy feeling initially. Otherwise, it will feel too big." And although she likes to talk with the director at length when she is finding her "map," on the set she prefers focused and limited discussion. "I've had directors who tell me too much. I had a director once who, between every take, would kneel down and say in my ear 'Now, don't forget that this moment, she's very angry. However, at the same time, she has to control herself, and . . .' You just have to say, 'That's too much information, because this is my "rolling-speed-marker-action" moment, where you've just got to trust me.'"

When this actor-director interaction works well, it can become very intuitive. With Juliette Binoche, late in the shooting of *The English Patient*, Anthony found that "by that point, our communication had become monosyllabic, because we just understood where we were in the filming process and we were so comfortable with each other. I would open my mouth and she'd say, 'I know. I know what you're going to say.' " Collaboration between actors and a director can be as exciting and rewarding as creative filmmaking gets. Anthony concludes that for him "the best moments in movies are acting moments. They're not shots, they're not locations, they're not effects. When I think about the moments in movies that I have loved, it's always about an actor revealing himself or herself." The elusive, intangible nature of this process is also a vivid example of how all filmmaking interaction must remain fluid, open to discovery and surprise, if a film is to "come alive."

Arguments Worth Having: *Responding to Creative Differences*

Hanif makes a distinction above between a productive collaboration that involves creatively pushing one another with "good arguments" versus one that is "a pain in the ass." It's a cliché of filmmaking that when someone leaves a production, the reason given is "creative differences." And certainly, the ideal model of balance between creative leeway and guided control our filmmakers have described can be difficult to achieve. When collaborators find their creative ideas overridden, how do they handle the rejection? How much should they fight for what they think is the best creative choice, even if they don't have final say? And how does a director or producer override an idea and yet not stifle the openness of the creative process or the collaborator's sense that their ideas are wanted and valued?

For the director, it's important to find people to work with who are sufficiently on the same wavelength, and not, as Hanif said, advocating "ideas which are too different, too diverse." Kimberly conveys the critical importance of these decisions about choosing collaborators when she says that "whenever you hire somebody, there's always a fear that they're not going to really see what you see. You might as well be on a lifeboat, because if that person is not understanding what you're seeing, you're dead, you know? You are relying on them, no matter how domineering you may be. They bring you back stuff they can do that you can't do."

Anthony agrees that "it's desperately important to find people whose opinions you can respect and value. You need as many people around you as possible who can help you identify how to improve something." In fact, once Anthony finds collaborators that are right for him, he wants to work with them over and over: "The team on *Cold Mountain* is exactly the same team, apart from the production designer, that was on *Ripley*, which was the same team that was on *The English Patient*."

Anthony's desire to keep the same team together doesn't mean that he has assembled a group with whom he has no disagreements, or who don't challenge him. He finds instead that he has "gravitated towards very strong personalities. I've surrounded myself with people who are slightly tougher than my own particular temperament. It's almost as if I need to be in a place where I have to prove myself to those people, and satisfy them. I don't know what the psychology is, I just know that when I look at this parade of bad-tempered, demanding souls, I think, well, I collected these people, and I need them. They've made me do better work."

One of those people is Walter Murch, sound designer and film editor on *The English Patient* and *The Talented Mr. Ripley* and *Cold Mountain*. Anthony describes Walter as "very tough on me. He's enormously, *enormously* hard on me. And impatient with me. And challenging of me. I adore him and I think he's one of the most important filmmakers in American film history. Walter, more than anybody, has taught me about film. And he's also done things which have made me crazy, in which I have walked out of the cutting room. And he's walked out of the cutting room on me, where we've knocked heads because it's such an intense relationship." When we reminded Anthony of Walter's story (in **Intuition**) about Anthony acquiescing to his idea for a montage of the "Yes, We Have No Bananas" song in *The English Patient*, he responded "I'm sure that Walter will also have told you that there were things that he wanted to do, that I couldn't have been less flexible about. And I hope we continue not always to agree."

KIMBERLY PEIRCE, writer-director

You use yourself as a barometer for making all your choices, and most of the time you're going to be right. But sometimes you're just going to get attracted to what you personally want. And that's why you need to surround yourself with strong-minded people, who, every now and then, remind you. I arm myself with people who I respect and admire, and I empower them to really stand up to me.

For *Boys Don't Cry*, Lee Percy, the editor, constructed the movie. He decided which line you actually cut out on, and he decided which image you actually go to. I had designed the emotional architecture of it, but having him put the pieces together allowed me to come in fresh, look at it and say "This is working. That's not working. That's great." I find it's a process of layering. I throw the ball out there. They

"A Process of Layering"

pick it up, throw it back. I pick it up and throw it back, each time laying down a new layer.

One challenge we had was to get the portrayal of class right, because class informs everything—your ambitions, your opportunities, your emotional state. Particularly in this story, I needed that to be authentic and emotionally accurate. The farmhouse we used as the main location was a real farmhouse. There had been one beautiful farmhouse that I wanted, and Christine Vachon, my producer, was, like, "Kim, you have to go for the ugly-looking one." She and my editor convinced me. It was the same economic class as the people we were writing about, and therefore everything made sense. The paint was screwed up in the way it should be. The view was right. And then I was saying, "Oh, this is the best thing in the world." So, it's sometimes letting go of what you think is beautiful in order to do what is right.

There are these enduring themes in each of our lives, and I think when you're making the work, you're tapping into them. You keep bringing people into the process. If they're tapped into these themes, you and they come closer and closer to this thing that already exists. I don't think that I invented that story. I think that story passed through me—I helped unleash its truth. Andy Bienen, my writing partner, Lee, my editor, and the audience all helped me see it and construct it. We were all responding to the same thing. It's not about being arbitrarily interesting. It's not "Oh, does that look good? Is that an attractive color or shot?" None of that matters. It's, "Is it right?"

We emphasize the importance of developing good collaborative skills at USC. The second semester production class, for example, is designed around a partnership: the two students coproduce, and one student writes, directs and designs sound while their partner shoots and edits picture. Halfway through the term, they reverse roles and make a second film. Jed's syllabus for this class reads: "At the core of this course is the partnership. A good partnership involves open communication, collaboration, shared responsibility and mutual trust. You will be expected to resolve disagreements in a constructive manner." Some of the working relationships formed in classes and on crews at USC have resulted in long-lasting and successful professional alliances after graduation.

Occasionally, these student collaborations are abrasive and challenging, but they can nevertheless be good learning experiences. Professional interaction can be contentious as well, and our filmmakers have found that greater experience and psychological insight can keep conflicts from becoming counterproductive. Lisa, for example, notes that "the editing room is a very naked place for two people to be. You're there together thinking, 'Oh my god, what do we do now?' Because people feel very vulnerable in the editing room, they play out the key relationships in their lives there." She finds that "gender really matters, the sexual dynamic between the two people matters. But what the content of that dynamic is depends totally on the individual person, whether it's a sexual tension, or whether I come to represent the director's sister or their mother. It's very complex and unpredictable, but it's almost always very intense as well as rewarding."

Kathy finds that the first time she meets with a prospective director, she can usually size up very quickly what kind of collaboration she would have. She may sense that " 'whatever they say is going to be fine,' or 'I'd have to watch myself with this one.' It has to do with eye contact, and whether or not they're really listening. I've been on interviews where the director just tells me all about himself, and his movie, and then says, 'Thank you very much,' and I go, 'Well, how's he going to know who I am, or what I'm doing?'"

Group collaborations may have potential pitfalls quite different from those of one-to-one interactions. Individuals within the group might have tendencies to show off, put other people down, or jockey for position and power. For John Wells, criticism within a creative group can be candid and still be productive, as long as it's "aesthetically based" rather than "self-serving." And, he adds, "you always know the difference." With the writing staffs on his television series, John likes to have a "let's all talk about where the series should go" session at the start of each new television season. "We have a process that happens at the beginning of summer before we start writing again on the show. We sit down, I hand out index cards, and everybody puts down five or ten things they hated the most about the previous year—the moments they thought were the least successful, the things they were embarrassed to be associated with—and then the five or ten things that they were most happy about. And everybody's ox gets gored. But it leads to a really open conversation, where we're honest about each other's work." His model for these sessions comes from classes he remembers as "the best thing from film school, in which people are not trying to demean each other, but are actually trying to make themselves better filmmakers by understanding what somebody else is doing."

Equally hard to learn is judging how to fight for what you think is right, even if you don't have the final say. Lisa notes that as an editor, she is constantly presenting her work for critique. "The director or the producer or the studio may say, 'No, no, no, I like this, but I don't like that' or 'That's wrong, start over,' and sometimes I agree and sometimes I may be completely opposed. It happens on every movie that you win some battles and lose others." She will continue to fight for her ideas, and if she loses the argument, "I often still feel in the end that I'm right and they're wrong and the movie is less than it should be. But I try not to take it personally. I think I've gotten to this Zen place where my ego is less tied up in it." She believes that filmmakers who don't have final say have to find a way to reconcile themselves to holding strong opinions and caring deeply, even when their ideas may be overridden, because "if you don't allow yourself to take that risk, then you can't do anything."

Cinematographer Conrad Hall describes a typical situation where the director has an idea for how to shoot a scene, but Conrad doesn't agree that the director's idea is "a wonderful way to do it." In that case, "I articulate my feelings. If the director decides that he wants to do it his way and not mine, I go ahead and make it happen. At least he's heard my way, and usually tells me why he likes his way better."

As Conrad's example makes clear, it's important for a director overriding a creative choice to make sure that the collaborator has a chance to be heard, that their idea is genuinely considered. If possible, directors should offer reasons for their decisions. Depending on the situation, it may be appropriate for a director to have a full discussion of an idea before making a decision, or even agree to try something more than one way. But sometimes, particularly when there's time pressure, a director has to quickly but respectfully say, "That doesn't work for me," and the collaborator needs to bear in mind, as Conrad does, that "the director is my boss and who I listen to. He's the storyteller, and I'm his or her helper."

Documentary editor Kate Amend also emphasizes the need to fight for the creative choices you think are right, and yet be able in the end to let go. In a sense, Kate preselects the creative atmosphere when she chooses what projects to work on, since she "probably wouldn't work with a director who was dogmatic or authoritarian." Once she's cutting a film, she doesn't like "to show a scene to the director until I feel like I've done everything I possibly can. There's nothing more frustrating than getting notes on things you already know are wrong. I want to present my best possible cut, and if it gets criticized, well, I can handle it." When disagreements do come up, "it's all give and take. I'll express my opinion, but if the director feels very, very strongly, I'll defer to that." Sometimes these disagreements aren't resolved right away. "Maybe two weeks or two months later we'll go back to the original way it was cut, or maybe not. The one thing you really have to develop is the ability to let go of things."

Trust is a word that cropped up several times when our filmmakers talked about working through disagreements with their collaborators. When a level of trust has been established, it's easier to recognize and acknowledge that sometimes you're wrong and they're right. If you're in serious conflict with someone you trust, you may want to step back and ask yourself why. Kathy Baker told us with chagrin about the "first and only fight" she had with *Picket Fences* executive producer and writer David E. Kelley. She had received a script for an episode in which Jill Brock hit her eldest son: "Matthew almost causes Zack to be in this terrible car accident. He's fine, but I'm so mad at Matthew that when I run to the accident, I slap him."

Kathy went into Kelley's office and said " 'I won't do it. I don't hit my kids. I don't believe in hitting kids. Jill would never do it.' He was quite upset with me for that. And he was absolutely right. I didn't trust him. I was out of line. It was the end of a season, I was exhausted, and mostly I was scared. Any time I don't want to play something, within the parameters of something I already trust, it's because I'm scared. I didn't want to go to the place you have to go, in order to be so mad at your own child that you would hit them."

Kelley explained to her all the reasons he wanted her to do it: "He said it was *precisely* because Jill wouldn't do it, precisely because an educated doctor wouldn't hit her child, precisely because I didn't hit my own children. He wanted it to be about people who don't hit their kids, but they are so upset, they're so out of control, that they do. And then, the whole rest of the episode was about Jill feeling terribly, and making it up to the rest of the family, because it permeated the whole family that Mom hit Matthew. It was a wonderful episode. I won an Emmy for it! And I got down on my knees and begged his forgiveness. He had seen my work, and he had figured out that he wanted me to try this. It was a trust thing—he was giving me a gift."

Kathy Baker with Tom Skerritt, Justin Shenkarow and Adam Wylie on the set of *Picket Fences*

James Newton Howard finds that as a composer, it's particularly important for him to not get defensive when a director doesn't like something he's written, since "people respond to music so unpredictably. I can play something that I think is so perfect, just the right shade of whatever, and they hear it, and it's just dead silence in the room after I play the cue. It's that horrible moment where you just know it's not going to fly and you've got to start over." Music is so subjective that if someone says to James of a cue "that's not ironic to me, that's feeling sad," he doesn't argue. "I've learned a long time ago that I can't talk anybody into liking something. I save myself a lot of trouble and just figure out why they don't like it, and try it again." This doesn't mean that James gives up on his own distinct creative approach to the score: "I have just as much chance of doing something different from what they expected and having them like it, as not, because it's so subjective, you just never know."

Sometimes it's the director who has pushed James in an unexpected direction. "For *Snow Falling on Cedars,* Scott Hicks played me a few of his music ideas against picture, and they were so 'out,' so wild, and in many ways, so wrong. He was playing music that was like 'you've got to be joking, this is just so irritating, how can you even score that?' " James and Scott started off with such different sensibilities that they had "huge confrontations." But James tried to open up to and explore these choices that at first seemed entirely wrong. "What was magnificent about it was, what was he liking about it? The more I thought about the angular quality of the things he was playing for me, there was an icy, kind of remote, wintery quality, way below the surface—you had to really dig at it to find what it was doing and sort of experience it. It was used as a sound effect in conjunction with the wind and the geography of where this story took place." James suddenly found himself "without any familiar touchstones, trying to throw away every preconception I had about this movie, and think about it completely differently. And that's when I started writing what became the final score." He ended up feeling that he'd created one of his best scores ever, for "a really wonderfully ambitious and beautiful movie. It was an exploration that I didn't think I was capable of surviving, and I almost didn't. It took me to a place that I had never been before and I think it elevated the quality of my work since. I've never had another experience like *Snow Falling on Cedars.*"

Everyone Is Telling the Story:
Establishing a Creative Environment

Productive, respectful, aesthetically based collaborations, even those between two filmmakers in private, have a way of rippling through and permeating the entire production, just as their opposites—bullying, back-biting, self-serving, ego-tripping and demeaning attitudes—can seep through and poison the well for everyone. From the top down, filmmakers need to work to create an overall environment in which honest and open creative interaction flourishes.

We have focused on the more prominent creative collaborators, but ideally everyone working on a film should feel that they are participating in the creative fluidity our filmmakers have described. Conrad notes that within the camera department, "the assistants are all storytellers, and the operators are storytellers, and I'm a storyteller." He wants his camera crew to have "a lot of input, ideas that they communicate to me that I use when I think they're appropriate, and when I can sell them to the director." He adds that they always "have a lot of freedom about focus and that kind of thing. When an operator's working, I set up the shot and they know what I want, but then actors don't always do what they're expected to do and something will happen, and they have to make decisions on their own. So I urge everybody to feel that they're telling the story as importantly as anybody, and that feeling makes their job interesting and keeps us all focused on doing the good thing for the scene."

Similarly, production designer Jeannine Oppewall wants everyone who works for her, including the painters and the carpenters building the sets, "to have room to add their own creativity. You have to establish an environment where people can create. A good boss makes everybody feel that their contribution is invaluable." Reflecting the way she herself wants to be treated, she says that "if you dictate, if you just go in there and say 'now paint the walls blue,' then people go 'fine, tell me what you want, I'll do it,' but they're not going to bring anything extra to the party." Jeannine emphasizes that "you're hiring them for those personal extras, a spirit, a feeling for the material, a sense of humor, a doggedness that you first saw in them."

As self-evident as these arguments for mutually supportive and respectful creative interactions may seem, the reality is that insecure and incompetent people do get into positions of power and feel threatened by those they fear are more talented than they are. Animation writer-director

John Lasseter describes the anticreative atmosphere he encountered when he first worked at a couple of animation studios early in his career where "the managers at the time were not talented people. They were second-rate animators that had gotten to their leadership positions through attrition. All these young, talented people were coming in, and the managers did everything they could to keep us down. They told us, 'We don't want to hear your ideas. If you don't want to do it this way, there's a line of people outside the door that would love to do what you do.' They actively made you feel like a cog in a wheel."

John contrasts that atmosphere with the one he encountered when he went to work for Ed Catmull in the early days of the Lucasfilm Computer Division. "Ed had the premier computer-graphics research people. I said, 'How did you get these great people here?' And he said, 'Oh, it's easy. I just try to hire people smarter than myself.' And Ed, you have to understand, is one of the best, smartest people that's ever been in computer graphics."

John has tried to apply this lesson to his role as head of creative at Pixar Animation Studios. "One thing I've found is that you never know where the good idea is going to come from. In a creative meeting, as we're listening to all these ideas coming up, I recognize that my job as the director, as the leader, is to just go, 'Oh! Oh! That's good, that's good,' and 'Oh, you could do this, and this, and blah-blah-blah-blah,' you know. And everybody's laughing, and saying 'Oh, this is great.' "

Anthony Minghella with producer Saul Zaentz on the set of *The English Patient*

Andrew Stanton, one of John's writer-director colleagues, likes to compare this creative ferment to the experience of the Beatles: "When you get us all together, it's magic. And when we're apart, it's just harder."

Just as John had a mentor, Ed Catmull, who modeled how to create a good environment for interaction, Anthony Minghella had a similar experience with the legendary producer Saul Zaentz. After seeing Anthony's first feature *Truly, Madly, Deeply*, Zaentz became "so convinced of my talent that he made it possible for me to make *The English Patient*. He had no reason to believe I could make a film of that scale, but he had much more confidence in me than I had." As a result, Anthony felt "enormously empowered by him. I felt as if he had such confidence, that there must be some basis for that confidence. He never let me, for one second, think that I was doing badly, which I think was very smart of him." In turn, Anthony has sought to "hand over a certain amount of empowerment" to the people he collaborates with, and he recognizes that "most of us work best when we feel cherished."

The producer is often in a key position to help create this "cherishing" environment. Ismail Merchant says that actress Madeleine Potter [who had roles in the Merchant Ivory productions *The Bostonians, Slaves of New York* and *The Golden Bowl*] calls him " 'the godfather'—not in the same sense as in the film *The Godfather,* but in a way where people feel they can come to you." Ismail first sets this tone by hosting at the beginning of production "a dinner for everybody that works on the set. They are all there, and I cook for them. And I feel that helps you to establish that the smallest job and the biggest job are treated in the same way. You have respect for a production assistant, as well as the stars of the film." He finds that as a result, "they can speak their minds. If something is not happening in the proper way, you hear from them. A producer must know every depart-ment—he must know costumes, he must know production design. If there is some flaw in any of the departments, or some setback, you go and correct it."

It's easier to have a supportive atmosphere when things are going well. The more crucial test comes when serious problems arise. Conrad remem-bers that on *American Beauty,* "Our first day of shooting was a disaster. It was the scene with Annette Bening and Peter Gallagher at the fast food place. My work just was amateurish. And the place that was picked was to-tally wrong. The actors were forced to go into a scene that was deep into the story. Everybody looked at the dailies and jaws dropped and they said, 'This is Conrad Hall's work? That's [director] Sam Mendes and Annette Bening?' Everybody was just really, really way off the mark." The dailies went to Steven Spielberg (cofounder of DreamWorks SKG, the studio producing the film) who "realized how you can make mistakes, and gave us another whole day to redo the scene, which we did much later on in the picture. The scene turned out to be wonderful. Great scene. And though we had made the mistake, DreamWorks allowed us to do it over again without firing any-body or being too judgmental of us."

Unfortunately, studios are not always understanding and supportive. Corporate and other commercial forces can undermine the creative interactions that a film needs. Directors and creative producers have to try to shield themselves and those working with them from these pressures. John Wells believes "that's really the job that a writer-executive producer in television is most responsible for doing, making certain that the entire creative team is protected and has the opportunity to do their best work." This is not an easy task, because in the hierarchy of the studios, networks and parent corporations, "there are a lot of people with a lot of opinions. I refer to it as 'the world at the other end of the telephone,' and it doesn't have a lot to do with what you're actually doing. You've got to kind of keep it separated out. Nobody's going to remember who the current executive from Warner Bros. was who gave you the notes to change the script. Their name isn't the one up on the screen. The writer, the director, the actors, and the executive producers are the ones who are held responsible for the quality of what it is that you do."

Sometimes the only way to protect the film and its creators is to take strong, even drastic, measures. When Ismail produced *The Golden Bowl,* distributor Miramax Films had them preview the film "at a mall in New Jersey and about half the people gave unfavorable responses." The studio then asked for changes in the film, cuts that Ismail found "abominable. Miramax said, 'If you don't agree to these things, either you pay us $4 million to promote it, or we are going to put it directly onto television, and that's the end of it.' So we said, 'We'll pay you back and take the film.' They never thought that would ever happen, but it did happen. We raised the money—we hocked our things in England and all of that." Ismail sees this decision as "a victory of the artist over money—money is not the main thing in life." He finds that a creative producer "has to fight the battles against people who try to impose their will on filmmakers. There are always battles when you are making a film."

Coincidentally, writer Hanif Kureishi also had a confrontation with Miramax cochairman Harvey Weinstein, who "had lots of ideas for *My Son, the Fanatic,* which in fact were not very good ideas. I had to say to him, 'Look, it wouldn't be my film, it won't be anybody's film. It'll just be bland. It'll have no edge to it if you do that.' In the end, it's the voice of the artist that makes the piece of value."

And yet Harvey Weinstein and Miramax have often been lauded by filmmakers for supporting risk-taking projects that other studios wouldn't touch. Anthony Minghella notes that in backing *The English Patient,* Weinstein "was prepared to give up common sense in the face of hearing real passion, and encountering real passion. He thought, 'Well, this guy has a film there somewhere, and it's worth taking a gamble.' That's what I felt, that he was prepared to gamble."

Juliette Binoche and Ralph Fiennes in *The English Patient*

Anthony tries to look at the process from the perspective of the studio executives who are listening to someone like him argue, "but I believe this movie in which a burnt man is lying on a bed, talking to a nurse in Italy, will be very important!" He remembers it sounding a little absurd even "as I was saying it in the rooms of Paramount, or Fox, or wherever I was trying to enlist support." Skeptical executives would respond: " 'So, let me get it clear: he's burnt, so you can't really recognize him, and he's lying there. And there's a nurse, and she's not American, either, and he's—and—and then what?' 'Well, then he dies, and everybody sort of dies, and . . .' "

Anthony believes that what in the end convinces executives is your passion and your vision. But then, paradoxically, as soon as the backers have their money at stake, "the very thing that attracts a studio or a producer to a filmmaker is often the thing they try to annihilate once they've got that filmmaker on board. They don't want the thing that they bought. They want something else. They're frightened."

At that point, Anthony cautions, "you have to be very careful as a filmmaker not to bend your own taste or lose your own compass." The studios, he believes, expect a good director to fight for what's important to the film. "You have to know that when they say you can't go and shoot in New York, what they mean is, they want to know how desperately you want to shoot in New York, not for you to say, 'All right then.' " At some unconscious level they're testing the filmmaker again, "to make sure that they really are dealing with somebody with a passion and a will and a sensibility, and they've invested wisely."

"We Share the Sensibilities and the Creativity"

ISMAIL MERCHANT, producer

This is the fortieth year of Merchant Ivory Productions. We are all three together [Ismail, director James Ivory and screenwriter Ruth Prawer Jhabvala] although we don't interfere in each other's work. We share the sensibilities and the creativity together, but we never impose our will, that this has to be done this way, because each artist has an independent idea, and their contribution is larger if they're left free. We respect each other. Most of the time we have harmony, because we know what we want as the end result.

We leave Ruth to come up with an idea and a story, or a first draft, you know. We don't interfere when she's writing. Then after she's given it to Jim and myself, then we talk about it, the things that could be worked out so that it could become better. We have suggestions of things to improve, and that really is the best way. She listens to it, and sometimes she may not agree with it. But most of the time, we don't have disagreements.

The director has the complete vision, and is responsible for everything that happens in a film. As a producer, you depend on the director to get his vision—the casting, the look of the film. During the editing, we see the first cut of the film that Jim and the editor make. And then we don't like something, and maybe we have a tremendous fight, so much so that you go out of the editing room and must never be seen again. And then back again.

In *The Bostonians,* there was a scene with Vanessa Redgrave and Christopher Reeve which was a very nice scene, but it didn't add to the thing we wanted. So, we convinced Jim, and then it was eliminated. You have to convince him, you know. It's a slow process, but it's a very worthwhile process.

Ismail Merchant with James Ivory on the set of *Heat and Dust*

However unwieldy it can be, we've seen how interaction is one of the keys to creative filmmaking. If you learn to invite and to feed off the fluid collaborations that can take place, to cherish your collaborators and handle creative differences with trust, honesty and respect, to foster a creative environment, and to convey your passion and determination, then the result has a chance to be, in Jeannine's words, like "a great piece of architecture." Superlative buildings, she believes, "are usually the result of a great collaboration between a client and an architect where the marriage was really good, the fit was good." As a production designer, she's always looking for that good fit. "You find a story and a director and a producer where the sensibilities overlap as much as possible, and it gives you the freedom to do your best work. It's something about the script that inspires you, it's something about a working relationship with the director, it's about the producer fighting for what needs to happen to make the movie the best it can be, a combo."

LIMBERING UP

1) The Ground Rules

Think about the best and worst collaborative experiences you've had in your life—backpacking, playing in a band, working on a political campaign. Make a list of ten or more personal qualities and work habits you've found to be key to successful interaction (e.g., communicative ability, enthusiasm, drive, lack of egotism, experience, talent, mutual trust, dependability, honesty, sense of humor, etc.) Rearrange them in the order of your priorities.

Ask a colleague or friend to create their own list. Share your lists and discuss how you would work with the different collaborative priorities on a project. For example, for you it may be important to be able to be bluntly candid and outspoken with a collaborator, while another person might place a high value on politeness and avoidance of confrontation. Think as well about how your work habits might or might not mesh with their habits. Do you like to work right up to a deadline, while others are sticklers for being finished in advance? Are you orderly and detail oriented, and bothered by people who are less organized? How do you handle differences about money? Evaluate your own adaptiveness, flexibility and directness in working with other people.

2) Elements of a Creative Environment

Are you currently working in a collaborative environment (regardless of whether it feels creative)? If you are not in one at the present, think of one from the past. It can be any experience—a school science project, a classroom, a community garden design or a local theater production. What qualities or elements in this environment helped you work creatively? Use the following questions to help you consider this relationship between environment and creativity: Does everyone involved feel that they can make a contribution? Do even risky ideas get an open reception? Is it okay to fail while trying to discover something or solve a problem? Do your colleagues feel that their work is valued and appreciated? Did you actually tell the people who worked with you or for you how much you valued what they did? Make a resolution of something you will do differently the next time you collaborate.

3) Deep Listening

Good listening skills are essential to successful collaborations. Here is a way to check your own skill level. Ask a longtime colleague or close friend a probing question in an area where you already have strong opinions. Focus on listening carefully to their answer without interrupting once. Repeat back to them the essence of what they just said, and ask if your summary is accurate. ("Let me see if I understand what you mean . . .") If there are holes in your understanding, ask questions ("Can you tell me more about . . ."). Is this a challenge for you? If it is, ask this person to point out to you when you interrupt in conversation, and also to tell you when you appear to be listening attentively and with interest. Good listening skills are critical to successful collaboration.

five impact

Conrad Hall told us that when he went into filmmaking, "I knew it was something very powerful. When I saw films, they influenced me, so I knew they must influence other people as well. It was a heady feeling to know that you had such power to create emotion, to move people, to make them feel and to think." Like Conrad, you have certainly experienced the power of film, and of art in general, to make us feel and think, and you probably hope as a filmmaker to work on films that have that same kind of impact on others—if not, you probably would have stopped reading this book long before now. Our fifth and final "I" is **Impact,** the way in which creative filmmaking can produce work that resonates deeply, touches our common humanity, stirs and even changes an audience.

The power of film comes in part from its being a storytelling medium. Theologian Anne Foerst has said that our most distinctive quality as human beings is that "we are capable of creating stories about ourselves and others that give our own life and the lives of others meaning." This gift for narrative seems to be wired into us at a primal level. As Jeannine Oppewall puts it, one of her joys as a filmmaker is "being with people who want to tell the stories that I want to tell because that's what it's all about, telling stories to each other. It's deep in our genes, sitting around the fire, barbecuing meat, talking about whatever."

At the same time, film combines storytelling with the modes of expression of many other art forms: the body language, vocal tone and facial expression of performance, the arrangement of light, color, shape, and line within a frame, the motion, depth of field and point of view of a shot, and so on with music, dialogue, sound, architecture, location, decoration, props, costuming, the juxtaposition of images through editing and all the other expressive elements of filmmaking.

This confluence of narrative, visual and aural expressiveness has resulted in a medium of unparalleled power, one that can communicate with an audience on the deepest metaphorical and archetypal levels. Film can move, illuminate, broaden and provoke. It can implant in the minds of its viewers a convincing representation of the experiences and feelings of other people, other cultures, other times, other realities.

The impact of a film is greatest when deep, universal layers of meaning and resonance lie beneath the specificity of its events and characters. This more fundamental point of entry is key not only to the eventual response of an audience, but to the ability of the filmmakers themselves to connect to the material creatively—if a film has nothing going on below its surface, it can be very difficult to do good work on it. Production designer Jeannine Oppewall told us "I turn down a lot of scripts because there's no subtext— the story is just what you read when you read the script. They're solely about the lives of coke dealers or people whose only motive in life is revenge. There's nothing below or above the story, and I can't work on those." Actor Kathy Baker has turned down roles because "I was just 'the Mom.' If she's just a cardboard mom, I'm not interested. A friend told me I have a great bullshit meter. I simply can't do it if it's bullshit." Writer-producer John Wells says that a television series will quickly "run out of steam if the premise isn't deep enough. There just isn't enough to write about. There are only so many medical stories you can tell, or cop stories you can tell, or whatever it is." If there's no deeper premise, "they get repetitive, no matter how you change them around." And editor Lisa Fruchtman sees this deeper level as so essential to the creative process that she "can't imagine working on a movie that has no kind of meat to it. It could be a comedy, but there has to be some kind of vision to latch onto." **The Undercurrent:** *Finding the Soul of the Film,* the first section of the chapter, explores this layered-ness of good filmmaking. We see how our filmmakers seek out "what the film is *really* about," and use it as a guide in their creative decision-making.

One of the many paradoxes of creative filmmaking is that to produce work with this kind of impact on our audiences, we must start with our own connections and what we find compelling. Then, if we have "latched onto the vision" of the film, as Lisa says, and applied it in our creative choices, postproduction offers an opportunity to test whether the film is "working" with audiences, if it is having the impact we had hoped. **Fresh Eyes:** *The Power of the Audience* looks at test screenings, which are often painful for the filmmaker and which have developed an odious reputation because of the destructive potential of studio marketing screenings. Yet our filmmakers make clear the great creative value of screenings—provided they are set up and interpreted properly—for both refreshing and enriching our perspective, so that we can revise and fine-tune the film before completion.

Finally, we turn to **Taking Responsibility:** *Owning the Images We Create.* Author Alice Walker has written: "I believe movies are the most powerful medium for change on earth. They are also a powerful medium for institutionalizing complacency, oppression and reaction." Recognizing that our films have an impact on others imposes on us, as artists and human beings, a responsibility. Wrestling with the "heady power" that Conrad described is the last act of creative filmmaking on any project, something to be digested and incorporated into our being as we move on to the next instance of creating from the inside out. It brings us back to the beginning of this book, to our introspection about why we are filmmakers, what stories we want to tell, and how and why we express and reflect ourselves through the work we create.

The Undercurrent: *Finding the Soul of the Film*

The idea that a film can be about more than "just what you read when you read the script," as Jeannine says above, is something we easily sense. We know that some films stay with us long after we have seen them, gratifying us, challenging us, haunting us, enlarging our sense of the world. They feel complex, reverberant, truthful on the deepest level. Others leave our minds as soon as they are over, and seem superficial, hollow, trivial. But it's easier to feel the impact of this multi-layered richness than to pin down just what it is or where it comes from.

The late Polish filmmaker Krzysztof Kieślowski said of his ten-episode series based on the Biblical Ten Commandments: "The best idea I had in *Decalogue* was that each of the ten films was made by a different lighting cameraman . . . In one the camera is hand-held, in another a tripod is used. One uses a moving camera while the other uses a stationary one . . . Yet despite everything, the films are similar. It seems to me that this is proof, or an indication, of the fact that there exists something like the spirit of a screenplay, and whatever resources a cameraman uses, if he's intelligent and talented, he will understand it, and this spirit will somehow get through . . . and determine the essence of the film."

Kieślowski counted on his collaborators, in this instance his cinematographers, to sense this "spirit" and then use it in their own creative work. Conrad described to us going through just such a process of discovery as a cinematographer: "It's finding the soul of the story, and deciding what that is. And then all of the scenes develop from the roots of this tree, which is a philosophical understanding of the story."

Filmmakers use many different terms to try to talk about this elusive deeper level. Jeannine spoke above of "subtext," and John Wells of a "deep premise." Kieślowski used the words "spirit" and "essence" while Conrad talks about finding the "soul" of the story. Our filmmakers also refer to the theme, spine, and through-line. Screenwriter William Goldman has famously written that after you ask "what's the story about?" you next have to ask "what's the story really about?" British director Sam Mendes says that "in a good movie, there is always a shadow movie underneath the text. . . ." Taiwanese-born director Ang Lee talks about "the juice, the core emotion . . . whether the whole film works at a deep level . . . There is no word for it." We believe they're all trying to describe the same elusive, intangible thing. We've chosen to call it the "undercurrent" of the film, a word that we think captures the sense of something submerged yet very powerful, singular but flowing and difficult to define precisely.

Where does this undercurrent come from? Anthony Minghella spoke in **Inquiry** about doing research to "feed and nourish those deeper layers" of the story. In the writing stage, he feels that he constructs a largely unseen "architectural design" for the film. "Architecture and film, to me, are very connected. If you try to fudge the groundwork in architecture, there's no amount of painting or decoration that will help you. What it's really about, to me, is the three weeks when you're just trying to find a brick that nobody will ever see, that is your brick, and then a course of bricks, and another course of bricks."

As a documentary writer, Renee Tajima-Peña actually tries to sketch this structure out: "I always have a schematic with the central theme and its branches. It's surprising, when I look back on the original one, that it's pretty clear what's central, what's off to the side, what's related. It's almost like a Rorschach test of associations."

The writer is the person who must first imbue the screenplay with this deeper layer. If the foundation is not there in the screenplay, it's unlikely that a rich, powerful film will emerge in the production phase. But that doesn't mean that a screenwriter starts out with a clear, concrete idea of the undercurrent. Although some books on screenwriting and filmmaking advise starting off with a clearly stated "theme," we have found that when our students attempt to state a theme too early in the process of writing or production, they usually come up with no more than an overused aphorism— "what goes around, comes around," "be careful what you wish for," "count your blessings," "put yourself in the other person's shoes"—that doesn't capture a good story's depth of meaning and implication.

The undercurrent that our filmmakers talk about is unlikely to be clear at the beginning, nor is it fixed and immutable. It and the filmmaker's understanding of it both evolve as the film develops. Hanif Kureishi says that "you don't have an idea until you've rewritten it twenty-five times. For me, all writing is really only rewriting. You just keep going, and you develop and you develop and you develop. You never stop."

Kimberly Peirce calls this underlying element the "through-line," and her image for it is that "you're building a train and getting it moving on the tracks." In her metaphor, you begin without actually knowing the route you are going to take. "When you start to build those tracks, then you start realizing what you can't realize in the beginning: 'Oh my God, if we take that turn, we'd go way over here, we'd lose the forward motion of the story.' But you don't know what the story is until you keep going down the path, back and forth."

Kimberly remembers that on *Boys Don't Cry,* "we always had a problem: is it a story of identity, or is it a tragic love affair? When we were shooting it, I

Hilary Swank (Brandon) and Chloë Sevigny (Lana) in *Boys Don't Cry*

thought, well, it's a tragic love story because in the end, Lana helps bring out Brandon's ability to love, right? His whole identity gets shattered, and then she's still there for him. So, I thought, that's what it's really about." But then, much later in the process, Kimberly "realized that, even more than that, it's about conquering the terror of intimacy. Brandon learns that the only way to love is to unveil himself, allow her to see him, allow her to touch him. I said, 'Well, now, that's what the movie's *really* about, finally being able to take that risk.' But I think sometimes you only get to that final, final crystallization at the very end of the process."

An audience seeing *Boys Don't Cry* would be unlikely to come out with an articulate intellectual awareness of this undercurrent that Kimberly took years to understand fully. The force of a film's undercurrent is emotional and subliminal, and often not apparent from what the story is about on a literal level. John Lasseter describes *Toy Story 2* as, on the surface, "a rescue picture with Buzz Lightyear and the other of Andy's toys trying to rescue Woody." But the undercurrent of the story is something more profound— Woody is being given a choice between love and immortality. He can be "a collectible and go on to a museum, and therefore live forever. He will never again have to worry about growing old. But, he realizes later on, if you choose that, you will never be loved again. So, the choice is, to live forever and never to be loved, or to go back to where you're really loved and yet may not last another week."

The previous chapter, **Interaction,** referred often to the director's "vision," without defining exactly what that meant. This vision and the undercurrent are really two sides of the same coin. The director is the principal interpreter of the script, building upon the undercurrent while at the same time starting the process of transposing its underlying structure into specifically cinematic visual and aural elements. By the time other collaborators join the project, the range of potential choices has narrowed considerably. Anthony says that when shooting begins, "I feel like I've already had my say so distinctly—I've been able to choose the material if I'm adapting, write the screenplay, cast the film, find the locations—so many things have already been determined, the possible courses of decisions, the possible options have become prescribed."

In episodic television, the filmmakers lock many creative decisions in place during the making of the pilot for the series. In that situation, John Wells told us, the need for continued creative fluidity within these limitations becomes particularly pressing: "If you trot out a cookie-cutter product every week, audiences feel as if they can miss it, because it's always the same." As the series continues, John looks for ways to allow and encourage "other voices to really enter—directors, actors, other writers, so that you don't feel like you've lost track of what the show's supposed to be, but you improve on it." His metaphor is that the series pilot "is like you've written the bass line for a melody in a jazz combo, and then everybody else gets to play off that melody. You want to be careful that it doesn't go completely off, but you also want to make sure that the ability of the other artists to improvise and to contribute isn't stymied by your own imaginings of exactly what it should be."

John looks for the right balance by having creative meetings that are wide open at first to any ideas. "You don't want to contain the initial conversations. You want people to come up with outrageous ideas. So, I try to let it get really out of hand, and then I'll rein it back in a little bit. If you try to contain it from the beginning within too small a vessel, you never get the great ideas, the crazy ideas that actually work, or the extraordinary ways of trying to do things that ultimately may not work, but lead you to something else."

PAMELA DOUGLAS, writer

*B*etween Mother and Daughter started because my daughter had a close friend whose mother had breast cancer. And I noticed that the girl was walking around saying "Everything is fine. Nothing's wrong." What was really going on, on an underlying level, was the whole issue of a woman's image for a teenage girl. "If my mother has no breasts, is she still a woman? And what about me if I've got a mother who isn't a woman? And also, by the way, is this inheritable, am I going to get it?"

I hadn't seen that treated anywhere. I called the network and said, "Let's do something about breast cancer that addresses how it is for a teenager and her mother." And the network said "Fine." And all of a sudden, there I was with a project, and actually no way in. It wasn't at that point coming from a personal passion. I did a good deal of psychological research, consulted a national association of social workers, read

"That Was My Way In"

Pamela Douglas and her daughter Raya Yarbrough

several books. But having done all that, I still really had nothing.

But then I realized that the film was not really about breast cancer, that's just the arena in which the relationship exists. I know a lot about relationships of mothers and daughters, and that was my way into it. Usually teenage girls are as distant and independent as possible. I know I was. And I think that the struggle of this mother and daughter to find each other is what it is really about. Breast cancer was simply the occasion to deal with what happens between two women of different ages who happen to be a mother and a daughter, where one is entering this world with a lot of bravado and is really fearful, and the other one is trying terribly to give what she can to someone who doesn't want it. And that's richer, you know.

Once the essence of the undercurrent is in place (at least for the time being), the other collaborators can begin to work from it. Our filmmakers describe thorough, repeated readings of the script and conversations with the director as the starting point for their own understanding of the undercurrent. Conrad told us: "I study the script really well, read it over and over again. I study it so that it's in my bones." He knows that by the time he comes aboard, the director may have a point of view that goes beyond what's apparent in the script, "and so the director and I talk about that early on." Similarly, Jeannine has discussions with the director "about each character and what metaphor or feeling they may represent."

James Newton Howard describes how a director communicating their sense of the undercurrent can completely alter the contribution of a collaborator. Working on the cue for the main title sequence of *Grand Canyon*, a pickup basketball game in an African-American neighborhood of Los Angeles, "I wrote a piece that I really believed in the first time. It was much more urban." Director Lawrence Kasdan heard it, "and he said it didn't feel portentous. You didn't get the feeling that the music was describing some irresistible force that's going to move through these people's lives, that when everything seems cool, calm and collected, the most unexpected thing can occur. He wanted the music to relate to that somehow." The piece of music that came to James as a result "was, in a way, totally disconnected from the visuals, but that was what made it work as well as it did, I think—it was like a Greek chorus chanting, with these guys playing basketball. And the effect was, at once, disconnected, but ultimately, incredibly connected, it made the picture bigger somehow. And it made my music sound better."

Not every filmmaker likes this sort of explicit discussion with the director, preferring to let the undercurrent emerge without intellectualizing about it. Lisa Fruchtman remarked that she finds such things are "better left unsaid" during the making of the film. And yet, she constantly seeks the undercurrent while she edits, first for the entire film and then as a guide to understanding the deeper meaning of each scene: "When I start working on a scene, I respond to it in terms of what is literally happening. But I also get a gut feeling for what the scene is really about—not the apparent action or plot, but the core, the meaning of the scene." For the opening of *The Doctor,* a scene of emergency heart surgery, Lisa found that the deeper layer was that William Hurt's character "is a great surgeon, but he's indifferent to the patient as a person." As a result, "I discovered I needed to hold off showing the patient—in fact, I never showed him until the very end. The doctor sees pieces of the patient but never really sees the person. So the audience doesn't either. It's a small editing decision, but I think a crucial one. I'm not sure how much of this was intellectually clear to me at the outset, but it became clear as I worked on it."

As Lisa's and James's examples indicate, our filmmakers' sense of the undercurrent informs in turn their creative choices about each scene, shot, camera setup, edit or music cue. By tuning into and enhancing these deeper resonances in their specific choices, our filmmakers help to build a film that is purposeful and coherent.

When Walter Murch, for example, worked as editor and sound designer for *The Conversation,* he and writer-director Francis Ford Coppola "talked about the idea of 'returning,' which is essential to the whole film—structurally returning to the same material periodically, but because of what you've learned from point A to point B, you're seeing it in a different light." This continual shift in the meaning of the same material resonated with the film's undercurrent, which Coppola has described as "how you never know anything . . . you never know what's going on." Walter notes that "there was a progression of that idea through the film, and we tried to find any resonances we could. Francis built a huge amount of them into the script and into the shooting, but also we looked editorially for anywhere we could get those resonances."

As with Lisa for *The Doctor,* and James with *Grand Canyon,* Walter found a way to begin to introduce this undercurrent of incomplete understanding in the opening scene. "A key part of the story is that Harry Caul is not able to record a perfect soundtrack. He misses a crucial moment the first go-round. So during the very first shot of the movie, which is a very long shot, both optically with a long lens and the fact that it's a very slow zoom-in, I started to introduce, without any explanation, distorted sounds which are unresolvable by an audience at that moment."

As a production designer, Jeannine describes her ultimate goal as having the background of every shot in the film serve as "a metaphor for what is happening in the scene or overall in the film emotionally." She starts, like all our filmmakers, by "internalizing the story as much as possible. You just put what you're looking for inside yourself." Then she seeks inspiration in the "world of visual metaphor that we all live through, walk through and experience every day. We may not always be aware of it, but like the literary world, a character or action can often have another layer of meaning, a subtext or metaphor that comes out of the deep genetic history of humanity. It seems to be something we all share, and therefore, visual metaphors can have real power in storytelling."

For the motel that serves as the main location of *Tender Mercies*, a place where Robert Duvall's character arrives at as an alcoholic drifter, Jeannine drew first on the research she'd done for years on motel design. She then "drove the old main highway from Dallas to Fort Worth to see more of the really old ones." But she wanted a design that answered the deeper question: "What is it about the motel's architecture that would make that character want to stay there?" She ended up creating a design she'd never seen in real life: "I laid out the Mariposa motel buildings in a 'Y' shape. It's a welcoming thing, in this flat landscape of nothing. You can drive in and it's encircling you in some way, like the huddled wagons on the trail, an encampment somehow." Jeannine worried that this metaphorical layout would stand out, and "somebody might say, 'You stupid fool, nobody has laid out motels like that.' But not one person has ever noticed that."

Often, our core sense of the undercurrent is present in our very first thoughts and impressions about a project. Lisa told us that when she begins editing a film, "I always note my strongest first responses to the material, and I work from those very heavily. You get dull to the material and I feel that my initial responses are the purest." Similarly, Stanley Kubrick once said that your "first impression is the most precious thing you've got, you can never have it again—the yardstick for any judgment that you have as you get deeper and deeper into the work."

For that reason, as teachers we often ask our students to keep a production journal from the earliest moments of developing or working on a project, and encourage them to refer back to these beginning entries to help them find their way later on. Howard Leder, who developed a documentary film in one of Doe's classes, wrote her after the end of production that "looking back now, I can really see the documentary taking shape in the journal entries. There was one entry in particular that I was quoting all the way up to picture lock. I even read it to the editors so they could help me remember it. It was so clear a thought, that every time I got lost, I would go back to it, reread it, think about what it meant in relation to where we were at that moment, and then forge ahead. The moments of clarity are, in the end, really quite simple and should be latched onto and not forgotten."

Of course, as Kimberly indicated above about *Boys Don't Cry,* our sense of the undercurrent may also evolve so much that we ultimately arrive at a completely different understanding of what the film is really about. When Kate watched the dailies for *Asylum,* a documentary directed by Joan Churchill about people in an institution for the criminally insane, "the theme that emerged the most strongly was that every one of those people had had a very traumatic childhood, abusive parents, alcoholics, criminals for parents. They all suffered huge traumas in their childhoods." So for the first cut, she had every character telling their childhood story. But "it was way, way too much. I think my original take on it was too simplistic—it's much more complex than that. In the end, the film was really about their healing process, how the environment nurtures them, how they connect with the other patients and create a community for themselves." She adds that despite "all the stages and permutations the film has gone through, at the end you think that this is the only way it could have ever been, this is the way it was meant to be."

As Kate makes clear, the undercurrent is something that may continue to evolve as the fluid interaction of the production process proceeds. James L. Brooks has described how it was two years after he had finished writing, producing and directing *Broadcast News* that he looked at the film and realized " 'Oh, my God, that movie was about three people who missed their last chance at real intimacy in their lives.' I never set out to make that movie, but . . . a lot of people chip in on that, a lot of people create these things with you."

The elusive quality of the undercurrent may mean that it never emerges as a succinct, easily stated concept. The best the filmmaker may be able to do is pose a series of questions or provocative ideas. Jeannine says that for *Pleasantville,* "the movie that Gary [Ross, the director] and I wanted to make is really a riff on American cultural consciousness. Who are we, where are we, and how did we get here? What's stuck in our heads and what should we change? It's a movie about the nature and meaning of art, and how cultural nostalgia and art, or tradition and culture, relate to each other. It's about certain incendiary qualities that art can have, and is that a good thing or do you want to stop it? Can you stop it? Can you go back? I think that's what the movie was trying to convey."

Jeannine Oppewall on the town set she designed for *Pleasantville*

It may be that the questioning process itself is what's essential. The late John Cassavetes described being bored while making the movie *Gloria* for Columbia Pictures "because I knew the answer to the picture the minute we began. All of my best work comes from *not* knowing." Listing his films *Husbands, A Woman Under the Influence* and *Opening Night,* he concluded: "You have to think about those pictures. I'm still thinking about them."

Walter agrees that "you struggle to answer questions in films, and films can be good simply through the quality of your struggle to answer those questions. Whether you actually succeed or not is sometimes irrelevant." He believes, in fact, that it is requisite in a good film to have an underlying question that is unanswerable: "The audience needs to use the raw material of the film, and the struggles of everyone involved in the making of the film, to come up with their own answers." Or, as documentary filmmaker Errol Morris said about his film *Mr. Death: The Rise and Fall of Fred A. Leuchter Jr.,* "I prefer to have people look at it and see what they make of it, in the way I did it thinking: 'What am I doing? What am I *really* doing?' "

Fresh Eyes: *The Power of the Audience*

Filmmaking is a medium of communication with an audience. As filmmakers, we hope the characters, events, images and sounds we have interwoven will have an impact on those who see our films. And yet, as our filmmakers have exemplified, the best films tend to come out of a process of self-expression and self-discovery, without trying to anticipate the taste of the audience. They are likely to be deeply felt, idiosyncratic, complex, perhaps challenging or even disturbing to an audience—the antithesis of films designed to be palatable to and popular with everyone.

Many great films are also very successful at the box office, but few filmmakers would consider blockbuster grosses to be a reliable index of quality. For those for whom a film is strictly a commercial venture, pleasing the largest possible audience is going to be the ultimate goal. However, if we as filmmakers set out to make such a film, it is far more likely to end up being simplistic, formulaic, puerile, and unsatisfying (if not excruciating) to work on. Yet if we make a film so obscure that it speaks to no one else, that only leads us to another creative dead end. Where each of us intends to land on this continuum is one of the most basic issues of creative filmmaking.

How then do we stay true to our authentic voices and yet take into account the effectiveness of our communication with an audience? Hanif Kureishi captures the delicate balance needed, emphasizing that he writes "about things that matter to me, that I'm thinking about, that are in my mind. I don't think, 'Now what does the audience want today?' I do what I'm interested in and I hope that other people might be interested." At the same time, he notes that "audiences can remind you of how interesting something is—you show it to people and they get interested in it, and you think, 'Oh, that's kind of worked.'"

The question we hear filmmakers ask over and over is "is it working?" If, as Hanif says above, an audience "getting interested" is an indication that something has "worked," then involving an audience was clearly a goal all along. There's no contradiction here, just a trick of the creative mind. If we start out focused on what will please an audience, rather than what intrigues us, our work is likely to go astray. But at some point, we want to know if others find it intriguing (or moving, funny, resonant, beautiful, shocking, meaningful, etc.) in the way we ourselves did. If they don't, we may be able to close that gap without sacrificing the integrity of the work.

As Walter stated above, films can and should leave room for the audience to have varied responses and interpretations—those that tell us exactly what to think and feel usually come across as heavy-handed and blatantly manipulative. Krzysztof Kieślowski expressed his pleasure that viewers would come up with interpretations of his films "that had never occurred to me. Film has a life of its own and can take on meanings the director didn't consciously put there. This is a very magical and wonderful thing." But if you intend your audience to be engrossed and they're bored, or you expect them to be laughing and they're somber, or you want them to be distraught and they're exhilarated, you will have missed your creative goals. Just in terms of story clarity, we find that students are frequently shocked that an audience has entirely missed or completely misunderstood something they thought was obvious and clear.

Rather than wait until the film is finished, discovering too late that it isn't working, filmmakers use test audiences to provide vital information for the creative team in the final shaping of the film. Test screenings have developed a very bad reputation among filmmakers because of a Hollywood studio system of market research previews that can be extremely destructive creatively. But a correctly designed test screening can allow the filmmakers to see the film through the eyes of the audience, sensing what they're feeling even before they give us any specific comments. Kate finds that "your perception changes if you watch the film with five people as opposed to sitting in a room by yourself. You need to keep bringing fresh eyes in." Kimberly has been "amazed by the power of an audience. When the lights go down and they're there, it's like they communicate with each other, and they communicate with the screen. Everything moves." Lisa "feels the pulse of the audience—are they with the movie or not, are they laughing or not, are they moved?" And Walter has described "those 6 or 600 strangers sitting with you, whose muffled presence alters and magnifies in an unquantifiable way the nature of what you see."

This shift in perception often has a dramatic impact on the filmmaker, both in discovering specific problems and in refreshing a perspective that has become stale. Lisa notes that "once you've gone through a few cuts of the film, you don't really know if you're achieving what you think you're achieving. So then you show the movie to people coming in to see it for the first time." Kimberly "would hit a point in post-production where I didn't know how to make the movie any better. And it was still three hours long, so I knew it wasn't fully working. And then we would screen it, and I'd sit in the back, and they'd laugh, or react, and all of a sudden I could participate again in the creative process. Now I had all these new ideas about things I could cut, and things I could rearrange. I was back in the game."

As a composer, James feels that he can only do his best job if he has the time and opportunity to write a score, create temporary "demo" music cues, and then use them as the temp music for the film's test screenings: "That allows me to see the construction of my score before I record it—listening to it with an audience, seeing if we're using too many themes too many times, if the spotting's good, where we're coming in, where we're coming out. Is there too much music? Are there barren patches, where there's not enough music? Is one of my cues hurting one of the laughs of the joke, am I obscuring the moment, is my timing off?"

James refers to the importance of timing when dealing with humor, something that is best judged through a test screening. For most comedy, audience response is the crucial indicator: do they laugh or not? And if so, for how long? Humor is notoriously unpredictable without an audience as a gauge. Kathy Baker has found that when a stage production is first performed for an audience, "You go, 'Oh, my God, there's a laugh there!' " about a line that hadn't seemed comic in rehearsal. Similarly, for her quirky role on *Boston Public,* "I didn't even know it was funny sometimes until I was watching it with people and they'd laugh." Even the most experienced comedic filmmakers are surprised in this way—Woody Allen is known for testing his films and then recutting them or even reshooting sections to enhance the humor.

Despite these positive results, test screenings have the potential to be painful, and filmmakers often approach them with dread. Kate says that she hates "the first screenings with the audience. It's hard to relax. I'm always worried about technical things like whether something's going to be out of sync. I worry about everything you can possibly worry about. I always try to get humor into the cut whenever I can. When I get the first laugh, then I relax. If I don't get it, I'm usually a wreck. But once you feel like the audience is with you, it's great. There's nothing like it."

The choices of when to screen, and to whom, are key. Kimberly warns that if the cut is four hours long, "you can't show it to a normal human being. They don't know how to look at it." Renee agrees that "you have to be really careful about what point in the rough cut you show it to people, because there's a lot of finessing still to be done. Earlier rough cuts I just show to other filmmakers—they're able to see what can be, as opposed to what's there. I show non-filmmakers later cuts, because by then they can see the rough story." Director Sidney Lumet has written that for the first screening he relies on "a small, devoted brain trust: five or six friends who know me and my work and wish us both well."

It can be dangerous to show a cut to filmmakers whose skill at giving feedback hasn't been tested, or whose taste may not be in sync with yours. They can be opinionated critics who argue for the film *they* would have made. One student we know waited until the night before picture lock to show a cut of the film he had directed to a group of other film students he didn't know well. They gave him pages of notes that called for a massive revision of the film. In a panic and ready to stay up all night with the editors attempting a last-minute overhaul of the film, he phoned Doe, who had seen the cut. She advised him to trust his own judgment and leave it the way it was. Subsequently, he realized that he had, in fact, made just the film he wanted to make, and felt greatly relieved that he had not butchered it in a moment of doubt.

"The Last Creative Act in Filmmaking"

WALTER MURCH, sound designer and editor

Screenings are essential. The film is not really complete until it is in the theaters being watched by people. That's the last creative act in filmmaking. So you want to get a prefiguration of that ahead of time. For *The Conversation*, there was a relentless hammering on our part—Francis, me, Richard Chew who was editing with me—to try to communicate what really happened in this story. And that's primarily because the film is told rigorously from Harry Caul's point of view. You don't see anything in the film that is not something he also is seeing or is part of. Your knowledge of the events is no greater than his. And the small audiences that we would show the film to—we never had what would qualify as "previews" by today's standards, but there were ten people at these screenings—Francis would use them to kind of figure out how far off the mark he was in achieving his goal.

The story twist at the end, that these innocent-looking people, the boy [played by Frederic Forrest] and the girl [played by Cindy Williams], were really the plotters of the murder of the Robert Duvall character, that just flew over people's heads. They just didn't get it. So we eagerly grabbed and put into the film anything that would allow this to sink in. And at a very late stage when I was mixing the film, I remembered a line reading that Fred Forrest had given when I was out with him and Cindy Williams in a residential park in San Francisco walking around and around in circles. I had a Nagra tape recorder and they were saying the conversation just like they said it in Union Square. The problem with Union Square is it's very noisy, so as a backup I got this wild track, and I would use that in many situations in the film. But on the third take, Fred read this line wrong and I heard that reading and said to myself, "Oops, wrong reading, wrong inflection" and almost a year later I recalled it again, thinking, "Hmm, maybe that would be a good thing to do at this point," because the emphasis isn't "he'd *kill* us if he had the chance," but instead it's "he'd kill *us* if he had the chance," meaning therefore we have to kill him. And so that's the last reading of the line that you hear in the film, and it is a different reading than you have heard up to that point.

We've always had test screenings, but what's happened is that previewing the film has acquired a structure and utility in the marketing of the film, a product of more corporate thinking. What is said is "we're just trying to help make the film a better film by showing it to the audience and getting reactions." The unspoken agenda is that the numerical score the film gets at the preview determines the amount spent in the advertising campaign. "Look, we got a score of ninety, that means we, the studio, can now go to our bosses and say we want to spend twenty or thirty million dollars," but if the film gets a forty, there's no way that anyone is going to spend ten million dollars on advertising that film.

I still get a tremendous amount out of previews. It's more nerve-wracking when you're showing the film and the studio is there and four hundred people are looking at it rather than what we did on *The Conversation*, "Let's have a screening in the screening room for twenty people." But I always learn something about the film when I show it to anybody. Even if there's only one other person looking at the film, I will look at the film in a slightly different way, knowing that somebody else is looking at it.

Gene Hackman, Cindy Williams and Frederic Forrest in *The Conversation*

It can also be important to check back later with colleagues to see how their response to the film has evolved. Danish writer-director Thomas Vinterberg found that when he screened *The Celebration*, his viewers would respond "with deep, deep silence and darkness," but then would phone days after to praise the picture. His other films, he believes, "appealed to an emotion that's closer to the surface. . . . This one apparently lies several layers down."

The creatively invigorating test screenings our filmmakers prefer are quite different from the highly formalized previews the studios like. These studio tests, run by market research companies, are too often slanted toward producing a mass-marketable "product," a film that has a simple premise conveyable in a thirty-second television ad, so that it can be "pre-sold" to open on thousands of screens and make a lot of money the first weekend, regardless of how good it may be. Anthony describes the painful shock of this moment when the film "ceases to be treated as a piece of art, and becomes an industrial activity. I feel your life is shortened incrementally by studio previews. They're horrible, disgusting things."

One of the most destructive aspects of these screenings, Lisa notes, is that "filmmakers understand how to use an audience screening, but there are some executives who don't understand it. If ninety percent of the audience is saying 'I hate the ending,' or 'I hate that character' or 'I'm bored,' then the executives might say 'well, we have to reshoot it. We have to do what that twenty-year-old in the focus group said we should do, instead of coming to our own conclusions.'"

In contrast, Lisa doesn't take suggestions too literally. "I listen between the lines. If they're saying 'I think you should do this,' or 'I hated that,' instead of my responding 'oh, I'll go and reedit that scene,' I think to myself, 'what's wrong with the structure of what we've done up to this point that they feel that way?' If they're bored in a certain sequence or in a certain part of the film, it usually isn't because there's something wrong with that part. It may be ten minutes earlier that you've done something wrong, and they're tired out by then or not involved. You've lost them somewhere, so when you get to this place where they should be really moved, they're not."

Even though this market research is supposedly designed to be scientific, a single negative comment can be blown up all out of proportion. James describes how "someone in the focus group afterwards might say, 'The music was really horrible.' And of course, one person can say that, and all of a sudden everybody's in a tizzy about the score." He adds that when a studio screening is over, "I feel like I've survived some terrible ordeal, a potential death threat."

Apart from the inappropriateness of following the specific suggestions of nonfilmmakers, testing can be problematic in the broadest sense, because it may well be wrong even on the most basic level of audience enthusiasm. Many movies and TV series have tested badly and gone on to be huge successes, and vice versa. John Wells told us that in television "the people around you spend a tremendous amount of time talking about what the audience wants, and they have research. When we took in *ER,* every network passed on it. They gave us a lot of research they had done, showing that people wouldn't watch a hospital show." He had a very similar

experience trying to launch *West Wing*.
"So in some ways, if someone tells me it's
a bad idea, I actually perk up a little bit.
They think it's a bad idea because it's not
what you've already seen or something
that you know. And it's very difficult to
have an extremely successful series that
hits into what people already know, because they feel they've seen it or they've
got it."

An emergency room scene
from *ER*

In battling against this literal-minded,
commercial, play-it-safe mentality, Anthony believes that what "finally separates those filmmakers who survive from
those who don't is finding a purchase po-
sition where you can say, 'I can use this testing process because I can make
the movie better. I mustn't be intimidated by this." Similarly, Kimberly
found it essential to stand up to the studio in negotiating what kind of testing would be done on *Boys Don't Cry*: "We were not taking the movie out to
New Jersey and testing it with a studio test audience."

In **Interaction,** Ismail Merchant similarly disparaged a test of *The
Golden Bowl* at a mall in New Jersey (page 112). This resistance, of course,
has nothing to do with the residents of New Jersey per se, but with the idea
that every film should be designed to be popular with a suburban shopping
mall multiplex audience. Rather, filmmakers need to ask themselves, "Who
is *my* intended audience?" It may well be a broad suburban audience, or it
might be something quite different.

We encourage students to think about a specific target audience. You
may hope to reach a much broader audience, but you want to begin with a
more specific one made up of people who, if they don't feel what you want
them to feel, if they're not affected by what's on the screen, you can be
pretty certain you haven't yet succeeded in realizing what you envisioned.
Kimberly describes how her first screenings for *Boys Don't Cry* started with
a very select audience and then broadened out: "At first, it was just me and
the producers, who I was on a pretty similar wavelength with. Then we
would open it up to, like, fifty people that we'd invited, who were smart,
who were maybe gay, who were at least progressive, who were in New
York—people that we knew understood movies, right? We would get the

questionnaires back. I would read every single one and write down all the questions and answers. 'Do you like Brandon?' 'No, I hate him.' 'Why do you hate him?' 'He's irritating in this scene.' 'Do you understand the story?' 'I think the story's too long' or 'I think it's repetitive.' You get one comment like that, you ignore it. When you see the same comment over and over, something's usually off, even if the comment is unspecific or wrong. I don't think it's a matter of homogenizing at all—it's learning how to read comments to find problems, and then using what you know and feel, and using your craft, to make it better."

Kimberly's point that you ignore one comment but pay attention when several people respond the same way is echoed by Anthony, who keeps in mind the saying "When nine Russians tell you you're drunk, lie down." Nevertheless, he adds that "sometimes twelve people have told me that I'm drunk, and I haven't laid down. The only way I've ever been able to properly articulate it satisfactorily to myself is that you need to have one 'hearing ear' and one 'deaf ear' "—one that's open to other people's advice and wisdom, and one that is closed to tastes and preferences that aren't your own. Kate agrees, saying "you get to the point where you know what to take and what not to use, as well as what you can do something about and what you can't."

How do you know when to listen and when to disregard what people say? There's no sure-fire answer. Anthony finds that occasionally "you listen to bad advice, and act on it. And you ignore good advice, and don't act on it. We're all frail, and hubristic, and screw up all the time." Doe tells her students how, when she herself was a graduate student at USC, she directed a film that included a problematic scene. Many people she screened the film for told her this scene stopped the story and was irrelevant, but she had an intellectual rationale for why the film needed it, and essentially argued herself into a corner where she would not budge. Keeping it unchanged became a kind of test of her will—usually the wrong reason to stick to your guns. Years later, she agrees that the film would have been better had she found a more creative way to address the problem.

Focusing on what isn't working is usually challenging and daunting even with the best-designed test screenings. A different kind of knowledge comes from seeing your finished film with an audience that has come not to critique it, but to enjoy and be swept up in it. At that point, if you have worked creatively from the inside out and stayed true to yourself, you may discover that, through the specificity and distinctiveness of the filmmaking, you and your collaborators have transcended a specific audience and tapped into something deep and universal.

Renee was delighted to discover that non-Asian-American audiences laughed at the humor in *My America:* "For me, that's very profound, that I can be true to my own experience and people will understand it." She also received e-mails "from every corner of America, many that weren't Asian-American. People would send me two- to three-page e-mails with their life stories." Even though Renee had consciously sought "this universal kind of idea, how the Asian-American experience can be a microcosm for the American experience," she was still delightfully surprised when the film turned out to work on that broader level.

Similarly, with *Boys Don't Cry* Kimberly had always "wanted more than anything to depict Brandon so that people would understand and identify with him, but I didn't know if that would be possible." Then when she traveled around the country with the finished film, "I was shocked and happy that people got it—they dealt with the gender issue not just as a gay thing, but as everybody's thing." She also found that the movie resonated with a widespread revulsion against the violence "erupting across America at that time—the murder of Matthew Shepard, the shooting at Columbine, the one at the Jewish daycare center. Many of the things triggering Tom and John in the movie—anger and terror over the fragility of their own masculinity, their own sexual and gender ambiguity, their hatred of difference—were behind those other atrocities. The movie revealed what was boiling up inside the culture."

In *Pleasantville,* contemporary teenagers travel back to a past that seems both idyllic and suffocating. Jeannine went to see it during its theatrical run "with a couple of different audiences and privately asked some of the people what they thought. Some people were cheering 'yeah, we can't look back, we have to look forward.' Others were saying 'shit, well we liked it the way it used to be.' " Jeannine found that arguments broke out, "and that's what the movie was supposed to do, to make you think a little bit. It's not mere entertainment, it's also edifying in some way. I hate to use sermonizing terms, but that's really what it is. It's a movie that has something on its mind rather than just parting a teenager from his parents' $8.50." One man said to her " 'Gee, why can't more Hollywood movies be like this? I know I'm going to wake up tomorrow thinking about this movie.' That's what I wanted. And he wasn't someone who was particularly intellectual. He had gone to the movie thinking it would be a comedy, and it *was* funny, it paid off. But it also had a serious tone to it that he got sucked in by."

People frequently come up to Kathy to tell her how much they were helped by *Clean and Sober,* in which she plays a cocaine addict."I am so proud of that. And there's this little code where people say 'I saw *Clean and Sober* seven times.' And I used to think, 'Wow, they must have really liked the movie!' And it's actually because they saw it seven times in rehab."

The number of people who saw *Clean and Sober* in rehab may be much smaller than the number who saw it in theaters or on television and video, but the impact among that particular audience was understandably quite high. Marlon Riggs, the late documentary filmmaker, was especially interested in reaching such nontheatrical audiences: "I make [films] to provoke people in some way, to be used in discussion, to be used in classrooms, to be used with students, to be used among counselors, to be used by organizations and business enterprises, in human relations studies and personnel management. That kind of stuff has real impact."

Hanif, who started our discussion by saying "I do what I'm interested in and I hope that other people might be interested," vividly remembers walking into *My Beautiful Laundrette* in Edinburgh when it opened "and just seeing people laughing and responding. We'd made this film, we'd looked at it ourselves, but you have no idea that anybody, en masse, is going to like it at all. There's no way you can know until you actually stand in the cinema and see people responding to it. And that was amazing to me."

Taking Responsibility: *Owning the Images We Create*

Although as filmmakers we know that others who see our films will be affected by them, that understanding is often just an intellectual one until we come in direct contact with a real-life audience experiencing a film we have made. That contact can be a delightful surprise, as several of our filmmakers have just described. It can also be an unsettling jolt of recognition as we come face-to-face with the responsibility we have as artists and human beings working in an immensely popular and powerful medium.

Producer David Puttnam has described the audience response to his film *Midnight Express* as a cathartic moment for him: "When I traveled with the film and saw the audience reactions, I got the shock of my life. We talked long and hard about the scene where Billy Hayes bites the tongue of one of the other prisoners. The reason we'd done it was to try to give the impression that he'd become demented. We thought the audience would vanish under their seats. But the opposite happened. They got up in their seats and they were cheering him . . . That's when I said to myself: 'Never again.' I don't ever want to sit in a cinema and look at a film that I've had any responsibility at all for and be stunned and shattered by the reaction it's getting from the audience."

Sometimes this recognition of impact and responsibility comes as the result of seeing one's film in a new context and perspective. Gale Anne Hurd, the producer of *The Terminator* and executive producer of *Terminator 2: Judgment Day,* had no problem with the audience response to her blockbuster action films until she took a trip where she "was on a boat and I happened to visit islands that are rarely visited by tourists. These people fish out of dugout canoes . . . When I found out they had all seen *Terminator 2,* it was terrifying. I didn't want to invade their culture with something that would impact them the way that it did. Here were these peaceful people living in paradise, but with no running water, indoor plumbing, or telephones. And they had all become fans of Arnold Schwarzenegger and urban, action-oriented entertainment. At that moment I realized that whatever you may think your responsibility is, it's overwhelming. It changed my perspective on the influence I have as a producer."

Sometimes, it is many years after the fact that filmmakers realize they have included something in their films that they wish they hadn't. Steven Spielberg, in 1995, told an interviewer that in the final sequence of *E.T. the Extra-Terrestrial* (1982), he regretted "that a gun was used as a threat to stop children on bicycles. And I regret that last cut, before E.T. opens his eyes and the bikes take off, of the gun coming up . . . I think those were, you know, distasteful moments to me." Spielberg decided to use computer graphics to change the guns to walkie-talkies for the twentieth anniversary re-release of the movie.

JAMES NEWTON HOWARD, composer

I think initially, when you start off, you're so hungry to work, to get a job, that you'll score anything. In the early days, I was guilty of not being as picky as I should have been. Now, I'm a lot pickier.

You live a duality of existence between what's on the surface and what your soul is speaking to you, what your inner self is speaking to you. You try intuitively to make choices that pay attention to the more subtle instinct within yourself, but that's a hard

"What Your Soul Is Speaking to You"

thing to do in the middle of Hollywood, because Hollywood's very seductive. It's a lot just to get offered a movie and to have people want you to do the movie. At that point, it's hard to hear that little voice in you saying "That's not what I'm comfortable doing, or what I can do the best."

John Schlesinger has always been one of my favorite directors, so when I had the chance to work with him on *Eye for an Eye,* I was really excited about it. And then when I saw the movie, I felt it was such a nasty, mean-spirited movie. It's basically about a vigilante played by Sally Field—her daughter gets brutally raped and murdered, and she goes out and buys a gun, and kills the guy. And it's just horrible. When I saw a cut of the movie, I'd already made a deal to do it, and I called my agents and said, "I can't do this movie. I think it's just so offensive to me in every way that I just don't want to be involved." So I called Schlesinger, and he basically charmed me into doing it. He said, "Oh, you must think this movie is positively dreadful." And then I felt so bad for him, and I said, "Oh, no, John, I don't! I think it's really a great movie. I'm just not musically connected with it," all this crap. I ended up doing the movie. And I wrote a bad score. It was uninspired work. I worked hard and did the best job I could do—I wasn't blowing it off in any sense of the word. But all those great, wonderful moments of connection—none of that happened.

Notably, all these examples of second thoughts by filmmakers about the stories and images they have created are focused on violence. Certainly, depictions of violence, along with other "hot button" issues like scenes showing sex or drug use, have been at the center of a heated debate in our society about social responsibility in filmmaking. As teachers and filmmakers, we find the polarized nature of this debate and its focus on controversial images to be limiting and often misleading. The issue of responsibility for the images we create is both more complex and more pervasive than is usually acknowledged by either "side."

To begin with, we believe that all films, however innocuous and uncontroversial they may seem, are embedded with countless values, morals, assumptions and judgments that affect their audiences. Every scene of every film is filled with these messages, but they are often unintentional and invisible, so culturally familiar that they are transparent to us, both as filmmakers and as audience members. Some touch on big issues: What is true love? How do you best settle a conflict? Is money a good or bad thing to want? Why do people behave the way they do and what makes them change? Who is considered "normal" and who is treated, either explicitly or through invisibility, as insignificant, exotic or deviant? Which is more powerful, individual or collective action? Do the ends justify the means?

But values are also embedded in such prosaic questions as whether or not it's hip to live in the suburbs, wear boxer shorts, own a cell phone, study hard, pierce your nose, sit in the back of the classroom, or use words like "hip." As film writer Peter Biskind has said: "Even the most apparently innocent aspects of script and casting, costumes and camera angle, are charged with meaning." And John Lasseter, whose family-oriented films have hardly been controversial, told us "I am fully aware of the impact of our films, more so than I was when we first made them."

The impact of these embedded values and messages may sometimes be very apparent and quantifiable, yet seem of limited societal significance. The sales of Ray-Ban sunglasses and Reese's Pieces candy skyrocketed after they were featured in *Risky Business* and *E.T. the Extra-Terrestrial* respectively. The impact may at other times be quite profound, even life-changing—often in a positive way—and yet be very difficult to pin down or quantify. As we said at the beginning of this chapter, for those of us who so love and respect films that we want to devote our lives to making them, it is certain that they have influenced us, and helped shape who we are.

The recognition that all films are carriers of values that affect their viewers can be liberating. Once we accept that the film we're making, *whatever* it is, will "say" something whether intended or not, we may be less likely to shy away from embracing the full, deep impact of our own filmmaking. Rather, we are likely to feel a greater need to explore how accurately our films are reflecting our own values and points of view. As a result, our work may become a more truthful reflection of who we are.

Even when it comes to controversial topics like violence, it is key whether a filmmaker works from their authentic voice on a story that is about more than just what's on the surface. That more than anything makes the difference between films with artistically valid portrayals of violence—in, for example, *Raging Bull* or *The Godfather*—and those that use violence to get an easy primal response from an audience, creating images that are often demeaning, exploitative, inhumane and desensitizing.

As with all creative choices, working from the undercurrent helps guide filmmakers to representations of violence that are valid for the film being made. Conrad has made many pictures that contained scenes of violence—*American Beauty, Butch Cassidy and the Sundance Kid* and *In Cold Blood* for example—and he believes that in those films the violence was depicted appropriately because the filmmakers were thoughtful and true to the undercurrent of what the film was really about. As he told us, "there's violence and then there's violence that's gratuitous in order to appeal to people's worst instincts. I know how that kind of violence affects me: I'm affected physiologically and I hate it." Conrad believes that "we have a responsibility to pay attention to the violence in films, to understand what we're doing, and to certainly not have violence in order to bring people into the theater because the violence appeals to them."

As an example, Conrad described how Richard Brooks, the director of *In Cold Blood,* "knew that he didn't want to see visual violence—he wanted psychological violence." In the film "you don't see any violence at all, but you feel the violence when somebody's going into a room and disappearing, and you see a flash of light and hear a loud noise and they come running out. It's horrifying because you know what happened. Your mind fills in the visual violence and it's more horrifying than seeing it. Now, if you went in with him, in the room and saw him point a gun, and then shoot, and you see somebody explode or splatter blood all over, it becomes something different."

Another key question in presenting violence is how invested the audience is in the characters, both the victims and the potential perpetrators, who we may hope will not resort to violence. Walter has found that, if the audience is not asked to invest in the specific humanity of characters on screen, the result is a scene "like in *Total Recall,* where people get used as human shields, the Schwarzenegger character grabs them at random, and they die in front of him, you see lots of blood and bullets tearing through people." But despite the graphic violence, there's no emotional repercussion or meaning, just primal visceral sensation. "Whereas a film like *The Talented Mr. Ripley,* you really don't see much when Ripley kills Dickie Greenleaf on the boat, and yet people come up and say 'it was so violent.' Well, yes, I agree, it was violent, but it's violent because you weren't expecting that kind of violence in this film at that time, and because you were invested in the characters. But if you just simply made some kind of objective scale of blood and guts shown per frame, and contact of deadly instruments with human flesh, it would score very low."

For John Wells, it is crucial to show the aftermath of the actions his shows depict. He has argued with NBC "because they don't ever want us to have any teenager commit or attempt to commit suicide on *ER.* They have research that shows that any time you bring it up on television, there are copycats. And we've said, 'but the thing that *ER* does differently is that we show consequence.' We show not the romanticized vision of what the teenager assumes the family's response will be to it—they have an image of everybody at their funeral feeling sorry—but the actual consequence of having your stomach pumped, and that's not what they've got in mind." The result, John believes, is a drama that will help prevent rather than encourage suicides. He emphasizes that while there is "a tremendous amount of violence on *ER,* and also on *Third Watch,* it is never violence without consequence, and it's never frivolous. It's never romanticized in any way, shape, or form."

John also stresses the importance of starting with the story you want to tell and believe in, and only then addressing the issues of depiction and impact that arise. He notes that the Kaiser Family Foundation "has done a lot of research on how much health information *ER* disseminates. Last year they believe that *ER* was the primary disseminator of medical information in the country. Now I can't come into a meeting with the writers and say, 'Well, as the primary disseminators of public-health information in this country, what should we do this year?' You go in and say 'Where are the good stories?' "

Kimberly found the story she wanted and needed to tell, Brandon Teena's murder, and then she struggled with these issues of depiction and impact right through the post-production of *Boys Don't Cry.* "It was really important to me," she told us, "not to be gratuitous and abusive with the violence, and not encourage violence." At first when she got back screening questionnaires that said "too long, too violent," her response was anger at the audience, because she felt they were "not paying attention to what this movie's about. It's *about* the violence. You should have been there for the real rape—*that* was too long and too violent." But then she started to

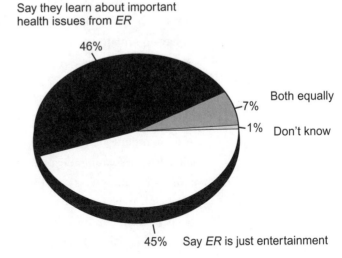

Many *ER* Viewers Learn Important Health Information From the Show

Percent of viewers who...

Say they learn about important health issues from *ER*

46%

Both equally —7%

—1% Don't know

45% Say *ER* is just entertainment

Source: Kaiser Family Foundation, *ER* Emergency Contraception Surveys, April–June, 1997

realize "that they were turning away and becoming desensitized because of the violence. I was looking for a human response, and if I was burning out their nerve endings, then I was really going against the whole point of the story, which was to include people in Brandon's journey, not to alienate them and numb them out. And so we started cutting it down, cutting it down, cutting it down, until we finally got it to the point where the audience pays attention." In other words, the depiction on the screen had to communicate the undercurrent, "what the film was really about." Kimberly emphasizes that "it's not a political question, it's a question of bringing people as deeply as possible inside the story. Even though the film is tough, the overwhelming response of audiences is that they appreciate that we respected them in choosing how much violence to show. If we had used less, it wouldn't have honored Brandon or brought the audience inside what he went through, while more would have alienated them, and we'd have lost them."

As we can see with our filmmakers, the fact that someone may detest cruelty or war or violence doesn't mean that those subjects are inappropriate for their films. George Lucas has said that "movies have a big voice, and what we filmmakers have to do is to set a good example." But there are many ways to set an example. Stories that probe the shadow aspects of human behavior—manifested as the "dark side" in Lucas's *Star Wars* movies—can create just as strong a moral context portraying our demons and failures as stories that emphasize our ideals and aspirations.

You may even find that your voice and point of view lead you in the direction of transgressive art. Long before film was invented, there were artists who, in order to more fully express, lament or rage against darker aspects of life such as isolation, despair, hypocrisy and cruelty, used form and content that broke taboos and upset the status quo. Such work may be vilified at the time, only to be praised, honored, even beloved, by later generations. Again, we believe an authentic creative voice and deeper resonance is what distinguishes the valid challenge that art can make to society, and separates it from work that is meaninglessly shocking just so it will get attention, pandering to the worst instincts of audiences.

Are there impulses so dark or primal that while they may indeed be authentic, they are nevertheless potentially destructive in their impact when put on the screen? Is there a difference between art that challenges society and that which is an oblique way of trying to exorcise troubling personal demons and obsessions? Are films so powerful, either individually or cumulatively, that our own concern about their potential negative impact may at times transcend or supersede our creative expression? And is there a possibility that, even though we have been true to our own voice, we have inadvertently created something that is likely to be "read against the grain" by an audience, taken in ways we didn't intend? Might we, for example, have created a scene of violence so compelling or kinetic that we have unintentionally glorified and made exciting something we ourselves believe to be reprehensible? And what, in turn, are our criteria for judging this? How many people need to read a film in a way we didn't intend for us to decide that we have misjudged? Half? Ten percent? One percent? One in a million? And what is our responsibility in any case? Do we change our work?

These are questions with no obvious or clear-cut answers, nor will one person's answers necessarily be right for anyone else. As filmmakers and educators, we are opposed to any form of censorship and are dedicated to the open exploration of film as art. Yet we feel a constant tension between those beliefs and our deep concern over the pervasiveness of films in our culture that we find sensationalistic and morally numbing, films that engender fearfulness for oneself and apathy about the suffering of others. Nor are we only concerned about the potential impact on the audience of the films we make. When a documentary or a drama depicts real people and events, filmmakers must confront the ethical issues that arise from its potential repercussions on those portrayed. Finally, our filmmakers have offered several examples in the course of this book of how working on a film that violates who we are can undermine our own creativity and even damage us personally.

The social impact of the images we create and our responsibility as artists and human beings for them is an extraordinarily complex issue, one without easy answers. We would hope that every filmmaker would wrestle with these concerns as an intrinsic part of their creative process. One of the goals of this book is to encourage you to be more thoughtful and aware in all aspects of filmmaking, including the decisions you will make (or make by default) about how to deal with the impact of the films you help bring into the world.

LIMBERING UP

1) In Your Bones

Conrad Hall describes reading a script "over and over again. I study it so that it's in my bones." Choose a short story, short screenplay or documentary treatment that you haven't written yourself—it might be for a project you intend to crew on or a short story you want to adapt as a film. Read it at least five times over a period of days or weeks. Each time, try to get to a deeper layer of understanding about the undercurrent of the story. Circle key images, sounds, moments. Write notes in the margins. What do you see of the "bricks," the underlying architecture that Anthony Minghella has referred to? Are there universal emotions and ideas to be found beneath the specifics of the story? What is the story *really* about? What is each scene *really* about? Once you feel that the script is truly "in your bones," jot down ideas about creative choices in the production process—casting, design, camera style or sound backgrounds that would be consistent with and would strengthen the film's undercurrent.

2) Filtering the Feedback

How are you at judging and filtering advice? Are you overly open to feedback? Are you resistant to the opinions of others? Take something creative that you've done and are proud of—a sketch, a poem, a song, a script, a special meal, etc.—and present it to a friend for feedback. Ask for in-person constructive, candid, specific suggestions. When you get this feedback, don't argue and don't agree. Just thank your friend and go away to think about it for at least a day. Then decide for yourself what you agree with and what you don't. If there is a specific response that keeps nagging at you, explore it more deeply. On the surface it may seem "wrong" or confusing, but probing it may give you a clue to something elusive and hard to pin down.

Think about your emotions when you were getting suggestions. If you felt tense, anxious, or defensive, you're not alone. If you felt you were too quick to agree with the feedback, you are also in good company. Try this process again with another friend, and keep trying it until you feel somewhat easier about and more experienced in judging what to listen to and what to ignore. The goal of this limbering is finding an appropriate balance for yourself.

3) "Things I Learned from the Movies or Television"

Make a list of ten things you have learned about life from watching films—perhaps some aspects of life that were new to you or ideas that changed your mind. Don't include what you learned about filmmaking. You might try to find a few that are humorous, and others that are quite serious. Does thinking about how films have affected you have any impact on your approach to filmmaking?

4) Embedded Values

Tape five or ten minutes of the opening of a television show or rent a feature that seems completely innocuous and uncontroversial (when we do this in our classes, we show an early section from the movie *Beethoven,* a comedy about a family that adopts a St. Bernard puppy). Watch the film analytically, looking for every instance of an embedded value you can spot—every implied assumption, judgment and lesson conveyed not only by the story but by the choices made in casting, locations, lighting, set design, music, etc. You might try imagining you were watching this film within another culture, perhaps the Pacific Islanders Gale Anne Hurd described above, to see if that makes the embedded values more visible.

Once you have made your own list, look through the catalog of story-oriented values in the **Embedded Values Questionnaire** (page 189). Does this give you more ideas for your list? Do you agree or disagree with the assertion that all films are carriers of embedded values? If you agree, think about how that might influence your approach to being a creative filmmaker.

introspection

inquiry

intuition

interaction

impact

six workouts

Federico Fellini believed that "the cinema, like all other manifesta-tions of creativity, ought to be in a state of combustion, a metabolism of the unconscious, a journey toward the center of ourselves and the world." We hope this book has heightened your desire to embark on just such a journey. While the *limbering ups* were designed to warm you up and get your creative juices flowing, the *workouts* will take you deeper into each stage of production, from generating an idea to listening to your audience:

Down on the Page guides you in discovering distinctive ideas and turning them into rich, resonant treatments, scripts and creative approaches to a project. **Into the Can** has workouts for preproduction and production. **Up on the Screen** covers post-production, screenings and looking ahead to future projects. For classroom use, our website (creativefilmmaking.com) provides additional *workouts*.

This chapter is not intended to cover comprehensively every aspect of the production process. Rather, it will suggest how you might apply the concepts in the first five chapters to a specific film project. Do any of the workouts that appeal to you, including those that are outside your current creative role. Consider doing some with a partner or a production team. Adapt them to your needs and to the time and space you have available. Come up with your own workouts for aspects of the production process that aren't dealt with here.

Down on the Page

PEOPLE-WATCHING

We saw in **Inquiry** the central importance of real-life observation in the creative process. The French screenwriter Jean-Claude Carrière has described sitting with actor-director Jacques Tati on a café terrace. "We would watch passersby. . . . Suddenly someone would appear, riveting us with some detail; a look, something special about clothes or body . . . you have to watch and *see,* and at once start imagining . . . try to hang upon this chance encounter a story . . . that seems to fit that person."

Try doing the same. Observe people in a public place and notice their expressions, gestures, body language and all the other nuances of their behavior and interactions. Think about how they have chosen to present themselves to the world through their clothes, hairstyle and makeup. Look for clues to the kind of work they do, and the life they lead. Try to guess "their story."

Keep a notebook with you to write down observations and to draw sketches that will remind you of what you saw (refer to the "Taking Note" *limbering* at the end of **Inquiry,** p. 70). Allow this notebook to evolve to suit your own interests and needs. Carroll includes still photographs of compelling places and notes on evocative sound images in her notebook. She has a section for "Wild Ideas," "Undercurrents," and "Questions That This Film Is Trying to Answer." Her "Yellow Pages" are for contacts and resources and she has graph paper for diagrams, pocket pages for "found" items, and colored tabs to highlight ideas she wants to find easily.

After a while you will become more attuned to your own distinctive responses. What catches your eye? What do you find compelling when you look at your notes later? Think of your notebook as both a storehouse of ideas and an emerging map of who you are as a filmmaker.

MEMORY IMAGES

Personal memories can play a key role in creativity, as we saw in **Introspection.** The images, characters and stories in our minds can be the seeds for film ideas that are rich with personal resonance. When Kasi Lemmons wrote and directed *Eve's Bayou,* she created a world for the film that drew upon a wealth of memories from her childhood as part of an upper-middle-class African-American family in Louisiana: "I was trying to recreate what my parents and their friends looked like to me as a child. They looked like gods. . . . If I look at pictures of them, they were gorgeous."

To find your own memory images, try the following. Find a comfortable and quiet place, perhaps outside. Close your eyes; breathe deeply for a minute, relaxing your whole body. Let this workout carry you to a place that feels fluid and unself-conscious. Slowly think back over the last week, the last month, or the last year of your life. Let a single image float into your thoughts, an image that captures a vivid scene or moment. Bring to mind as many of the physical details as possible—the quality of light, the landscape of sounds, the scents, colors, shapes and movements, the tastes and textures—as well as the emotional mood and tone. Then continue to let other images appear.

Over time, try this memory process with other years and time periods in your life. Think of different ways to spark memories. Student Monique Zavistovski, in a course Jed teaches on originating ideas for films, thought of trying to remember things from her childhood that signified adulthood to her: "A stack of mail with official stamps, one's name written in type; a set of keys; a wallet; a bag of makeup; eyeglasses; sedate, patient conversation; strong odors." She asked her husband Adam King to do the same thing and he recalled "veins that stick out on one's arm; hair on the back of one's hand; choosing neutral colors as opposed to vivid colors (in clothes mostly); coffee and alcohol; newspapers; clipboards."

Once you have brought these memory images to the forefront of your mind, you may find them reappearing in your consciousness, popping up in creatively provocative and helpful ways. Begin to explore them as possible ideas for images, settings, characters or moments in a film. If you are planning a fictional screenplay, try at first to stay away from plot, which tends to veer quickly toward cliché and formula. First develop a strong feeling for the world of your possible film, its characters, locations, moods, emotions, themes and specific dramatic situations. Use your emotional and sensory intelligence as well as your intellect.

CAPTURING DREAM IMAGES

The film *Un Chien Andalou* developed out of a collaboration between the Spanish surrealists Luis Buñuel and Salvador Dalí. Buñuel later recalled telling Dalí "about a dream I'd had in which a long, tapering cloud sliced the moon in half, like a razor blade slicing through an eye. Dalí immediately told me he'd seen a hand crawling with ants in a dream he'd had the previous night. 'And what if we started right there and made a film?' he wondered aloud." They wrote the script in less than a week, following one rule: "No idea or image that might lend itself to a rational explanation of any kind would be accepted. We had to open all the doors to the irrational and keep only those images that surprised us, without trying to explain why."

Keep a notebook and pen next to your bed, and when you first awake in the morning, try to remember the images from a dream and write them down. Or use any method of representation that allows you to capture them visually— watercolors, chalk, etc. Focus on the images themselves and the emotions you felt, rather than trying to interpret the dream.

Choose several dream images and write a short description or sketch a rough storyboard for a film scene based on them. Feel free to deviate from the actual dream but keep in mind how you actually experience dreams—maintain the dreamlike quality and resist analyzing it or imposing a conventional narrative plot. Imagine how you might use the elements of cinematic expression (such as performance, production design, camera, lighting, editing, sound design, music, etc.) to create a sense of structure and coherence.

WORKING FROM MUSIC

Australian-born director Peter Weir has said that music "helps me think of the film . . . it's music that unlocks the images for me." As a film evolves he puts together "three, four, five cassettes that seem to give me the whole picture . . . that rock and roll, that aria, that piece of Mozart or that African drum . . . Somehow they've tied together all the emotional moments of the picture, and have all given me images. They influence the casting, the entire film."

Select three pieces of music in different styles (preferably without lyrics) that create an emotional response in you. As you play each piece of music, listen with your whole body, not just your ears. Recognize the state or feeling that this evokes. Don't rush this stage of the workout.

When you are ready, write without stopping or even pausing. Let the words come in a stream-of-consciousness manner, and don't judge or think about what you're writing. Allow the music's structure, rhythms, and energy to influence what happens in your writing. Be open to associations of emotion with sound and image. When you have done this with all three pieces, look back over what you have written for bits and pieces that seem intriguing, and think about how you might develop them.

THE IMAGE WALL

Create a quilt of strong and resonant images on a wall, a bulletin board or room divider. The Image Wall may start out as a repository for exploratory ideas. Antonia Kao, a former USC student, has created a "wall of movement" in

Antonia Kao designs her "wall of movement"

her apartment: "Currently, it is less about a specific project than about the entire project of my life and the hoped-for discovery of projects to hone in on. I've hung up journal entries from turning points in my life on sheets of opalescent and colored cellophane and a few photos that felt expressive or stimulating. My goal with this wall was to have it shift constantly. I've strung the stuff on fish line so it can slide horizontally."

You might try using swatches of fabric, palettes of color, drawings, key words and phrases, photographs of faces, found objects, anything that seems evocative. As you begin to develop initial ideas into a treatment or script, the Image Wall can shift in its function from a "brainstorm" of fragments to a more focused group of chosen elements. Gather whatever seems to belong to your emerging idea and take away anything that no longer seems appropriate. As you begin to develop a documentary or fictional treatment or to write a screenplay, stand in front of the wall on your coffee break or while listening to music and let your collection speak to you.

Photograph your entire wall as it evolves. In pre-production, the wall might become a space for ideas about casting, locations, production design, wardrobe, sound, music or cinematography. As we've seen, Walter Murch uses a version of the wall in post-production. If your wall is in a collaborative space where a creative team meets, this visual mosaic of images can encourage each collaborator to see and spark off each other's ideas.

FIRST IMPRESSIONS

As you begin to research a project, keep track of your strong first impressions of places, people and events. Some of Martin Scorsese's most powerful images in *Raging Bull* came out of his first visits to a boxing ring: "The first evening, even though I was far away from the ring, I saw the sponge red with blood, and the film started to take form. The next time I was much closer, and I saw the blood dripping from the ropes." Try to make your research a mix of both alert intellectual questioning and vivid sensory impressions. Notice your emotions—what surprises, dismays or awes you? What demands your attention? What creeps up on you? What has to be flushed out of hiding? Use poetic and sensory words to write down impressions.

INVISIBLE ANGEL

The angel Cassiel (Otto Sander) listens to the thoughts of a mortal human in *Wings of Desire*

In the film *Wings of Desire,* angels can listen to the private thoughts of mortal people, but are invisible and cannot interact. German director Wim Wenders has described his experience making the film: "As soon as we started shooting, it became obvious how vast the possibilities of innovation were because of the invention of the guardian angel and the point of view it implied."

Imagine you are an invisible angel and follow in your mind a fictional character you are writing about. Don't think ahead, don't impose anything, just follow this character and observe where they go and what they do. Now you can hear their thoughts—what are they thinking?

STARTING WITH SOUND

Ethnographic filmmaker Robert A. Gardner, in his documentary *Forest of Bliss,* opens the film with haunting sound motifs. Dogs are barking, water is lapping, and crows are flying overhead. Each sound seems authentic and intrinsic to the location, the river Ganges in India, and yet the sources of the sounds are not all shown. Collectively, this "soundscape" evokes a world just waking up. Separately, the specific sounds are echoed later in the film as they carry ideas about the spiritual life of the river and the journey of the dead.

Design an opening for the film you are writing based entirely on sound cues. Imagine an audience watching a black screen for a full minute and listening to a landscape of sounds that evoke a sense of the story or subject. Then bring in your opening visual images. Do the sounds suggest new ideas or connections to the visuals? Do they provide a counterpoint? Do they deepen the mood and meaning of the moment or evoke the story's undercurrent? Consider the possibility that these sound motifs might recur throughout the film.

Try this workout again, and focus on finding some non-literal sounds (ones that would not actually be present in real life in your setting) to mix in with your other choices. You might also see if different ideas emerge if you do this workout when you first wake up in the morning or as you drift off at night in that half-asleep dreamy state.

REALITY CHECK

Describe the story or the ideas of the project you are working on to several people who actually live the kind of lives portrayed in it. Notice what you change, embellish, emphasize, or leave out as you talk. Do you experience a bit of discomfort or embarrassment at times? Do you sense a real connection with your listener at other moments? Imagine this audience watching the film you have in your mind—regardless of whether they like it or not, are you confident of its truthfulness? If this film were to become a principal source of information about the people or events depicted, would an audience come away with a better, truer understanding?

While you are getting feedback on your script or documentary treatment, and before you start pre-production (and still feel free to make changes), use the questions in the **Embedded Values Questionnaire** (p. 189) to give you a clearer sense of the values that are currently ingrained in the project. Try this again later with decisions on casting, locations, production design, wardrobe, camera placement and other areas of creative choice. Do these embedded values truly reflect your own point of view (including your shadow side), or have they appeared because they are familiar, faddish or seemingly commercial?

"LOCKS START OPENING . . ."

Frank Daniel, the late Czechoslovakian-born filmmaker and teacher, used to tell his students about a technique for breaking a creative logjam that he'd learned from old-time screenwriters. While you are still in the prime of inspiration on your project, he advised, write yourself a secret letter that includes "everything that you can tell about it: why this script will be the greatest piece ever written, how it's going to shake the world." As you write, "some strange things will begin to happen. There will be some ideas that still may not have any specificity, but they'll still be ideas that express the push and pull of the story." Later, if you reach a point where you have lost track of what you're doing and why, open the letter and read it: "You'll be surprised. The tormenting problems that you have had with your script have been there in the envelope, solved. You begin to see answers, keys, the locks start opening."

Creative work does not come without periods of blankness, or "blackness" as Kimberly Peirce described in **Intuition.** Trust that these periods do not mean the end of your creative work, but are part of the whole experience. If you come to a point of feeling truly lost or disconnected, it may be comforting or inspiring to consider Federico Fellini's account of his anguish as he tried to begin *8½,* Ingmar Bergman's similarly despairing state that led to *Persona,* Martin Scorsese on grappling with his demons before making *Taxi Driver* or Francis Ford Coppola recalling his struggles during the production of *Apocalypse Now* (see **Endnotes**).

Into the Can

POETIC SCRIPT

Stuart Dryburgh, cinematographer on *The Piano,* has described the visual look of the film in poetic terms of color and metaphor: "the blue-greens of the bush and the amber rich mud . . . 'Bottom of the fish tank' was the description we used." The use of poetic language can help open filmmakers to fresh images and actions. In his book *Film Production Theory,* Jean-Pierre Geuens argues for the benefits of using freer, more expressive formatting and language at the screenwriting stage.

As you go over the script or treatment for the project, identify essential sensory elements in every scene. Do this whether you are the cinematographer, director, production designer or sound designer. In your imagination, enter every scene. Have all your senses alert. Feel the textures and temperatures, smell the scents, taste the air, see the quality of light and the impending weather, listen for distant sounds, close and subtle sounds, defining emotional sounds.

Conventional Script

EXT. ALASKA FISH CANNERY DOCK- DUSK

It has just finished raining in this gray and isolated cove. A long wooden dock extends out from the only old cannery building left standing.

At the end of the dock a large, slow moving old boat is edging in. This is the *Uncle Sam*, the local mail boat.

A few gulls overhead dive bomb the boat and then pull up at the last minute, COMPLAINING.

MARGE KENNER idles the engine as she eases the boat in. Her deck is loaded with white Styrofoam boxes, a bicycle, fishing gear and an antique dresser. On the edge of the dock a mangy, half-blind dog looks up.

Marge looks around. The dock is deserted. She frowns and shuts off her engine. The mutt struggles to balance on his arthritic legs and eagerly walks in her direction.

Write sensory details into your script and let them affect the behavior of your characters.

Re-write the moment or scene in a poetic version, using only these expressive, sensory words. Use non-technical terms if you want to indicate camera movements or sound elements. Write with fragments of sentences. Spread them out intuitively over the page, leaving plenty of white space between these fragments. Your version will look and sound more like poetry than a traditional scene description. Read it aloud and listen to its rhythms. Let the rhythms evoke new images that convey the essence of the scene.

Consider how you would shoot this scene if this were your actual shot list with parallel sound design cues. How is the resulting scene in your mind different from the conventionally formatted scene you started with?

Poetic Version

Silver gray dampness

Steaming mist

warm lumber

scent of motor oil and kelp
screaming gulls
salty air

a frowning face

shuts down

A dog pants

A head lifts

lips whistle,   ears respond

a woman smiles

OPEN-CLOSED CASTING

Walter Murch's idea of being "open-closed" in making creative decisions (**Intuition,** p. 75) can be used in many areas of pre-production and production. One example is in casting, where it is essential to have a clear idea of the qualities an actor needs to play a certain character, and yet remain open to being surprised. Film history is filled with stories of actors who turned out to be superb in a role, and yet were initially considered wrong for the part.

One particularly common problem we see is that filmmakers go into the casting process with a fixed idea of the physical appearance of a character, and miss out on fine actors who might bring something fresh and unexpected to a role. Jane Campion, the New Zealand–born writer-director of *The Piano,* at first thought that Holly Hunter (who subsequently won the Best Actress Academy Award for the role) "was not my image of Ada at all . . . Originally, I had an almost clichéd, romantic view of this tall, statuesque, black-haired, black-eyed beauty. In many ways, she wasn't a very real human being, and when meeting Holly, I was not very willing to see her as Ada . . . Holly read the opening prologue and I started to tape her. I immediately realized she was doing something for me that I wasn't expecting."

Write casting notices for the film's characters that avoid all physical characteristics except those that are truly essential to the story. Emphasize what is distinct, intriguing and surprising about the character. Imagine you are trying to convince a great actor that this will be a challenging and rich role to play. When you subsequently go through head shots and then audition actors, try to stay open-closed, ready to have your own conception of the character enlarged by a performance you weren't expecting.

TEAMBUILDING

Director Mira Nair has a voluntary yoga session for cast and crew every morning before shooting, in part because it breaks down hierarchies and puts everyone on an equal footing: "It genuinely promoted a sense of democracy on the set, a great sense of egolessness. . . . We all saw each other gripping our thighs and with our bums in the air."

Plan both one-time and ongoing activities for the entire production or your specific creative department that will help engender a sense of mutual respect and collaboration. You might even consider bringing in a specialist to lead teambuilding exercises. When Carroll worked as one of the producers on the independent feature *Raven's Blood,* there was concern that, in addition to the common tendencies toward division along the lines of departments (camera, sound, lighting) and authority hierarchies, there were other possible conflicts. The crew could divide between old timers and newcomers to Alaska ("that's not how we do it here") or between interns and experienced crew ("that's not how it's done").

Just before production started, the cast and crew spent a day on teambuilding, led by Suzanne Blue Star Boy, one of the producers, who was also an organizational development trainer. A series of "mapping" exercises uncovered and explored both diverse and common values within the group. In the middle of an open area, individuals placed themselves in constantly shifting configurations that reflected the many facets of their identities in response to questions like "What part of the country/world were you born in? How long have you known you were a storyteller? What spiritual tradition would you place yourself in?" There was always the option to not define oneself in a particular category. The overall effect was heightened interest in each other's backgrounds and a sense of mutual respect on the set as differences arose.

NURTURING A CREATIVE ENVIRONMENT

As Anthony Minghella remarked in **Interaction,** "most of us work best when we feel cherished." Jazz trumpeter Wynton Marsalis has eloquently described how he and his fellow musicians collaborate with each other and then indicate their appreciation for one another onstage: "Make room for someone else, help them sound good, then use a part of what they are playing to sound good yourself. Whenever somebody plays something good on our bandstand, we jokingly cup our hands together, reach down and scoop up the sound and pour it all over our faces like we're bathing in it."

On your current production, have you made an effort to "make room" for someone else's efforts, as Marsalis describes? Have you helped someone "sound good"? Have you let others know the ways in which you were "bathing" in the good work they were doing? Make a specific effort to actually tell a collaborator about something they created or contributed that you particularly admired, enjoyed, or benefitted from in terms of having your own creativity sparked.

BLOCKING FOR RELATIONSHIPS

In **Impact,** several of our filmmakers talked about how they draw on the film's undercurrent to make detailed creative decisions such as where to place the camera for a shot or when to make an edit in a scene. As they explore their understanding of what the film is *really* about, they can then ask what a particular scene or a single moment is really about. This process of working from the deeper layers of the story is applicable in innumerable ways, but this and the following three workouts provide a few examples for the production phase.

The physical positioning of actors in a scene is just one of many visual cues to the deeper levels of their characters' relationships, revealing such aspects as who has power at any given moment. Canadian writer-director Atom Egoyan has said that "the amazing thing about the construction of any dramatic scene is that it's really about defining territory, and how you use the camera, how you use the actors, to somehow establish the shifting relationships to power." He has specifically described how, in certain scenes of *The Sweet Hereafter,* changes in the blocking of the actors reflect these shifts in who has power.

To consider more fully your own ideas about power and its role in the story you are telling, first read the "Power" section of the **Embedded Values Questionnaire** (p. 189). Then, if you're making a documentary, pay attention in your dailies to where your characters position themselves relative to one another and to the camera. Begin to explore how you might frame and film them to provide a stronger visual representation of their relationships.

If you are directing a fiction film, think through the power shifts within each scene before rehearsing it. Don't impose preconceived blocking on the actors, but encourage them to explore their characters' "shifting relationships of power" through their movements, physical proximity and body language.

THE CAMERA'S POINT OF VIEW

Once the action of the characters is blocked (or becomes apparent when shooting a documentary), the next major decision is where to put the camera. The camera serves as the eyes of the audience, and gives powerful cues about who in the scene to identify with, as film critic Andrew Sarris has humorously noted: "If the story of Little Red Riding Hood is told with the Wolf in close-up and Little Red Riding Hood in long-shot, the director is concerned primarily with the emotional problems of a wolf with a compulsion to eat little girls. If Little Red Riding Hood is in close-up and the Wolf in long-shot, the emphasis is shifted to the emotional problems of vestigial virginity in a wicked world. Thus, two different stories are being told with the same basic anecdotal material."

As you prepare a scene's shot design or plan a documentary shoot, consider the ways that camera placement might help convey the ideas and emotions of the story. Ask questions like "Whose scene is it? Whose needs or goals are driving the action and consequences? Is there a particular character's perspective with which the audience should primarily empathize? What is the storyteller's perspective?" In advance of shooting a fictional film, work with rough storyboard sketches. On the set or location, use a director's viewfinder or the lens of a still camera to explore point of view.

FRAMING THE STORY

Max Pomeranc as chess prodigy Josh Waitzkin in *Searching for Bobby Fischer*

The movie *Searching for Bobby Fischer* is based on the true story of Josh Waitzkin, a young chess prodigy. Cinematographer Conrad Hall felt that, in essence, it was "a story about genius, and how to treat it." To explore this undercurrent of extraordinary mental capacity, Conrad wanted to "look into the mind of the boy when he's playing chess and see his thought process in his eyes." He accomplished this with unusual framing: "I did things with moving his eyes very close to the top of the frame. If the eyes are close to being out of frame, then it's maybe worrisome that you're not going to see them, and that focuses your attention on them."

In advance of shooting, work with your storyboards and a movable frame of two L-shaped pieces of paper. What would be the emotional result of having more symmetry and balance, or less, in the composition? Are there elements in the frame that need greater or less emphasis? Ask similar questions about such choices as focus, depth, camera movement and movement within the frame.

LIGHT AND SHADOW

Lighting is another major storytelling tool for the filmmaker. Italian cinematographer Vittorio Storaro, for the film *The Conformist,* worked from his concept that "the Fascist period in Italy was very closed, very claustrophobic, without any real communication between shadow and light." After shooting the scenes in Italy with sharp definition between lit and unlit areas, he began to shift the design at the point in the story that the main characters board a train to France: "I wanted to express a sense of freedom by letting the light go into the shadows, very gradually, and to have colors [appear] that were not in the film before."

Try using the "clustering" *limbering* (in **Intuition**) with your creative collaborators to look for adjectives and adverbs that resonate with the film's undercurrent, and nouns that seem to be metaphors for the story. How might they become part of the light and shadow of the film? Supplement these ideas with photographs that you shoot or collect, or reproductions of paintings or art work that capture the essence of what you are looking for. Share them with others or hang them on the Image Wall.

SIMPLIFY, SIMPLIFY, SIMPLIFY

Jeannine Oppewall noted in **Inquiry** that taking away is "much stronger than adding." James Newton Howard, when working with writer-director M. Night Shyamalan on the scores for *The Sixth Sense, Unbreakable* and *Signs,* found that the limitations imposed by Shyamalan stimulated him to find innovative approaches to the music: "He says, 'You can only use this. You can only use that. I'm taking away all these different things, and you can't use those.' He pushes you into an area where, because you don't have those familiar tools, you're forced to come up with alternatives you might otherwise not have thought of."

Try peeling back or losing a number of elements that you are working with and see if they are essential. Trim dialogue, limit the number of colors in the film's palette, subtract props and set decoration, reduce the number of music cues. While working on the lighting for a set, many cinematographers and gaffers turn off all their lights except one and then gradually turn on another one and then another, looking for the simplest lighting solution, which is often the most elegant and effective.

Up on the Screen

RANDOM SAMPLING

Sound can be a deeply intuitive and emotional (and often nonliteral) element in a film. Many filmmakers find great value in getting into a nonintellectual, associative state when working with it. Sound designer Frank Warner finds it helpful to roll randomly through the reels of his extensive collection of original sound effects when he starts a new project, open to unusual choices and juxtapositions for the scenes he is working on. Similarly, sound editor Midge Costin likes to go through the catalogs of sound effects libraries (increasingly available through online sources and CDs) to trigger new ideas. She listens to samples of specific effects ("rain on a tin roof, rain on gravel, rain on pond water") in the order they appear in the catalog. The randomness of order takes her out of her specific expectations and helps clarify and deepen her sense of the sounds and moods she is seeking.

Try these intuitive exploratory techniques as you research and organize sound cues, and begin to edit sound. Look back over the notes you took and any associative work you did when you were writing, or first reading, the script or documentary treatment. Let these initial responses help refresh and clarify your current direction.

You may also want to try a version of Walter Murch's photo wall (**Intuition**) to spark associative thoughts during picture editing. He uses digital prints of the first three or four frames from each shot or setup and arranges them not in the film's actual story order but in a more random way, the order they were actually shot during production. If you don't have access to digital prints, use index cards with sketches or evocative descriptions. You may find your own system for organizing your wall in a way that opens your mind to new possibilities. Cruising quickly through digitized footage can give you access to the same "dreamy" and associative state of mind.

SENSING THE UNDERCURRENT

It is easy to lose one's way during the making of a film, to get off track or become bogged down in the details. That's particularly the case in post-production when the process of looking at the same footage over and over again, perhaps hundreds of times, can cause it to seem flat, opaque and meaningless. Writer-director Oliver Stone talks about the need to have a "Theseus-like thread" if one is to find one's way out of the "six-month to one-year maze" of picture editing (in classical mythology, Theseus used a thread to find his way out of the Labyrinth). That thread, in Stone's words, is "the thing within the thing," what we have called the undercurrent.

When you feel you are in danger of losing your way during editing, go back and look at photos of the Image Wall from the pre-script conceptualization phase onward. Reread notes and journal entries that captured initial impressions or attempted to wrestle with what the film is really about. Perhaps now is the time to reread the letter you wrote and sealed early in the process (see the workout **"Locks Start Opening . . ."**, p. 155). Try to recapture a Zen-like "beginner's mind" by listening to the sound tracks without the picture, and then watching the picture without sound. If the footage is in color, flip the image to black and white on your monitor if you can. You're not trying to pin down the undercurrent like a specimen under glass, but rather to refresh your sense of the flow and continuity of your understanding—how you got from there to here, and what has remained constant.

USING THE SCORE TO TELL THE DEEPER STORY

Composer Elmer Bernstein has said that music "can express what [the story's characters] are not willing to express, or are unable to express. For that very reason, the music can supply an emotional rail, so to speak, for the film." In creating the opening music cue for *To Kill a Mockingbird,* he found that "what was going on here were a series of real-world adult problems seen through the eyes of children. That led me to the basic sound of the score: the piano being played one note at a time. Music box–type sounds, bells, harps, single-note flutes were all things that suggested a child's world."

Working from another facet of a film's undercurrent, composer Tan Dun and director Ang Lee approached *Crouching Tiger, Hidden Dragon* by focusing on its blend of Chinese and Western storytelling genres. They explored music that would, in Tan's words, "serve as a bridge . . . between East and West. That's why we decided to cast the cellist Yo-Yo Ma [born in Paris of Chinese parents, raised in the United States] as that bridge."

What instruments and musical styles might echo and enhance the deeper themes or points of view embodied in your film. Consider unexpected instruments and sources of rhythm. Use recordings as temporary music in editing, as points of departure for the score, or just as an evocative background while you work on any aspect of production or post-production. Instead of using music to reiterate what is already on the screen or in the soundtrack (which often creates a sense of the film being overscored), use it sparingly, looking for moments where music might add new layers of nuance.

A SCREENING QUESTIONNAIRE

When Kimberly Peirce organized test screenings for *Boys Don't Cry,* she used a questionnaire that included open-ended questions such as "Give your feelings about the beginning and the end of the film," and "Please give your impressions about the following: Lana and Brandon's love affair . . ." (see **Endnotes** for the complete set of questions). She then carefully read all the answers herself, and wrote notes in the margins.

Well before test screening your film, start keeping track of the information you hope to get from the audience. Avoid questions that attempt to get the audience to agree with you. The eventual questionnaire should be a collaborative effort of everyone involved in the final creative choices. If you are planning a big screening, try out the questions with a small group first. Once you have the responses, consciously try to get into a nondefensive frame of mind and then read all the answers carefully. Don't make up your mind right away, but come back to them over a period of days, especially the ones that seem to touch a nerve or that reappear several times. If you have more than one screening, keep revising and improving your questionnaire.

THE LAST CREATIVE ACT

Your learning process on a film can continue even after the film is completed as you reexperience your work through screenings with audiences. With *The Talented Mr. Ripley,* Anthony Minghella made question-and-answer appearances at screenings in many countries: "Brazil, Australia, Norway—and it's fantastic because you just learn what's speaking and what isn't speaking, where you're going wrong, where people see what you hope they'll see. It's good to stand up and take responsibility for what you've done."

Get feedback from audiences in as many different types of venues as possible. If the film is in theatrical release, engage people in conversation as they leave the theater as Jeannine Oppewall did with *Pleasantville* (see **Impact,** p. 137). Submit it to festivals, and if it's accepted, try to attend some with audiences that may provide an alternative take on your film. Arrange and attend screenings for groups and communities represented in the film. At all screenings, make yourself available for questions afterward whenever possible.

PERSONAL METAPHORS

Akira Kurosawa often used metaphors when talking about filmmaking. For example, he compared the process to a tree: "The root of any film project for me is this inner need to express something. What nurtures this root and makes it grow into a tree is the script. What makes the tree bear flowers and fruit is the directing." He also drew an analogy to a military campaign: "If you compare the production unit to an army, the script is the battle flag and the director is the commander of the front line." At another moment, filmmaking seemed to Kurosawa like ceramics: "Things can happen without warning that produce a startling effect. When these can be incorporated in the film without upsetting the balance, the whole becomes much more interesting . . . similar to a pot being fired in a kiln. Ashes and other particles can fall onto the melted glaze during the firing and cause unpredictable but beautiful results."

What figures of speech have you used or would you use to describe the production process you have just gone through? Think about your choice of words and see if they give you insight into your deeper attitudes and beliefs about filmmaking. Does your vocabulary reflect how you want to experience filmmaking? Come up with a metaphor that reflects your own style and that you want to use in your next project. Let it influence the work you do and the people you work with. Ask other members of your collaborative team for their own production metaphors—perhaps as a teambuilding exercise at the start of a film. Have fun with the process and use it to open a discussion rather than to pin down an exact definition.

LETTING YOUR LAST FILM
HELP LEAD TO THE NEXT

Miriam Kim, a graduate production student at USC, created as one of her first films a fictional portrayal of the physical and emotional isolation of a bedridden old man. Later, she made a documentary at a retirement home for the elderly. After completing that film, she wrote in her production journal that her second film dealing with elderly characters "was actually a reaction to the first one. My view of old age had been narrow and biased. I felt the impetus to do another project and learn things, as I had not seen them before. What I learned is that fundamentally all human beings deal with the same basic issues independent of their age. Above all this film became about love and the need we have of it."

You may not have a future project grow quite so directly out of the one you have just finished, but take some time to reflect on what you have learned about yourself as a filmmaker, as a collaborator, as a creative person, and how that greater knowledge and experience might influence your subsequent work. What convictions do you hold even more strongly now? Is your "mysterious pre-disposition" clearer? We have circled around to **Introspection,** a good place to be as you consider where to go from here.

endnotes

Chapter One: Introspection

Page

17 *The artist Edward Hopper:* Quoted in Gail Levin, *Edward Hopper: An Intimate Biography* (New York: Alfred A. Knopf, 1995), pp. 460,486.

24 *"I found* The Art of Animation: Bob Thomas, *The Art of Animation* (New York: Simon & Schuster, 1958).

29 *Italian cinematographer Vittorio Storaro:* "A Journey Into Light: Vittorio Storaro in Conversation with Ric Gentry," *Projections 6: Film-Makers on Film-Making,* ed. John Boorman and Walter Donohue (London: Faber & Faber, 1996), p. 256.

30 *in the words of Indian-born filmmaker Mira Nair:* Ethirajan Anbarasan and Amy Otchet, "Mira Nair: An Eye for Paradox," *UNESCO Courier,* November 1998, p. 46.

37 *Glen Keane, the supervising animator:* Charles Solomon, "Time to Draw the Line," *Los Angeles Times,* July 18, 1999.

44 *But as documentary filmmaker and film historian Eric Barnouw wrote:* Eric Barnouw, *Documentary: A History of the Non-Fiction Film,* rev. ed. (Oxford: Oxford University Press, 1983), p. 313.

Chapter Two: Inquiry

Page

49 *Sound designer Ben Burtt:* David Wally, "Aural Surgery," *USC Trojan Family Magazine.* Autumn 2001, p. 67.

53 *video artist Bill Viola:* Bernard Weinraub, "A Video Explorer Who Sees Links to the Renaissance," *The New York Times,* December 9, 1997.

53 *Mexican director Alejandro González Iñárritu:* Sorina Diaconescu, "A New Independents' Day," *Los Angeles Times,* December 8, 2001. Iñárritu's reference to Nan Goldin's photography took place at the Independent Feature Project/West director series, Los Angeles, March 19, 2002.

55 *As German writer-director Tom Tykwer has said:* John Anderson, "New Language of Film: Quick and Fast," *Los Angeles Times,* June 30, 1999.

56 *But the late French filmmaker Jean Renoir:* Jean Renoir, *My Life and My Films,* trans. Norman Denny (New York: Atheneum, 1974), p. 171.

58 *The late Japanese filmmaker Akira Kurosawa: Interviews with Film Directors,* ed. Andrew Sarris (New York: Bobbs-Merrill, 1967), pp. 245–46.

60 *Renee has written about:* Renee Tajima-Peña, "No Mo Po Mo and Other Tales of the Road," *Countervisions: Asian American Film Criticism,* ed. Darrell Y. Hamamoto and Sandra Liu (Philadelphia: Temple University Press, 2000), pp. 245–62.

61 *Dylan Robertson:* Personal correspondence with Dylan Robertson, director of *The Size of It* (University of Southern California, 2001).

62 *As writer-director John Sayles has said:* Peter Biskind, "The Sweet Hell of Success," *Premiere,* October 1997, p. 100.

64 *He had gone through old magazines:* Curtis Hanson displays this collection of photographs, and describes how he used it, on the DVD edition of *L.A. Confidential* (Warner Home Video, 1998). From the main menu, select "Hush-Hush Headliners," then "Extra! Extra! Reel Shocking Evidence!" and then "The Photo Pitch."

69 *According to actor Helena Bonham Carter:* Ismail Merchant, *Ismail Merchant's Florence: Filming and Feasting in Tuscany* (New York: Harry N. Abrams, 1994), p. 35.

70 *In his book* Developing Story Ideas: Michael Rabiger, *Developing Story Ideas* (Woburn, MA: Focal Press/Butterworth-Heineman, 2000).

Chapter Three: Intuition

Page

71 *a nonconscious process:* We prefer the term "nonconscious" to "subconscious" or "unconscious." Antonio R. Damasio, in *The Feeling of What Happens: Body and Emotion in the Making of Consciousness* (New York: Harcourt Brace, 1999, p. 228) notes: "The unconscious, in the narrow meaning in which the word has been etched in our culture, is only a part of the vast amount of processes and contents that remain nonconscious, not known in core or extended consciousness." And J. Allen Hobson, in *The Chemistry of Conscious States: How the Brain Changes Its Mind* (Boston: Little, Brown, 1994, p. 207), states "We have all heard of the conscious, the subconscious, the unconscious, the nonconscious, the preconscious, the repressed unconscious, and so on. What a mess! All we need are two terms: conscious and nonconscious."

71 *Cognitive scientist Steven Pinker:* Steven Pinker, *How the Mind Works* (New York: W. W. Norton, 1997), p. 63.

72 *physicist and biologist Leo Szilard:* Quoted in Antonio R. Damasio, *Descartes' Error: Emotion, Reason, and the Human Brain* (New York: G. P. Putnam's Sons, 1994), p. 189.

80 *Composer John Cage:* Philip Guston, *It Is,* 5 (Spring 1960), pp. 36–38.

80 *Swedish writer-director Ingmar Bergman:* Ingmar Bergman, *The Magic Lantern: An Autobiography,* trans. Joan Tate (New York: Viking, 1988), p. 73.

80 *And the late Luis Buñuel:* Quoted in Anthony Minghella, "The House Is Dark, and the Children Are Afraid," *The New York Times,* August 12, 2001.

80 *Walter Murch notes that there is a paradox:* See also Walter Murch, *In the Blink of an Eye: A Perspective on Film Editing* (Los Angeles: Silman-James, 1995); and Michael Ondaatje, *The Conversations: Walter Murch and the Art of Editing Film* (New York: Alfred A. Knopf, 2002).

82 *Gore Vidal, coincidentally, has said:* "The Creators: How They Keep Going and Going and . . ." *Modern Maturity,* March–April 2000, p. 44.

Chapter Four: Interaction
Page

93 *as Walter Murch has written:* Walter Murch, "Summer Films: The Future; A Digital Cinema Of the Mind? Could Be," *The New York Times,* May 2, 1999.

96 *Federico Fellini, the late Italian writer-director:* Charles T. Samuels, *Encountering Directors* (New York: G.P. Putnam's Sons, 1972), p. 133.

Chapter Five: Impact
Page

117 *Theologian Anne Foerst: Science Friday,* National Public Radio, April 26, 2002.

119 *Author Alice Walker has written:* Alice Walker, *The Same River Twice: Honoring the Difficult* (Scribner, 1996), p. 282.

120 *The late Polish filmmaker Krzysztof Kieślowski: Kieślowski on Kieślowski,* ed. Danusia Stok (London: Faber & Faber, 1993), p. 156.

120 *Screenwriter William Goldman:* William Goldman, *Adventures in the Screen Trade: A Personal View of Hollywood and Screenwriting* (New York: Warner, 1984), p. 489.

120 *British director Sam Mendes:* Lynn Hirschberg "Just-High-Enough Art," *The New York Times,* July 7, 2002.

120 *Taiwanese-born director Ang Lee:* Rick Lyman, "Watching Movies with Ang Lee: Crouching Memory, Hidden Heart," *The New York Times,* March 9, 2001.

125 *which Coppola has described:* "Writing and Directing *The Conversation:* A Talk with Francis Ford Coppola," interview by Annie Nocenti, *Scenario,* Vol. 5, No. 1 (Spring 1999), p. 63.

126 *Similarly, Stanley Kubrick once said:* Francis X. Clines, "The Silent Celebrity and the Quotable Recluse," *The New York Times,* May 14, 1999.

127 *Howard Leder:* Personal correspondence with Howard Leder, director of *A Sound Education* (University of Southern California, 1999).

127 *James L. Brooks has described:* Unpublished interview by Laura Davis, October 17, 1997.

128 *The late John Cassavetes:* "A Man Under His Own Influence," excerpts from interviews by Ray Carney, *Visions,* Summer 1992, p. 29.

128 *Or, as documentary filmmaker Errol Morris said:* Peter Applebone, "A Taste for the Eccentric, Marginal and Dangerous," *The New York Times,* December 26, 1999.

130 *Krzysztof Kieślowski expressed his pleasure:* Kristine McKenna, "Past, Present . . . Future?," *Los Angeles Times,* February 12, 1995.

131 *Director Sidney Lumet has written:* Sidney Lumet, *Making Movies* (New York: Vintage, 1996), pp. 167–68.

133 *Danish writer-director Thomas Vinterberg:* Thomas Vinterberg, interview by Bo Green Jensen, *Weekend Avisen,* available at www.dogme95.dk/dogme/news/interview/index.htm.

138 *Marlon Riggs, the late documentary filmmaker:* Revon Kyle Banneker, "Marlon Riggs Untied," *BLK,* April 1990, p. 11.

138 *Producer David Puttnam has described:* David Puttnam, interview by Bill Moyers, *Bill Moyers' World of Ideas,* Public Affairs Television, September 12, 1988.

139 *Gale Anne Hurd, the producer of* The Terminator: Quoted in Linda Seger and Edward Jay Whetmore, *From Script to Screen: The Collaborative Art of Filmmaking* (New York: Henry Holt and Company, 1994), p. 83.

139 *Steven Spielberg, in 1995, told an interviewer:* Mark Caro, "Spielberg Alters Scenes in *E.T.* for 20th Anniversary Release," *Los Angeles Times,* November 5, 2001.

141 *As film writer Peter Biskind has said:* Peter Biskind, *Seeing is Believing: How Hollywood Taught Us to Stop Worrying and Love the Fifties* (New York: Pantheon, 1983), p. 2.

141 *The impact of these embedded values:* Sales of Ray-Ban Wayfarer sunglasses, worn by Tom Cruise in *Risky Business,* went from 18,000 pairs in 1981 to 330,000 in 1983, the year of the movie's release (Dave Karger, "Undie Film Movement," *Entertainment Weekly,* July 30, 1999); Reese's Pieces candy, which lured E.T. into Elliott's house, tripled in sales in the two weeks following the movie's opening (Joël Glenn Brenner, *The Emperors of Chocolate: Inside the Secret World of Hershey and Mars* (New York: Random House, 1999), pp. 277–78.

144 *George Lucas has said:* " 'I'm a Cynic Who Has Hope for the Human Race,' " by Orville Schell, *The New York Times,* March 21, 1999.

Workouts

Page

149 *Federico Fellini believed:* Quoted in Dawna Markova, *No Enemies Within: A Creative Process for Discovering What's Right About What's Wrong* (Berkeley, CA: Conari Press, 1994), p. 201.

150 *The French screenwriter Jean-Claude Carrière:* Jean-Claude Carrière, *The Secret Language of Film,* trans. Jeremy Leggatt (New York: Pantheon Books, 1994), pp. 158–59, 170.

151   *When Kasi Lemmons:* Kasi Lemmons, interview by James Mottram, *The Independent,* London, August 6, 1998.

152   *Buñuel later recalled telling Dalí:* Luis Buñuel, *My Last Sigh* (New York: Random House, 1984), quoted in *Roger Ebert's Book of Film,* ed. Roger Ebert (New York: W.W. Norton & Company, 1996), pp. 441–43.

152   *Australian-born director Peter Weir:* Michael Ventura, "The Nuts and Bolts of Peter Weir," *L.A. Weekly,* February 8, 1985.

154   *Some of Martin Scorsese's most powerful images:* "Raging Bull," interview by Michael Henry in *Martin Scorsese: Interviews,* ed. Peter Brunette (Jackson: University Press of Mississippi, 1999), pp. 97–98.

154   *German director Wim Wenders has described:* "Wenders' Method of Making Films: 'I Prefer Movies That Ask Me to See,' " in *The Cinema of Wim Wenders: Image, Narrative, and the Postmodern Condition* (Detroit: Wayne State University Press, 1997), p. 67.

155   *Frank Daniel:* Frank Daniel, unpublished address given at Columbia University School of the Arts, Film Division, May 5, 1996.

156   *If you come to a point: Federico Fellini: Comments on Film,* ed. Giovanni Grazzini, (Fresno: University of California State Press at Fresno, 1988), pp. 161–62; Charles T. Samuels, *Encountering Directors* (New York: Putnam Publishing Group, 1972), p. 186; "Raging Bull," in *Martin Scorsese: Interviews,* pp. 88–89; *Hearts of Darkness: A Filmmaker's Apocalypse,* prod. and dir. Fax Bahr, Eleanor Coppola, and George Hickenlooper. 1 hr. 36 min. Paramount Studios, 1991, videocassette.

156   *Stuart Dryburgh:* Jane Campion, *The Piano* (New York: Miramax Books and Hyperion, 1993), p. 141.

156   *In his book* Film Production Theory: Jean-Pierre Geuens, *Film Production Theory* (Albany: State University of New York Press, 2000), pp. 90–95.

156–57 *Conventional and poetic scripts:* Carroll Hodge, *Aleut Bay,* unpublished screenplay.

157   *Even Jane Campion:* "The Piano," interview by Miro Bilbrough in *Jane Campion Interviews,* ed. Virginia Wright Wexman (Jackson: University of Mississippi Press, 1999), pp. 118–19.

158   *Director Mira Nair:* Shanti Menon, "Profile: Director's Cut," *Yoga Journal,* August 2002, p. 76.

159   *Jazz trumpeter Wynton Marsalis:* Wynton Marsalis and Frank Stewart, *Sweet Swing Blues on the Road* (New York: W.W. Norton & Company, 1994), p. 14.

159   *Canadian writer-director Atom Egoyan has said: The Sweet Hereafter,* dir. Atom Egoyan, prod. Atom Egoyan and Camelia Freiberg. 1 hr. 59 min. New Line Studios, 1997. DVD audio commentary track, 1:10:17 to 1:13:30.

160   *as film critic Andrew Sarris has humorously noted:* Quoted in Louis Giannetti, *Understanding Movies,* 9th ed. (Upper Saddle River, NJ: Prentice Hall, 2001), pp. 379–81.

161   *Italian cinematographer Vittorio Storaro:* Storaro, "A Journey Into Light" in *Projections 6,* p. 256.

162   *Writer-director Oliver Stone:* Oliver Stone, "An Epic That Gets Better as It Gets Longer," *The New York Times,* November 29, 1998, p. 20.

163   *Composer Elmer Bernstein has said: Innocence and Experience: The Making of "The Age of Innocence,"* prod. and dir. Laura Davis. HBO premiere, September 8, 1993.

163   *In creating the opening music cue for* To Kill a Mockingbird: Jon Burlingame, "Hollywood's Scorekeeper," *Los Angeles Times,* November 8, 2001.

163   *They explored music that would, in Tan's words:* Daniel Schweiger, "Martial Artist: *Crouching Tiger* Composer Tan Dun Looks for Emotion in His Action," *Venice Magazine,* 2000. Available at http://www.venicemag.com.

164   *the complete set of questions:* Kimberly Peirce's screening questions for a preview screening of *Boys Don't Cry,* February 24, 1999:

> Please answer as thoughtfully and completely as possible.
>
> 1. Overall reaction. Please be as general or as specific as you like.
>
> 2. Give your feelings about the beginning and the ending of the film. When was it clear what the story was?
>
> 3. Which scenes did you like/dislike?
>
> 4. Please discuss the overall pacing of the film: Did the film move too fast or too slow in any particular area? Were there any parts of the film you found repetitious in terms of story or character? Please be as specific as possible.
>
> 5. Were you left with any factual concerns/points of confusion at the end of the film? Were there any scenes you felt were missing or unnecessary to tell the story?
>
> 6. Discuss your overall feelings regarding Brandon [the main character]. How would you describe him? How did you feel about Teena (as a girl) before she becomes Brandon? Did Brandon do anything that bugged you? Were there any times Brandon was unbelievable as a boy, as one of the kids of Fall City?
>
> 7. The following is a list of the main characters in the film: [list follows] Who were your favorite characters? Why? Who were your least favorite characters? Why?
>
> 8. Please give your impressions about the following: Lana and Brandon's love affair. Tom and John as characters, their turn against Brandon, their stripping of Brandon and their rape and murder of Brandon. The rape and its aftermath (cutting away from the rape and returning to it).
>
> OPTIONAL QUESTION
>
> Discuss the use of music in the film. How did the music work with or against the narrative and the characters? Any suggestions? Favorites?
>
> Thank you for watching the cut.
>
> How do you identify? Age? Gender? Sexual preference? Favorite movie last year?

164   *Anthony Minghella made question-and-answer appearances:* Richard Stayton, "The Talented Mr. Minghella," *Written By,* February 2000. Available at http://www.wga.org.

165   *Akira Kurosawa often used metaphors:* Akira Kurosawa, *Something Like an Autobiography,* trans. Audie E. Bock (New York: Random House, 1983), quoted in Ebert, p. 663.

Embedded Values Questionnaire

Page

189   *Embedded Values Questionnaire:* the questionnaire was inspired in part by Paul Jarrico, "What's Playing at Plato's Cave?," *Written By,* Dec/Jan 1998, pp. 80–81.

selected filmographies

Kate Amend

PANDEMIC: FACING AIDS (2002), Editor

Out of Line (2001), Editor

Into the Arms of Strangers: Stories of the Kindertransport (2000), Editor; **American Cinema Editors' Eddy Award,** 2000; (**Academy Award,** Best Documentary Feature, 2001)

On Tiptoe: Gentle Steps to Freedom (2000), Editor; (**Academy Award Nomination,** Best Short Documentary, 2001; **IDA Award,** Best Short Documentary, 2001)

Kiss (2000) (Season Premiere for VH1's *Fan Club*), Editor

A Man Is Mostly Water (2000), Editor

The Girl Next Door (1999), Editor

Free a Man to Fight: Women Soldiers of WWII (1999) (TV), Editor

Some Nudity Required (1998), Editor

Tobacco Blues (1997), Editor

The Long Way Home (1997), Editor; (**Academy Award,** Best Documentary Feature, 1998)

The Animal Is Out: The Making of Wolf (1994) (TV), Editor

Spread the Word: The Persuasions Sing Acapella (1994), Editor

Come the Morning (1993), Editor

The Making of The Age of Innocence (1993) (TV), Editor
Skinheads, USA: Soldiers of the Race War (1992) (TV), Editor
The Southern Sex (1992) (TV), Editor
Asylum (1992) (TV), Editor; **(Cable ACE Award Nomination)**
Legends (1991) (TV), Editor; (**Audience Award,** Sydney Film Festival)
How Will I Survive? (1992) (TV), Editor
Danger: Kids at Work (1991) (TV), Editor
Homesick (1989) (TV), Editor
Metamorphosis: Man into Woman (1990), Editor
Art for Our Sake, Producer, Director
From Darkness into Light: Creating the Holocaust Project (museum video), Producer, Director
Making a Difference, Producer, Director

Kathy Baker

Cold Mountain (2003)
Too Young to Be a Dad (2002) (TV movie)
Assassination Tango (2002)
Murphy's Dozen (2001) (TV series)
Door to Door (2001) (TV movie)
Boston Public (2001–2002) (TV series)
Ten Tiny Love Stories (2001)
The Glass House (2001)
Sanctuary (2001) (TV movie)
A Little Inside (2001)
Ratz (2000) (TV movie)
Chicago Hope (2000) (TV series) guest appearance
Touched by an Angel (2000) (TV series) guest appearance; **Emmy Award Nomination,** Outstanding Guest Actress in a Drama Series, 2000
Things You Can Tell Just by Looking at Her (2000)
Gideon's Crossing (2000) (TV series) guest appearance
Bull (2000) (TV series) guest appearance
A Season for Miracles (1999) (TV movie)
Shake, Rattle and Roll: An American Love Story (1999) (TV miniseries)
The Cider House Rules (1999); **SAG Award Nomination,** Outstanding Performance by a Cast in a Theatrical Motion Picture
A.T.F. (1999) (TV movie)
Oklahoma City: A Survivor's Story (1998) (TV movie)
The Practice (1997) (TV series) guest appearance
Not In This Town (1997) (TV movie)
Weapons of Mass Distraction (1997) (TV movie)
Inventing the Abbotts (1997)
Ally McBeal (1997) (TV series) guest appearance
Gun (1997) (TV series) guest appearance
To Gillian on Her 37th Birthday (1996)

Lush Life (1993) (TV movie)

Mad Dog and Glory (1993)

Jennifer Eight (1992)

Picket Fences (1992) (TV series); **Emmy Awards,** Outstanding Lead Actress in a Drama Series, 1993, 1995, 1996; **Emmy Award Nomination,** Outstanding Lead Actress in a Drama Series, 1994; **SAG Award,** Outstanding Performance by a Female Actor in a Drama Series, 1995; **SAG Award Nomination,** Outstanding Performance by an Ensemble in a Drama Series, 1995; **Golden Globe,** Best Performance by an Actress in a TV Series Drama (1993)

Article 99 (1992)

One Special Victory (1991) (TV movie)

Edward Scissorhands (1990)

Mister Frost (1990)

The Image (1990) (TV movie)

Dad (1989)

Jacknife (1989)

Permanent Record (1988)

Clean and Sober (1988)

Street Smart (1987); **National Society of Film Critics Award,** Best Supporting Actress, 1987

Mariah (1987) (episodic TV)

My Sister's Keeper (1986)

Amazing Stories (1985) (TV series) guest appearance

Nobody's Child (1986) (TV movie)

A Killing Affair (1986)

The Right Stuff (1983)

Pamela Douglas

Twigs and Ashes (2002) (fiction book), Author

Teen Violence (1998) (TV movie), Writer

All or Nothing (1997) (TV movie), Writer

Between Mother and Daughter (1995) (TV movie), Writer, Coproducer; **Humanitas Prize,** 1995; **Writers Guild of America Award,** 1996

Different Worlds (1992) (TV movie), Writer; **Emmy Award Nomination,** Writing; **Humanitas Certificate,** 1992; **25th Annual NAACP Image Award,** 1992

Ghostwriter (1992) (TV series), Creator, Writer; **Writers Guild Award**

Sexual Considerations (1991) (TV movie), Writer; **American Women in Radio and Television Award,** 1992; **National Education Association Award**

Star Trek: The Next Generation (1990) (TV series), Writer

A Girl of the Limberlost (1990) (TV movie), Writer

Tin Man (1989) (TV pilot), Writer

Paradise (1989) (TV series), Writer

TV101 (1988) (TV series), Story Editor; **Nancy Susan Reynolds Award,** 1989

Trapper John, M.D. (1979) (TV series), Writer

A Year in the Life (1987) (TV series), Writer; **American Women in Radio and Television Award,** Best Dramatic Show of the Year, 1988

Frank's Place (1987) (TV series), Story Editor; **(Emmy Award)**

Sojourner Truth (1985) (TV movie), Writer

Mike Hammer (1984) (TV series), Writer

On the Boulevard (1983) (TV), Writer

Rosa Parks (1982), Writer

Lisa Fruchtman

Normal (2003) (HBO movie), Editor

Technolust (2002), Editor

Point of Origin (2001), Consulting Editor

Witness Protection (1999) (HBO movie), Editor

Dance with Me (1998), Editor

Nothing Sacred (1997) (pilot for TV series), Editor

My Best Friend's Wedding (1997), Editor

Truman (1995) (HBO movie), Editor; **Emmy Award Nomination,** Outstanding Single Camera Editing for a Miniseries or a Special, 1996; **Cable Ace Award,** Best Editing, 1996

Shimmer (1993), Editor

Wrestling Ernest Hemingway (1993), Consulting Editor

The Doctor (1991), Editor

The Godfather, Part III (1990), Editor; **Academy Award Nomination,** Best Editing, 1991

Children of a Lesser God (1986), Editor

Captain Eo (1986), Editor

The Right Stuff (1983), Editor; **Academy Award,** Best Editing, 1984; **American Cinema Editors' Eddy Award Nomination,** Best Editing, 1984

Street Music (1981), Editor

Heaven's Gate (1980), Editor

Apocalypse Now (1979), Editor; **Academy Award Nomination,** Best Editing, 1980; **American Cinema Editors' Eddy Award Nomination,** Best Editing, 1980; **Film Award Nomination,** British Academy of Film and Television Arts, Best Editing, 1980

Conrad L. Hall

Road to Perdition (2002), Cinematographer

Career Achievement Award, Los Angeles Film Critics Association, 2000

American Beauty (1999), Cinematographer; **Academy Award,** Best Cinematography, 2000; **Film Award,** British Academy of Film and Television Arts, Best Cinematography, 2000

Sleepy Hollow (1999), Additional Photography: New York

A Civil Action (1998), Cinematographer; **Academy Award Nomination,** Best Cinematography, 1999

Without Limits (1998), Cinematographer

Love Affair (1994), Cinematographer; **American Society of Cinematographers Award,** Outstanding Achievement in Cinematography in Theatrical Releases, 1995

Lifetime Achievement Award, Camerimage, 1995

Searching for Bobby Fischer (1993), Cinematographer; **Academy Award Nomination,** Best Cinematography, 1994; **American Society of Cinematographers Award,** Outstanding Achievement in Cinematography in Theatrical Releases, 1994

Lifetime Achievement Award, American Society of Cinematographers, 1994

Jennifer Eight (1992), Cinematographer, Second Unit Director

Sharkskin (1991), Cinematographer

Class Action (1991), Cinematographer

Tequila Sunrise (1988), Cinematographer; **Academy Award Nomination,** Best Cinematography, 1989; **American Society of Cinematographers Award,** Outstanding Achievement in Cinematography in Theatrical Releases, 1989

Black Widow (1987), Cinematographer

It Happened One Christmas (1977) (TV movie), Cinematographer

Marathon Man (1976), Cinematographer

Smile (1975), Cinematographer

The Day of the Locust (1975), Cinematographer; **Academy Award Nomination,** Best Cinematography, 1976

Catch My Soul (1974), Cinematographer

Electra Glide in Blue (1973), Cinematographer

Fat City (1972), Cinematographer

The Happy Ending (1969), Cinematographer

Tell Them Willie Boy is Here (1969), Cinematographer

Trilogy (1969) (segment "A Christmas Memory"), Cinematographer

Butch Cassidy and the Sundance Kid (1969), Cinematographer; **Academy Award,** Best Cinematography, 1970; **Film Award,** British Academy of Film and Television Arts, Best Cinematography, 1971

Hell in the Pacific (1968), Cinematographer

Rogues' Gallery (1968), Cinematographer

In Cold Blood (1967), Cinematographer; **Academy Award Nomination,** Best Cinematography, 1968

Cool Hand Luke (1967), Cinematographer

Divorce American Style (1967), Cinematographer

The Professionals (1966), Cinematographer; **Academy Award Nomination,** Best Color Cinematography, 1967

Harper (1966), Cinematographer

Incubus (1965), Cinematographer

Morturi (1965), Cinematographer; **Academy Award Nomination,** Best Black and White Cinematography, 1966

Wild Seed (1965), Cinematographer

The Outer Limits (1963) (TV series), Cinematographer

Stoney Burke (1962) (TV series), Cinematographer

Pressure Point (1962), Camera Operator

Mutiny on the Bounty (1962), Camera Operator

The Adventures of Huckleberry Finn (1960), Camera Operator

Edge of Fury (1958), Cinematographer

Running Target (1956), Cinematographer, Cowriter

Sea Theme (1949) (short) Codirector, Coeditor, Cowriter, Cinematographer; **ASC International Prize for Cinematography**

James Newton Howard

Dreamcatcher (2002), Composer

The Emperor's Club (2002), Composer

Who Shot Victor Fox (2002), Composer

Treasure Planet (2002), Composer

Signs (2002), Composer

Big Trouble (2002), Composer

America's Sweethearts (2001), Composer

Atlantis: The Lost Empire (2001), Composer

Vertical Limit (2000), Composer

Unbreakable (2000), Composer

Gideon's Crossing (2000) (TV series), Theme Composer; **Emmy Award,** Main Title Theme Music

Dinosaur (2000), Composer

Snow Falling on Cedars (1999), Composer

Mumford (1999), Composer

The Sixth Sense (1999), Composer

Stir of Echoes (1999), Composer

Runaway Bride (1999), Composer

A Perfect Murder (1998), Composer

From the Earth to the Moon (1998) (TV miniseries, Part Six), Composer

The Postman (1997), Composer

The Devil's Advocate (1997), Composer

My Best Friend's Wedding (1997), Composer; **Academy Award Nomination,** Best Musical or Comedy Score, 1998

Father's Day (1997), Composer

Liar Liar (1997), Composer—theme

Dante's Peak (1997), Composer—theme

The Sentinel (1996) (TV series), Theme Composer

One Fine Day (1996), Orchestrator; **Academy Award Nomination,** Best Song "For the First Time," 1997; **Golden Globe Award Nomination,** Best Original Song—Motion Picture "For the First Time," 1997; **Grammy Award Nomination,** Best Song Written Specifically for a Motion Picture or for Television "For the First Time," 1997

Space Jam (1996), Composer

The Rich Man's Wife (1996), Composer—musical theme

The Trigger Effect (1996), Composer

Primal Fear (1996), Composer

The Juror (1996), Composer

Eye for an Eye (1996), Composer

Restoration (1995), Composer

Waterworld (1995), Composer

French Kiss (1995), Composer

Outbreak (1995), Composer

Just Cause (1995), Composer

Intersection (1994), Composer, Orchestrator

Major League II (1994), Composer—additional music

Junior (1994), Orchestrator; **Academy Award Nomination,** Best Music—Song "Look What Love Has Done," 1994; **Golden Globe Award Nomination,** Best Original Song—Motion Picture "Look What Love Has Done," 1994

ER (1994) (TV series), Theme Composer; **Emmy Award Nomination,** Outstanding Individual Achievement in Main Title Theme Music, 1995

Wyatt Earp (1994), Orchestrator

The Saint of Fort Washington (1993), Orchestrator

The Fugitive (1993), Composer; **Academy Award Nomination,** Best Achievement in Music, Original Score, 1994

Dave (1993), Composer, Orchestrator

Falling Down (1993), Composer, Orchestrator

Alive (1993), Composer, Orchestrator

Night and the City (1992), Composer—film score and songs

American Heart (1992), Composer

Glengarry Glen Ross (1992), Composer

2000 Malibu Road (1992) (TV series), Composer—theme

Diggstown (1992), Composer, Conductor/Orchestrator

A Private Matter (1992) (TV movie), Composer

Middle Ages (1992) (TV series), Composer

Grand Canyon (1991), Composer

The Prince of Tides (1991), Composer; **Academy Award Nomination,** Best Achievement in Music, Original Score, 1992

My Girl (1991), Composer

The Man in the Moon (1991), Composer

Dying Young (1991), Composer; **Grammy Award Nomination,** Best Instrumental Music from Television or Film, "Love Theme from *Dying Young*," 1990

Guilty by Suspicion (1991), Composer

King Ralph (1991), Composer

Sunday Dinner (1991) (TV series), Composer, "You'll Love the Ride"

Descending Angel (1990) (TV movie), Composer

3 Men and a Little Lady (1990), Composer

Marked for Death (1990), Composer

Somebody Has to Shoot the Picture (1990) (TV movie), Composer

Flatliners (1990), Composer

Revealing Evidence: Stalking the Honolulu Strangler (1990) (TV movie), Composer

Pretty Woman (1990), Composer—film score, Orchestrator

Coupe de Ville (1990), Composer

The Image (1990) (TV movie), Composer

The Package (1989), Composer

Major League (1989), Composer—film score and song, "Most of All You"

Tap (1989), Composer

Men (1989) (TV pilot), Composer; **Emmy Award Nomination,** Outstanding Achievement in Main Title Theme Music, 1989

Off Limits (1988), Composer

Promised Land (1988), Composer

Everybody's All-American (1988), Composer—film score and song, "Until Forever"

Go to the Light (1988) (TV movie), Composer

Some Girls (1988), Composer, Conductor

Russkies (1987), Composer

Five Corners (1987), Score Producer

Campus Man (1987), Composer

Elton John in Australia (1987) (TV show), Orchestra Conductor

Nobody's Fool (1986), Composer

8 Million Ways to Die (1986), Composer

Tough Guys (1986), Composer

Wildcats (1986), Composer

Cobra (1986), Composer "Hold on to Your Vision"

Never too Young to Die (1986), Composer

Nothing in Common (1986) Music Conductor, Music Arranger for Strings

Head Office (1985), Composer

White Nights (1985) Composer "Prove Me Wrong"

Hanif Kureishi

Intimacy (2000), Writer

Mauvaise passé (1999), Writer

My Son, the Fanatic (1997), Writer (also novel)

The Buddha of Suburbia (1993) (TV miniseries), Writer (also novel); **Television Award Nomination,** British Academy of Film and Television Arts, Best Drama Serial, 1994

London Kills Me (1991), Writer, Director

Sammy and Rosie Get Laid (1987), Writer

My Beautiful Laundrette (1985), Writer; **Academy Award Nomination,** Best Screenplay Written Directly for Screen, 1987; **New York Film Critics Circle Award,** Best Screenplay, 1986; **National Society of Film Critics Award,** Best Screenplay, 1987; **Film Award Nomination,** British Academy of Film and Television Arts, Best Original Screenplay, 1986

John Lasseter

Monsters, Inc. (2001), Executive Producer; **Academy Award Nomination,** Best Animated Feature Film, 2002

For the Birds (2000), Executive Producer

Toy Story 2 (1999), Story by, Director

A Bug's Life (1998), Story by, Director

Computer Illusions (1998), Actor

Geri's Game (1997), Executive Producer

Outstanding Achievement Award, ShoWest Convention, 1996

Toy Story (1995), Story by, Director, Visual Effects: modeling and animation system development; **Special Achievement Award,** Academy of Motion Picture Arts and Sciences, 1996; **Academy Award Nomination,** Best Screenplay Written Directly for Screen, 1996; **Annie Award,** Best Individual Achievement: Directing, 1996

Luxo Jr. in "Surprise" and "Light and Heavy" (1991), Animator, Director

Knickknack (1989), Writer, Director, Animator, Modeler

Tin Toy (1988), Writer, Director, Animator, Modeler; **Academy Award,** Short Film—Animated, 1989; **Golden Nica Award** Prix Arts Electronica, Austrian Broadcasting Corporation, 1988

Red's Dream (1987), Writer, Director, Animator, Modeler, **Golden Nica Award**

Young Sherlock Holmes (1985), Visual Effects: computer animator: ILM

Luxo Jr. (1986), Writer, Director, Producer, Visual Effects: models, animation; **Academy Award Nomination,** Best Animated Short Film, 1986; **Silver Berlin Bear,** Berlin International Film Festival, Best Short Film, 1987; **Golden Nica Award**

The Adventures of André and Wally B. (1984), Director, Character Designer, Animator

Mickey's Christmas Carol (1983), Creative Collaboration, Animator

Ismail Merchant

Le Divorce (2003), Producer

The Mystic Masseur (2001), Director

The Golden Bowl (2000), Producer

Cotton Mary (1999), Producer, Director

A Soldier's Daughter Never Cries (1998), Producer; **Independent Spirit Award Nomination,** Best Feature, 1999

Lifetime Achievement Award, Asian American International Film Festival, 1998

Gaach (1998), Executive Producer

Side Streets (1997), Executive Producer

Surviving Picasso (1996), Producer

The Proprietor (1996), Director

Street Musicians of Bombay (1994), Producer

Feast of July (1995), Executive Producer

Lumière et compagnie (1995), Director

The Remains of the Day (1993), Producer; **Academy Award Nomination,** Best Picture, 1994; **Film Award Nomination,** British Academy of Film and Television Arts, Best Film, 1994

In Custody (1993), Director

Howards End (1992), Producer; **National Board of Review Award,** Best Picture, 1992; **Academy Award Nomination,** Best Picture, 1993; **Film Award,** British Academy of Film and Television Arts, Best Film, 1993

The Ballad of the Sad Café (1991), Producer

Second Daughter (1991), Producer

The Perfect Murder (1990), Executive Producer

Mr. & Mrs. Bridge (1990), Producer

Slaves of New York (1989), Producer

The Deceivers (1988), Producer

Maurice (1987), Producer

Sweet Lorraine (1987), Executive Producer

My Little Girl (1986), Executive Producer

A Room with a View (1986), Producer; **Academy Award Nomination,** Best Picture, 1987;
   Film Award, British Academy of Film and Television Arts, Best Film, 1987

American Playhouse (1985) (episodic TV), Executive Producer for episode "Noon Wine"

The Bostonians (1984), Producer

The Courtesans of Bombay (1982) (TV documentary), Producer, Director, Coscreenwriter

Heat and Dust (1982), Producer; **Film Award Nomination,** British Academy of Film and
   Television Arts, Best Film, 1984

Quartet (1981), Producer

Jane Austen in Manhattan (1980), Producer

The Europeans (1979), Producer

Hullabaloo Over Georgie and Bonnie's Pictures (1979) (TV movie), Producer

The Five Forty-Eight (1979), Producer

Roseland (1977), Producer

Sweet Sounds (1976) (documentary short), Producer

Autobiography of a Princess (1975) (TV movie), Producer

The Wild Party (1975), Producer

Mahatma and the Mad Boy (1974) (documentary short), Producer, Director

Savages (1972), Producer

Adventures of a Brown Man in Search of Civilization (1971) (TV documentary), Producer

Bombay Talkie (1970), Producer

The Guru (1969), Producer

Shakespeare Wallah (1965), Producer

The Delhi Way (1964), Producer

The Householder (1963), Producer

The Sword and the Flute (1961) (short), Producer

The Creation of Woman (1960), Producer, Director; **Academy Award Nomination,** Best
   Short Film, 1960

Anthony Minghella

Cold Mountain (2003), Writer, Director

The Assumption (2002), Writer, Producer

The Quiet American (2002), Producer

Heaven (2002), Producer

Iris (2001), Executive Producer

Play (2000), Director

The Talented Mr. Ripley (1999), Screenplay Writer, Director, Score Producer, Songs Producer and Lyrics

The English Patient (1996), Screenplay Writer, Director; **Academy Award,** Best Directing, 1996; **British Academy of Film and Television Arts Award,** Best Film, Best Screenplay–Adapted

Mr. Wonderful (1993), Director

Truly Madly Deeply (1991), Writer, Director; **British Academy of Film and Television Arts Award,** Best Original Screenplay, 1991

Living with Dinosaurs (1989) (TV movie), Writer

The Storyteller (1987) (TV series), Writer

Inspector Morse (1987) (TV series), Writer, various episodes

Walter Murch

Cold Mountain (2003), Editor and Sound Rerecording Mixer

K-19: The Widowmaker (2002), Editor and Sound Rerecording Mixer

Apocalypse Now Redux (2001), Editor and Sound Rerecording Mixer

Dumbarton Bridge (1999), Consulting Editor

The Talented Mr. Ripley (1999), Editor and Sound Rerecording Mixer

Touch of Evil (1998 reconstruction), Editor and Sound Rerecording Mixer

The English Patient (1996), Editor and Sound Rerecording Mixer; **Academy Awards,** Film Editing, Sound; **British Academy Award,** Best Film Editing; **British Academy Award Nomination,** Best Sound.

First Knight (1995), Editor and Sound Rerecording Mixer

I Love Trouble (1994), Coeditor

Crumb (1994), Sound Rerecording Mixer

Romeo Is Bleeding (1993), Editor and Sound Rerecording Mixer

House of Cards (1993), Editor and Sound Rerecording Mixer

The Godfather Trilogy: 1901–1980 (1992), Editor

The Godfather, Part III (1990), Editor and Sound Rerecording Mixer; **Academy Award Nomination,** Best Editing

Ghost (1990), Editor and Sound Rerecording Mixer; **Academy Award Nomination,** Best Editing

Call from Space (1989), Editor

The Unbearable Lightness of Being (1988), Supervising Film Editor

Captain Eo (1986), Editor

Return to Oz (1985), Cowriter, Director

The Adventures of Mark Twain (1985) (animated film), Special Creative Consultant

The Right Stuff (1984), Documentary Editorial Researcher

Dragonslayer (1981), Sound Re-recording Mixer

Apocalypse Now (1979), Coeditor, Sound Designer, Sound Rerecording Mixer; **Academy Award,** Sound; **Academy Award Nomination,** Best Film Editing; **British Academy Award Nomination,** Best Sound

Julia (1977), Editor; **Academy Award Nomination,** Best Film Editing; **British Academy Award Nomination,** Best Film Editing

The Black Stallion (1979), Cowriter (uncredited)

The Godfather: Part II (1974), Sound Montage and Rerecording

The Conversation (1974), Coeditor, Sound Montage and Rerecording; **British Academy Awards,** Best Film Editing and Best Sound; **Academy Award Nomination,** Best Sound

The Great Gatsby (1974), Sound Technician

American Graffiti (1973), Sound Montage and Rerecording

The Godfather (1972), Supervising Sound Editor

THX 1138 (1970), Cowriter, Sound Montage and Rerecording

Gimme Shelter (1970), Cameraman

The Rain People (1969), Sound Montage and Rerecording

Jeannine Oppewall

Catch Me If You Can (2002), Production Designer

The Sum of All Fears (2002), Production Designer

Wonder Boys (2000), Production Designer; **Art Directors Guild Nomination,** Excellence in Production Design

Snow Falling on Cedars (1999), Production Designer

Pleasantville (1998), Production Designer; **Academy Award Nomination,** Art Direction, 1998; **Art Directors Guild Nomination,** Excellence in Production Design; **Los Angeles Film Critics Association Award,** Best Production Design, 1998

L.A. Confidential (1997), Production Designer; **Academy Award Nomination,** Art Direction, 1997; **Art Directors Guild Nomination,** Excellence in Production Design; **British Academy of Film and Television Arts Nomination,** Art Direction, 1997

The Rich Man's Wife (1996), Production Designer

Primal Fear (1996), Production Designer

The Bridges of Madison County (1995), Production Designer

Losing Isaiah (1995), Production Designer

Corrina, Corrina (1994), Production Designer

The Wrong Man (1993) (TV movie), Production Designer

The Vanishing (1993), Production Designer

School Ties (1992), Production Designer

Sibling Rivalry (1990), Production Designer

White Palace (1990), Production Designer

Music Box (1989), Production Designer

Rooftops (1989), Production Designer

Ironweed (1987), Production Designer

The Big Easy (1987), Production Designer

Light of Day (1987), Production Designer

Desert Hearts (1985), Production Designer

Maria's Lovers (1984), Production Designer

Racing with the Moon (1984), Set Designer

Love Letters (1983), Production Designer

Tender Mercies (1983), Production Designer

Cat People (1982), Set Designer

Blow Out (1981), Set Designer

Honky Tonk Freeway (1981), Set Design

My Bodyguard (1980), Set Designer

Hardcore (1979), Project Consultant

Blue Collar (1978), Design Consultant

Kimberly Peirce

Boys Don't Cry (1999), Director, Writer; **London Film Festival Critics Award; Stockholm Film Festival Critics Award; National Board of Review Award,** Best Debut Director; **Boston Society of Film Critics Award,** Best New Filmmaker; **Academy Award,** Best Actress (Hilary Swank); **Academy Award Nomination,** Best Supporting Actress (Chloë Sevigny)

Renee Tajima-Peña

The Journey Home (2003) (TV special), Coexecutive Producer, Director

The New Americans "Kansas, Stories" (2002) (TV series), Producer, Director

Labor Women (2002), Producer, Director, Covideographer

Skate Manzanar (2001), Director, Videographer

The Last Beat Movie (1997), Producer, Director, Writer

My America . . . or Honk if You Love Buddha (1996), Producer, Director, Writer; **Sundance Film Festival Documentary Cinematography Award; Best Overall Documentary Award,** Athens International Film Festival

Rockefeller Foundation Intercultural Film/Video Fellow in Documentary, 1994

Fellow in Film, New York Foundation for the Arts, 1994

Declarations: All Men Are Created Equal? (1993) (TV movie), Senior Producer, Segment Director for "The Ballad of Demetrio Rodriguez"

Jennifer's in Jail (1992), Director, Writer; **Cable Ace Award Nominations,** Directing and Best Documentary, 1992

Best Hotel on Skid Row (1990), Director, Writer

What Americans Really Think of the Japanese for Fujisankei (1990), Producer, Director, Writer

Yellow Tale Blues (1990), Director, Executive Producer

Wade H. McCree, Jr. Award for the Advancement of Justice, 1990

Rockefeller Foundation Intercultural Film/Video Fellow in Documentary, 1990

Asian American Legal Defense & Education Fund, Justice in Action Award, 1990

Monkey King Looks West (1989), Producer, Writer

James Wong Howe Media Award, 1989

Who Killed Vincent Chin? (1988), Producer, Director; **Academy Award Nomination,** Best Feature Documentary; **Peabody Award,** Excellence in Broadcast Journalism, 1990; **Dupont-Columbia Award** Silver Baton, 1991

Haitian Corner (1987), Producer; **Grand Prize,** Festival du Cinema "Images Caribes"

Fellow in Film, New York Foundation for the Arts, 1987

John Wells

Presidio Med (2002) (TV series), Executive Producer

Far from Heaven (2002), Executive Producer

The Good Thief (2002), Producer

White Oleander (2002), Producer

One Hour Photo (2002), Executive Producer

The Big Time (2001) (TV movie), Executive Producer

Citizen Baines (2001) (TV series), Executive Producer

The Grey Zone (2001), Executive Producer

Thunder Below (1999), Producer

Third Watch (1999) (TV series), Executive Producer, Writer

The West Wing (1999) (TV series), Executive Producer; **Emmy Awards,** Outstanding Drama Series, 2000, 2001, 2002

Trinity (1998) (TV series), Executive Producer

The Peacemaker (1997), Coexecutive Producer

Entertaining Angels: The Dorothy Day Story (1996), Writer

ER (1994) (TV series), Executive Producer, Director (various episodes), Writer (various episodes); **Emmy Award,** Outstanding Drama Series, 1996; **Emmy Award Nominations,** Outstanding Drama Series, 1995, 1997, 1998, 1999, 2000, 2001; **Emmy Award Nominations,** Outstanding Writing for a Drama Series, 1996, 1997; **Emmy Award Nomination,** Outstanding Directing for a Drama Series, 2000, 2002

ER (1994) (TV movie), Executive Producer

Angel Street (1992) (TV series), Executive Producer, Creator, Writer

Angel Street (1992) (TV movie), Executive Producer, Writer

The Nightman (1992) (TV movie), Coexecutive Producer, Writer

China Beach (1998) (TV series), Coexecutive Producer, Supervising Producer, Director, Writer; **Emmy Award Nominations,** Outstanding Drama Series, 1989, 1990, 1991; **Emmy Award Nomination,** Outstanding Individual Achievement in Writing a Drama Series, 1992; **Golden Globe Award,** Best Television Series—Drama, 1990; **Golden Globe Award Nomination,** Best Television Series—Drama, 1991

suggested reading

Berger, John. *Ways of Seeing.* London: British Broadcasting Corporation, 1972.

Block, Bruce. *The Visual Story: Seeing the Structure of Film, TV, and New Media.* Boston: Focal Press, 2001.

Bok, Sissela. *Mayhem: Violence as Public Entertainment.* Reading, Massachusetts: A Merloyd Lawrence Book/Addison-Wesley, 1998.

Boleslavsky, Richard. *Acting: The First Six Lessons.* New York: Theatre Arts Books, 1984.

Cameron, Julia. *The Artist's Way: A Spiritual Path to Higher Creativity.* New York: Jeremy P. Tarcher/Putnam Book, 1992.

Citron, Michelle. *Home Movies and Other Necessary Fictions.* Vol. 4 of *Visible Evidence.* Minneapolis: University of Minnesota Press, 1999.

Dancyger, Ken and Jeff Rush. *Alternative Screenwriting: Writing Beyond the Rules,* 2d ed. Boston: Focal Press, 1995.

Edwards, Betty. *Drawing on the Right Side of the Brain.* New York: Jeremy P. Tarcher/Putnam Book, 1989.

Geuens, Jean-Pierre. *Film Production Theory.* Albany: State University of New York Press, 2000.

Johnson, Claudia Hunter. *Crafting Short Screenplays That Connect.* Boston: Focal Press/Butterworth-Heinemann, 2000.

Johnstone, Keith. *Impro: Improvisation and the Theatre.* New York: A Theatre Arts Book, 1992.

Kagan, Jeremy, ed. *Directors Close Up: Interviews with Directors Nominated for Best Film by the Directors Guild of America.* Boston: Focal Press, 2000.

Karlin, Fred and Rayburn Wright. *On the Track: A Guide to Contemporary Film Scoring.* New York: Schirmer Books/Macmillan, Inc.

Kritek, Phyllis Beck. *Negotiating at an Uneven Table: A Practical Approach to Working with Difference and Diversity.* San Francisco: Jossey-Bass Publishers, 1994.

Maisel, Eric. *Fearless Creating: A Step-by-Step Guide to Starting and Completing Your Work of Art.* New York: Jeremy P. Tarcher/Putnam, 1995.

May, Rollo. *The Courage to Create.* New York: W. W. Norton & Company Inc., 1975.

Metzger, Deena. *Writing for Your Life: A Guide and Companion to the Inner Worlds.* New York/San Francisco: HarperSanFrancisco/HarperCollins Publishers, 1992.

Murch, Walter. *In the Blink of an Eye.* Los Angeles: Silman-James Press, 1995.

Nachmanovitch, Stephen. *Free Play: Improvisation in Life and Art.* New York: Jeremy P. Tarcher/Putnam, 1990.

Rabiger, Michael. *Developing Story Ideas.* Boston: Focal Press, 2000.

Rea, Peter W. and David K. Irving. *Producing and Directing the Short Film and Video,* 2nd ed. Boston: Focal Press, 2001.

Rico, Gabriele. *Writing the Natural Way: Using Right-Brain Techniques to Release Your Expressive Powers.* Los Angeles: J. P. Tarcher, Inc., 1983.

Seger, Linda and Edward Jay Whetmore. *From Script to Screen: The Collaborative Art of Filmmaking.* New York: Henry Holt and Company, 1994.

Seger, Linda. *Making a Good Writer Great: A Creativity Workbook for Screenwriters.* Los Angeles: Silman-James Press, 1999.

Von Oech, Roger. *A Whack on the Side of the Head: How You Can Be More Creative,* 3d ed. New York: Warner Books, Inc., 1998.

embedded values
questionnaire

We may spend a lot of time consciously giving our characters their names, their actions and their attitudes. Meanwhile our less conscious minds may be traveling down convenient and well-worn paths of assumptions, generalizations and stereotypes as our story and characters become clothed in a multitude of *unexamined* value-laden details. Ultimately, our films reflect and convey a worldview that is largely constructed from the values embedded in these details, whether or not we are aware of them. You might use the following questions (they are not in any order of priority) to heighten your awareness of ways in which films are carriers of values, and to help you deepen the intentionality and authenticity of your own creative choices. There are many more questions about values that could be asked; what questions and categories would you add to the list?

Class and wealth

Is money a problem or source of problems, taken for granted, a worthy goal, a sign of decadence? Are working class characters absent or portrayed only as side characters? Do "middle class" characters live a luxuriant lifestyle? Are wealthy characters all despicable, clueless, appealing? Does the size of a character's car or house exceed their earnings? Does the story challenge or reinforce class hierarchies and distinctions?

Authority

How are the people in authority—business executives, politicians, military personnel, police, religious figures, etc.—portrayed? With reverence? Scorn? How are institutions portrayed? As trustworthy? Corrupt?

Conflict negotiation

How do your characters deal with conflict? With physical force? Intimidation? Weapons? Personality? Money? Flight? Legal tools? Verbal or non-verbal negotiation? Denial? Delayed reactions? Does conflict have a central, recurring role? Is it comic? Deadly? Creative? Does it come into the story as an organic element arising out of the characters' struggles? Are there consequences that arise from the way the characters respond to conflict?

Power

Who has power? Who desires power? Who seems to have power but doesn't really? Who is condescended to? Who initiates conversations, drives the action of the scene? Who makes the story happen? Is having power seen as desirable or dangerous? Does power shift between characters, and if so, what causes that shift to occur? Does the ability to move the story forward and bring it to a resolution reside primarily in the actions of a heroic individual or in the collective efforts of a group (a community, a social movement, etc.)? If the story involves collaboration between an individual and a group, does one become empowered by the other?

Social and family relationships

How is close friendship indicated? By the sharing of confidences? Through teasing and bantering? How are families and family structure portrayed? How are children and older people represented? What constitutes a family? Are there two parents present? Alternative parents? Are family members part of the fabric of the story or nonexistent? Influential? Directly or indirectly?

Sexual expression

Is the sexuality of the characters acknowledged? How? What is the attitude of the film towards sex? The attitude of the protagonist? Is sexuality presented in a way that is sniggering, enjoyable, puritanical, sleazy, glorifying, raunchy, sensual, thrilling, perfunctory, voyeuristic, matter-of-fact, romantic? Are certain kinds of sexual behavior presented as deviant? Are characters' sexual identities portrayed in stereotyped ways?

Gender

Are the major players predominantly one sex? If so, is that essential to the setting and context of the story? Who has the subordinate role? Are women and men drawn as variations of types (e.g., virgins, prostitutes, sex goddesses, earth mothers for women, ineffective dads, macho warriors, oversexed adolescents for men)? Or do characters behave in ways that challenge or avoid gender stereotypes?

Race, ethnicity, diversity

Is every major character the same race and ethnicity? If so, is that essential to the setting and context of the story? If more than one ethnicity is represented, is the representation of anyone patronizing? Stereotyped? Celebratory? Matter of fact? Is someone of a different ethnicity in a role of being a sidekick to the protagonist? How do the same questions apply in terms of age? Are all the characters presented as having three-dimensional lives, ongoing romantic relationships? Is physical or mental difference or disability represented, and if so, how?

Time period

If the story is set in the present, is there a sense that we live in bad or good times? If it is set in the past, is the past presented nostalgically as a golden era? A less enlightened time? A quaint or pretentious or noble time? If the story is set in the future, is the vision utopian or dystopian? Is the past or future used as a mirror on the present, and if so, what are the implications? What values are assumed? Overt?

Background

How are people characterized in terms of where they come from—a big city, a suburb, a small town, a farm, the South, California, New York, France, Russia, Japan, etc.? How does their education, their upbringing, the significant events of their past define them? What do the differing vocabularies of various characters tell you about them? Have the characters made mistakes in the past or suffered hardships, and if so, how have they responded? Do they seem to have a past at all?

Profession

Do we know what the characters do for a living? Do we see them doing it? Do we see them in their workplace, but without any portrayal of what they actually do? Do they seem knowledgeable about their work? Is it important to them? Are they valued for what they do?

Character and appearance

Are the characters judged or valued according to how they look? By how sexy they are? Does everyone seem physically perfect? What traits of character—courage, compassion, toughness, loyalty, stubbornness, ambition, nonconformity, emotionalism, intellectualism, etc.—are put in an admirable light? Are ridiculed? Are made to seem villainous or evil? What cues are given telling us who we are supposed to care about and who we're not?

Worldview and belief systems

Is the view of human nature optimistic or pessimistic? Are religion and spirituality portrayed, and if so, how? Do characters make decisions that determine their fate or are they primarily subject to luck or the whim of fate? The environment? God? The supernatural? Their genetic makeup? Who wins and who loses? Who is rewarded and who is punished? Who lives and who dies? Do these outcomes reinforce or present alternatives to prevailing cultural norms?

Connections between your own personal values and the values in your material

What are your own beliefs and values in each of these areas? Do they jibe with or contrast with those of your characters or subjects? Is that similarity or difference intentional? Do you feel you really know the world and the people you are portraying?

index

material, 126; on "fluid process" of filmmaking and talented directors, 96–97; focused dreamy state, solitude, and editing, 85, 89; *Godfather III,* 97; on intuition, 71, 74–75, 82–83; intuition, dreams, and *The Right Stuff,* 82–83, 83*i;* problem-solving, 89; psychology of collaborative relationships, 104–5; researching *The Right Stuff,* 66
Fugitive, The, 15

Gallagher, Peter, 111
Gardner, Robert A., 154
"Gerald McBoing Boing" (cartoon), 20, *20*
Geuens, Jean-Pierre, 156
Ghostwriter (TV series), 2
Girl Next Door, The, 14
Gloria, 128
Godfather, The, 141
Godfather, The, Part II, 13, 26
Godfather, The, Part III, 12, 13, 97
Golden Bowl, The, 111, 112, 135
Goldman, William, 120
Grand Canyon, 15, 124–25
Grapes of Wrath, 53
Guru, The, 52
Guston, Philip, 80

Hackman, Gene, *133*
Haines, Randa, 85
Hall, Conrad, xvii, 10, *10; American Beauty,* 42, 76–77, *76,* 111, 141; camera department, environment in, 109; choosing his creative field, 25–26; director overriding his ideas for a shot, 106; director's vision and his job as cinematographer, 124; discovery of the "soul" of a story, 120; films and film history, influence of, 54; on intuition, 71, 76–77; mental notes of observations, 56; on the power of film, 117, 119; on pressure and performance, 90; *Searching for Bobby Fischer,* 90, 160; study of a script, 145; on violence in his films, 141–42
Hall, James Norman, 10
Hanson, Curtis, 64, 65, 97–98, *97,* 168*n.*
Heat and Dust, 8, *114*
Heaven's Gate, 13
Hicks, Scott, 108
Hill Street Blues (TV series), 54
Hitchcock, Alfred, 38
Hodge, Carroll, xix; notebook use and, 150; resonance with her childhood, projects and, 33–34; student on documentary assignment and, 61–62; on teambuilding, 158
Hopper, Edward, 17
Householder, The, 52
Howard, James Newton, xvii, 15, *15;* as art collector, 50; choosing his creative field, 24, 26–27, 27; creating theme for *The Sixth Sense,* 79–80; on *Dave,* 88; defensiveness, listening to other views, and *Snow Falling on Cedars,* 107–8; director's vision and music for *Grand Canyon,* 124–25; on fluid interaction with the director, 98–99, *99;* on focused work

and creativity, 88; on intensity of a production schedule, 90–91; intuition and composing, 75, 79; music and test screenings, 131, 134; painful childhood longings and composing, 42; researching music for *Snow Falling on Cedars,* 66; responsibility to audience and listening to your soul, 139–40; on working with M. Night Shyamalan, 79–80, 161
Howards End, 8
Hunter, Holly, 157
Hurd, Gale Anne, 139, 147
Hurt, William, 125
Husbands, 128

I Vitelloni, 53
Impact, xv, xvi, 31, 117–47; Baker on acceptance of scripts, 118; embedded values questionnaire, 172*n.,* 189–92; fresh eyes: the power of the audience, 119, 129–38; Fruchtman on deeper levels and the creative process, 118–19; Fruchtman on postproduction and testing impact, 119; Hall on, 117, 119; layers of meaning and resonance, 118; limbering up, 145–47; Lucas, George, on, 155; narrative and, 117–18; Oppewall on acceptance of projects, 118; Oppewall on film's narrative power, 118; power of film, 117–19; social responsibility of, 119; taking responsibility: owning the images we create, 119, 138–45; undercurrent, the: finding the soul of film, 119–28; visual, aural expressiveness and, 118; Walker, Alice, on the power of film, 119; Wells on depth in TV series, 118; workouts, 159–60, 164. *See also* audiences; undercurrent, multi-layers of film
Iñárritu, Alejandro González, 53
In Cold Blood, 10, 141, 142
Inquiry, xv, 47–70; breadth of knowledge: a preparation in the liberal arts, 48–56; doing the homework: researching a film, 48, 63–68; getting out of the car: observation of the world, 48, 56–63; limbering up exercises, 68–70; workout: people-watching, 150. *See also* education, preparing for filmmaking; observation of the world; researching a film
Interaction, xv, xvi, 93–116; arguments worth having: responding to creative differences, 95, 102–8; everyone is telling the story, establishing a creative environment, 95, 109–15; film as a collaborative medium, 93; as key to creative filmmaking, 114–15; Kieślowski, Krzysztof, on his *Decalogue,* 120; Kureishi on, 94–95; Lasseter on, 93; limbering up, 115–16; Murch on, 93–94, *94;* Oppewall on, 115; plenty of rope: the fluid collaboration, 94, 95–102; undercurrent and collaboration, 120; Wells on, 94; workout: nurturing a creative environment, 159; workout: teambuilding, 158. *See also* conflict and creative differences; directors and collaborators; environment, establishing a creative

photo credits

Page 1: © Miriam Berkley; Page 3: Brigitte Lacombe; Page 7: Tyrone Turner; Page 8: Gaspar Tringale; Page 9: © 1997 by Kenneth Hunter; Page 10: François Duhamel; Page 12: Jed Dannenbaum; Page 13: Cayce Calloway; Page 14: Alison Dyer; Page 20: © and TM UPA Pictures Inc., 1951; Page 27: Jed Dannenbaum; Page 35: Phil Bray; Page 37: © 2001 Kenneth Hunter; Page 40: Joth Shakerley; Page 52: © MIP; Page 56: Jeannine Oppewall; Page 57: Kenneth Hunter © 1997; Page 61: William Short; Page 65: *The West Wing* © 2001 Warner Bros. All Rights Reserved; Page 67: Bill Matlock, *Boys Don't Cry* © 1999 Twentieth Century Fox. All Rights Reserved; Page 75: Jed Dannenbaum; Page 76: *American Beauty* courtesy of DreamWorks L.L.C.; Page 83: © 1983 The Ladd Company. All Rights Reserved; Page 87: Jeff Jacobs; Page 90: Kerry Hayes; Page 92: Doe Mayer; Page 94: Jed Dannenbaum; Page 99: Jed Dannenbaum; Page 100: Bill Matlock, *Boys Don't Cry* © 1999 Twentieth Century Fox. All Rights Reserved; Page 107: Carin Baer; Page 110: Phil Bray; Page 114: Christoper Cormack; Page 122: Bill Matlock *Boys Don't Cry* © 1999 Twentieth Century Fox. All Rights Reserved; Page 124: Jed Dannenbaum; Page 128: © 1997 Kenneth Hunter; Page 133: Courtesy of American Zoetrope; Page 135: *ER* © 2001 Warner Bros. All Rights Reserved; Page 143: Kaiser Family Foundation, *ER* Emergency Contraception Survey, April–June 1997; Page 153: Jed Dannenbaum; Page 154: Courtesy of MGM Clip + Still; Page 156: Carroll Hodge; Page 157: Carroll Hodge; Page 160: Kerry Hayes, courtesy of Paramount Pictures. *Searching for Bobby Fischer* copyright © 2002 by Paramount Pictures. All Rights Reserved.

about the authors

CARROLL HODGE is an independent producer, documentary filmmaker and editor. She has taught film production at the University of Southern California School of Cinema-Television since 1987, following ten years as a producer with Alaska Public Television. She also travels to give workshops on the impact of film images and the development of self-awareness and creativity in student filmmakers.

JED DANNENBAUM is an award-winning writer, producer, and director of nonfiction films and is a Senior Lecturer at the University of Southern California School of Cinema-Television, where he teaches film production. His programs about the making of Hollywood movies have appeared often on HBO and Showtime and have been released on video and DVD.

DOE MAYER is the Mary Pickford Professor of Film and Television Production at the University of Southern California. She teaches documentary and narrative filmmaking, often functioning as the head of the Documentary Program for the Production Division. She has been working in film and television for the past twenty-five years and has produced, directed, and provided technical support for hundreds of productions in the U.S. and numerous developing countries. Much of this programming has been in the areas of family planning, basic education, health and nutrition promotion, HIV/AIDS awareness and prevention, population, and women's issues.